Britain's Greatest
Aircraft

Britain's Greatest Aircraft

ROBERT JACKSON

Pen & Sword
AVIATION

First published in Great Britain in 2007 by
PEN & SWORD AVIATION
an imprint of
Pen & Sword Books Ltd
47 Church Street
Barnsley
South Yorkshire
S70 2AS

ISBN 978-1-84415-383-1

A CIP catalogue record for this book is
available from the British Library.

Typeset by Concept, Huddersfield, West Yorkshire
Printed and bound in Great Britain by CPI UK

Pen & Sword Books Ltd incorporates the Imprints of
Pen & Sword Aviation, Pen & Sword Maritime, Pen & Sword Military,
Wharncliffe Local History, Pen & Sword Select,
Pen & Sword Military Classics and Leo Cooper.

For a complete list of Pen & Sword titles please contact
PEN & SWORD BOOKS LIMITED
47 Church Street, Barnsley, South Yorkshire, S70 2AS, England.
E-mail: enquiries@pen-and-sword.co.uk
Website: www.pen-and-sword.co.uk

Contents

CHAPTER ONE

The Sopwith Camel

or Captain John Trollope of No. 43 Squadron, Royal Flying Corps, 24 March 1918 began in much the same way as many other days on the Western Front, with a morning patrol into enemy territory. On the first patrol of the day, Captain Trollope, leading a flight of Sopwith Camels, sighted three DFW two-seaters and worked his way round to the east to cut off their line of escape. He closed in and fired at the first, but then his guns jammed. After clearing the stoppage he engaged the second DFW and fired 100 rounds at it, seeing it break up in mid-air; he at once closed on a third and set it on fire. Meanwhile, the first DFW had been engaged by Captain Cecil King and 2nd Lieutenant A.P. Owen, who continued to fire at it until it too broke up. Some Albatros Scouts arrived belatedly to protect the DFWs, and Trollope immediately shot one down. At a lower level, another flight of 43 Squadron Camels, led by Captain Henry Woollett, was engaging more DFWs, one of which Woollett set on fire. Lieutenant Daniel of Woollet's flight, losing contact during the engagement, joined up with No. 3 (Naval) Squadron, which attacked five Pfalz Scouts. Daniel destroyed one of them, bringing No. 43 Squadron's score on that patrol to seven.

That afternoon Trollope led a second patrol into action, despite deteriorating weather conditions. Soon after crossing the front line he sighted four enemy two-seaters attacking a pair of RE.8 observation aircraft; five or six German single-seat fighters were also in the vicinity. Trollope led his pilots down to the aid of the REs and he singled out one of the two-seaters, firing in short bursts as he closed in to almost point-blank range. He saw pieces fly off the enemy aircraft's wing, and then the whole wing collapsed. Turning hard, Trollope came round for a stern attack on another two-seater, running through heavy defensive fire from the German observer as he did so. A few moments later the German was dead in his cockpit and the aircraft spiralling down in flames. Almost at once, Trollope engaged a third two-seater which was flying at very low level; after a short burst of fire the enemy aircraft nose-dived into the ground, disintegrating on impact.

Pulling up, Trollope saw one of the squadron's Camels hard pressed by a dozen German scouts, so he climbed hard to assist, soon joined by 2nd Lieutenants Owen and Highton. He saw each of these pilots destroy an enemy aircraft and engaged one himself, but then his ammunition ran out and he was forced to break off. On another patrol, nine Camels led by Henry Woollett fired 6,800 rounds in strafing attacks on enemy troops, and Woollett also shot down two observation balloons. By the end of the day, Lieutenant 'Bert' Hull, No. 43 Squadron's records officer, could report to his CO, Major Miles, that the unit had broken all previous records, having destroyed twenty-two enemy aircraft without loss in the day's fighting, and that the destruction of six by Captain Trollope in a single day had created a new RFC/RNAS record.

No. 43 Squadron, now based at La Gorgue, had arrived in France fourteen months earlier. Equipped initially with Sopwith One-and-a-half-Strutters, it had begun to receive Camels in September 1917, and from then on its successes had continued to mount. On the Flanders front, flying operations were severely hampered by foul weather in the first weeks of 1918, but on the few favourable flying days there were some spirited combats between the opposing sides, the RFC crews often finding themselves outnumbered. Most of the activity took place in the second half of the month, and the following extracts from the operations record of No. 43 Squadron are fairly representative of fighter operations during this period:

> 17 February. Trollope's patrol of five Camels encountered an enemy formation of eight machines. As a result of the combat which ensued three enemy machines were driven down out of control.

> 18 February. Captain Trollope while on a special mission (alone) saw three Armstrong Whitworths under attack by six enemy machines. He at once attacked the enemy who were then joined by six more. Trollope fought the twelve for ten minutes until all his ammunition was exhausted, by which time the enemy machines had all flown away to the east.

> 19 February. Second Lieutenant R.J. Owen whilst on patrol on his own was attacked by five enemy scouts in the vicinity of the Bois de Biez. He fought the five, one of which according to the testimony of anti-aircraft gunners was seen to fall in flames.

> 26 February. Captain Trollope leading a patrol of nine Camels saw four DFWs escorted by fifteen enemy scouts. He led the patrol into the attack. Although gun trouble prevented him from joining in he stayed in the middle of the fight and saw two enemy machines crash and a third fall out of control.

Before the Armistice brought the carnage of the First World War to an end in November 1918, the formidable Sopwith Camel would destroy more enemy aircraft than any other Allied type. In the hands of a novice it displayed vicious characteristics that could make it a killer; but under the firm touch of a skilled pilot, who knew how to turn its vices to his own advantage, it was one of the most superb fighting machines ever built.

Designed by Herbert Smith as a successor to the Sopwith Pup and Triplane, the Camel prototype made its appearance in December 1916. Early production aircraft were powered either by the 130 hp Clerget 9B or the 150 hp Bentley BR1 rotary engine, but subsequent aircraft were fitted with either the Clerget or the 110 hp Le Rhone 9J. Armament comprised twin Vickers guns mounted in front of the cockpit, and four 9 kg (20 lb) Cooper bombs could be carried under the fuselage for ground attack.

The first unit to receive Camels was No. 4 Squadron of the Royal Naval Air service, followed by No. 70 Squadron RFC, both in July 1917. By the end of the year 1,325 Camels (out of a total of 3,450 on order at that time) had been delivered, and were used widely for ground attack during the Battles of Ypres and Cambrai. In March 1917, meanwhile, a shipboard version of the Camel, the 2F.1, had undergone trials; designed to operate from platforms on warships, from towed lighters or from the Royal Navy's new aircraft carriers, this differed from the F.1 in having a slightly shorter wing span, and, instead of the starboard Vickers gun, a Lewis angled to fire upwards through a cut-out in the upper wing centre section. The 2F.1's principal mission was Zeppelin interception; 340 examples were built, but the first of these did not become operational until the spring of 1918. By the end of the war, however, 2F.1 Camels were deployed on five aircraft carriers, two battleships and 26 cruisers of the Royal Navy. On 11 August 1918, a 2F.1 Camel flown by Lieutenant Stuart Culley, and launched from a lighter towed behind the destroyer HMS *Redoubt*, intercepted and destroyed the Zepplin L.53 over the Heligoland Bight.

Early in 1918, while the pilots of the RFC and RNAS in France learned how to master the Camel in combat, the type went into action over southern England against German night bombers. One of the biggest threats was posed by the Zeppelin (Staaken) R Type, known as the *Riesenflugzeug* (giant aircraft). This monster was capable of carrying a 2,200 lb bomb at 14,000 feet at 80 mph under the power of its four 260 hp Mercedes engines; moreover, it was defended by five machine guns, which made it a much tougher target than the Gotha, the other and more prolific bomber type.

The first German bombing raid of 1918 was mounted on the night of 28/29 January, when thirteen Gothas and two Giants were despatched to attack London. In the event seven Gothas and one Giant succeeded in doing so, killing sixty-seven civilians, injuring another 166, and causing damage of nearly £190,000. The raid was thwarted to some degree by fog, as far as the Gothas were concerned, while one of the Giants had engine trouble and was forced to turn back, having jettisoned its bombs into the sea off Ostende.

One of the Gothas involved in the London attack dropped its bombs on Hampstead at 9.45 pm and was then tracked by searchlights as it flew over north-east London. The beams attracted the attention of two patrolling Sopwith Camel pilots of No. 44 Squadron from Hainault – Captain George Hackwill and Lieutenant Charles Banks – who at once gave chase and independently picked up the glow from the Gotha's exhausts as it passed over Romford at 10,000 feet. Banks was flying a Camel with an unconventional armament; in addition to its normal pair of Vickers guns it also carried a Lewis, mounted on the upper wing centre section and using the new RTS ammunition. Designed by Richard Threlfall and Son, this combined explosive and incendiary qualities. It was Banks who attacked first, closing from the left to about thirty yards behind the Gotha and opening fire with all three guns. Hackwill meanwhile closed in from the right and also opened fire, effectively boxing in the German bomber and presenting an impossible situation to its gunner, whose field of fire was re-stricted. After ten minutes or so the Gotha caught fire and dived into the ground

The last view of many a German airman. This Camel, seen taking off from Hainault Farm in Essex, was flown by Major Murlis Green, night-fighting specialist. (IWM)

near Wickford, where it exploded. It would almost certainly have crashed anyway, even if it had not caught fire, for a subsequent examination of the crew's bodies revealed that the pilot had been shot through the neck. Hackwill and Banks were each awarded the Military Cross for their exploit.

An hour after the last Gotha had cleared the coast, the *Riesenflugzeug* was over Sudbury, having made landfall over Hollesley Bay, east of Ipswich, and was droning towards London via a somewhat tortuous route. By this time, at least forty-four fighters were searching for it. Shortly after it had released its bombs over London, the Giant was picked up east of Woolwich by a Sopwith Camel of No. 44 Squadron flown by Lieutenant Bob Hall, a South African. Hall followed it as far as Foulness, cursing in helpless frustration all the way because he could not get his guns to work. The Giant got away. The anti-aircraft barrage scored one success that night, but unfortunately its victim was a Camel of No. 78 Squadron flown by Lieutenant Idris Davies, whose engine was stopped by a near shell burst at 11,000 feet over Woolwich. Davies tried to glide back to Sutton's Farm, but he hit telegraph wires near the Hornchurch signal box and was catapulted out of the cockpit. He fell between the railway lines, amazingly without injury, but the Camel was a complete loss. Forty minutes later Davies was sitting in another Camel, ready to take off if need be.

The following night witnessed the most remarkable night battle of the war, when three Giants out of four despatched attacked southern England. The fourth, having developed engine trouble over the Channel, bombed fortifications near Gravelines before returning to its base, while the other crossed the English coast between Southend and the Naze. One of these, the R.26, developed engine trouble soon after crossing the coast and began losing height, so its crew jettisoned the bomb load and limped back across the Channel on two engines, eventually landing at Ostende. A second Giant, the R.39, came inland via the Blackwater estuary and approached London from the north-west at approximately 11,000 feet. It was sighted by Bob Hall of No. 44 Squadron, who pursued it until it became lost in the haze near Roehampton. Once again, Hall's guns gave trouble and he had no opportunity to open fire. Meanwhile, the Giant had dropped its bombs on residential areas between Acton and Richmond Park, the crew having apparently mistaken Hammersmith Bridge for Tower Bridge, which was several miles to the east.

South of the Thames, the R.39 was attacked briefly and with no visible result by Captain F.L. Luxmoore of No. 78 Squadron, flying a Sopwith Camel. He fired fifty rounds on his first pass, but as he made a second firing run one of his bullets struck the Camel's propeller and the brilliant tracer element flew back into his face, temporarily blinding him. By the time his night vision was restored, the bomber had vanished. Shortly after this the R.39, now down to 9,500 feet and travelling very fast, was located by Captain G.H. Hackwill of No. 44 Squadron, who was also flying a Camel. Hackwill gave chase and fired 600 rounds from long range before shortage of fuel compelled him to break off. The Giant was last seen as it crossed the coast near Hythe by 2nd Lieutenants F.V. Bryant and V.H. Newton, the crew of an Armstrong Whitworth FK.8 of No. 50 Squadron. They too gave chase, but lost the bomber in haze.

The third Giant, the R.25, crossed the coast near Foulness at 22.50 hours and was almost immediately attacked by 2nd Lieutenant F.R. Kitton of No. 37 Squadron, flying a BE.2e. Diving his aircraft at a shuddering 100 mph, he got under the Giant's tail and fired a complete drum of ammunition at it, observing several hits, but lost the bomber while he was busy rearming. The R.25 was next attacked by Bob Hall of No. 44 Squadron at 23.15 hours over Benfleet, but his guns kept on jamming as he pursued it. He was joined by 2nd Lieutenant H.A. Edwardes, also of No. 44 Squadron, who fired three long bursts before his guns also jammed.

By this time the R.25 was taking violent evasive action. The battle had now attracted three more Camels, all from No. 44 Squadron; the first on the scene was 2nd Lieutenant T.M. O'Neill, who fired 300 rounds before his guns jammed too. Next came the squadron commander, Major Murlis Green, who was flying a Camel equipped with two Lewis guns using RTS ammunition. He had already made one run, only to break away when he almost flew into O'Neill's fire. Now he closed in again to be greeted by the full attention of the Giant's rear gunner. Undeterred, he fired three quarters of a drum at the bomber before suffering a stoppage which he was unable to clear. As his second Lewis also refused to function, he had no choice but to return to base to have the trouble put right.

The R.25 was now in trouble. The Camels' fire had put one of its engines out of action and some of its instruments had also been smashed. Although unable to maintain height with a full bomb load, and with their speed down to about 60 mph, the crew decided to press on to London. The Giant's bombs fell in open ground near Wanstead. Up to this point the R.25 had been harried by Bob Hall, who was able to fire only five rounds before each stoppage; he now lost his target, but encountered the R.39 a few miles to the west. The R.25 scraped home to Ostende, having survived successive attacks by five fighters. They had collectively fired over 800 rounds at her, and after landing she was found to have taken no fewer than eighty-eight hits. Had the fighters not suffered continual gun stoppages, there seems little doubt that they would have brought down the bomber. However, there were other factors in their failure to do so; analysing the action later, the Camel pilots of No. 44 Squadron realised that the Giant's sheer size had led them to believe that they had been firing from a much closer range than was actually the case. Instead of closing to within fifty yards, as they had thought at the time, they must have been anything up to 250 yards away.

The last German aircraft raid on Britain in the First World War took place on the night of 20/21 May 1918. Twenty-eight Gothas and three Giants set out to attack London, and were met by a vastly more effective night fighter force than had been the case four months earlier, at the time of the previous night raids. Seventy-four Camels and SE.5s went up to intercept the bombers, shooting down three Gothas, while the anti-aircraft defences claimed two more and a sixth crashed in Essex after engine failure. It was the biggest loss suffered by the German bombers in a single night's operations over England, and it was to be more than two decades before they came again.

At the beginning of March, despite continuing bad weather, the enemy's air effort in Flanders intensified, with much activity by observation aircraft. There were some brisk engagements, and on 13 March seven Camels of No. 43 Squadron, escorting a pair of FK.8s, encountered a mixed force of fifteen Albatros and Pfalz Scouts and attacked them. Captain Henry Woollett fired at one, which broke up in mid-air, then engaged a second, which went out of control and crashed. Two more were shot down by 2nd Lieutenant Peiler, and one each by 2nd Lieutenants Lingham, Lomax, King and Dean. A ninth enemy aircraft was shot down by an observer in one of the FK.8s, which belonged to No. 2 Squadron, whereupon the remainder broke off the action and flew away.

On 16 March, seven Camels of No. 4 (Australian) Squadron, which was part of the 10th (Army) Wing, took off from Bruay to attack targets near Douai with 20 lb bombs. The attack was carried out without incident, but as the Camels were climbing to 16,000 feet to cross the front line they were hotly engaged by a formation of sixteen brightly-painted Albatros Scouts, readily identifiable as belonging to the Richthofen *Geschwader*. While four of the Albatros remained at altitude, ready to dive down and pick off stragglers, the other twelve attacked in pairs. The Australian flight commander, Lieutenant G.F. Malley, and Lieutenant C.M. Feez avoided the first pass and went in pursuit of the two Albatros, which were diving in formation. The Australians shot both of them down. Meanwhile, Lieutenant A.W. Adams, some 2,000 feet lower down, fought a hectic battle with two more scouts and destroyed one of them, while Lieutenant W.H. Nicholls, pursued down to ground level, was forced to land behind

The Camel could be a tricky aircraft to handle, as the pilot of this one discovered while attempting a forced landing. (via J.R. Cavanagh)

the German lines and was taken prisoner. Another Camel pilot, Lieutenant P.K. Schafer, was attacked by three Albatros of the high flight; as he was attempting to evade, the Camel flicked into a spin and fell 10,000 feet before the shaken Australian managed to recover. He landed at Bruay with sixty-two bullet holes in his aircraft. On the following day, Captain John Trollope of No. 43 Squadron sighted six enemy scouts while flying alone on an altitude test (a favourite ploy of pilots lacking the necessary authorization to carry out lone patrols over the front line). He climbed above them and attacked, sending one down out of control. The other five dived away. Shortly afterwards, while returning to base, Trollope sighted four more enemy aircraft and attacked one at close range. It caught fire and broke up. Trollope at once turned to engage the rest, but they flew away eastwards.

On 21 March, the Germans launched a massive offensive against the British Third and Fifth Armies. A magnificent defence by the British infantry divisions in the centre of the Third Army's sector, south-east of Arras, kept the line intact, but the right flank near Bapaume was hard-pressed and fighting a desperate rearguard action as the troops strove to maintain contact with the fragmented and retreating Fifth Army. It was in this sector, on the 23rd, that some of the most intensive air operations took place. The Camels of No. 4 (Australian) Squadron were in the thick of the fighting here. On the morning of the 23rd, the Squadron received orders to attack the Germans near Vaux-Vraucourt and along the Bapaume–Cambrai road. Two flight of six Camels took off just after 10.00 am, led by Captain Courtney, and flew to their objective at low level, keeping under 500 feet the whole way. The low-level attack took the enemy troops by surprise, the bombing and strafing throwing the Germans into confusion and panic. Top cover during the initial attack was provided by Lieutenant G.F. Malley's six Camels, which dived on several Albatros attempting to attack the strafing flight. Malley shot down two of the enemy fighters, and 2nd Lieutenant Scott destroyed a third. Bapaume was now in enemy hands, and later in the day No. 4 Squadron was ordered to attack British ammunition dumps there which had not been destroyed by the retreating troops. Whether the dumps were hit or not is not recorded, but the Camels were attacked by enemy fighters soon after dropping their bombs. One Australian pilot, Lieutenant A.E. Robertson, shot down one Fokker Triplane and 'drove two others down out of control'.

Strafing attacks by the Camel squadrons played a major part in containing the German offensive, which eventually petered out, and during the remaining months of 1918 the Camel established a degree of air superiority over the Western Front that it would never lose, even though the enemy now deployed formidable new fighter aircraft such as the Fokker D.VII, arguably the best fighter to see operational service in the 1914–18 War.

By the end of the conflict the Camel squadrons had begun to rearm with the Sopwith Snipe, which was built around the new 230 hp Bentley BR.2 rotary engine and was considered to be the best Allied fighter in service at the time of the Armistice. Ordered into production at the beginning of 1918 after a somewhat protracted development programme, the Snipe was issued to No. 43 Squadron in France in September, followed by No. 208 Squadron and No. 4 (Australian) Squadron. By 30 September 161 Snipe Mk.Is had been delivered. Over 4,500 examples of this very effective fighter were ordered, but there were heavy cancellations and only 497 were built.

The Sopwith Camel went on to see action after the Armistice of November 1918, in support of the Allied Intervention Force in Russia. In South Russia, the RAF deployed No. 47 Squadron from Amberkoj in Greece to Ekaterinodar in April 1918, and No. 221 Squadron, together with 'A' Flight of No. 17 Squadron, from Mudros to Petrovsk in December. No. 47 Squadron was commanded by a renowned air fighter, Major Raymond Collishaw, the third-ranking ace of the British Empire with sixty-two victories to his credit. The function of Nos 17 and 221 Squadrons, both of which were equipped with DH.9s, was to bomb the Bolshevik bases on the Caspian and provide air support for the Royal Navy, which was operating a small armada of vessels in the area. By May 1919, following a series of limited air-sea actions against the Bolsheviks, the whole of the Caspian with the exception of Astrakhan was in Allied hands.

The Camel's immediate successor was the Sopwith Snipe, which equipped the RAF's fighter squadrons in the immediate post-war years. (Source unknown)

Rare photograph of Sopwith Snipes in South Russia, 1919. (Source unknown)

No. 47 Squadron comprised three flights, two equipped with DH.9 and 9A bombers and one with Sopwith Camels, all of them war-weary. In March 1919, the squadron moved to Beketovka to lend direct support to White Russian ground operations, carrying out reconnaissance, ground attack and escort work, and in May the pilots were ordered to step up their operations and destroy as many enemy aircraft as possible in support of the White Russian advance on Tsaritsyn. Attacks centred on Urbabk airfield, where several red air units were based, and the squadron mounted a series of ground attack operations in the Tsaritsyn area. By the end of the month, No. 47 Squadron's aircrews had accounted for some twenty enemy aircraft in air engagements.

The squadron flew intensively during the summer months of 1919, carrying out attacks on enemy cavalry formations and river traffic. In September it moved to Kotluban, from where it continued attacks on the enemy's lines of communication. It was now the sole RAF unit operating in south Russia, No. 221 Squadron having disbanded on 1 September. In October No. 47 Squadron lost its identity, becoming known simply as 'A' Detachment, RAF.

By the last week in September the Red forces were advancing on all fronts. The RAF Detachment was earmarked to carry on the fight in support of General Mai-Maevsky's White Volunteer Army, engaged in bitter fighting around Kharkov, but both men and machines were swept up in the chaos of retreat and the detachment was disbanded, the crews making their way to Rostov. They were evacuated in March 1920, after destroying their few re-maining aircraft.

CHAPTER TWO

The Royal Aircraft Factory SE.5A

The SE.5 single-seat scout entered RFC service in the spring of 1917, being delivered to No. 56 Squadron in March. Although less manoeuvrable than either the French-built Nieuports and Spads, the SE.5 was faster and had an excellent rate of climb, enabling it to hold its own in combat with the latest German fighter types. The original SE.5 was followed into service, in June 1917, by the SE.5A, with a 200 hp Hispano-Suiza engine. Deliveries were slowed by an acute shortage of engines, but the pilots of the units that did receive the SE.5A were full of praise for the aircraft's fine flying qualities, physical strength and performance.

> The May evening is heavy with threatening masses of cumulus cloud, majestic skyscapes, solid-looking as snow mountains, fraught with caves and valleys, rifts and ravines ... Steadily the body of scouts rises higher and higher, threading its way between the cloud precipices. Sometimes, below, the streets of a village, the corner of a wood, a few dark figures moving, glides into view like a slide into a lantern and is then hidden again ...
>
> A red light curls up from the leader's cockpit and falls away. Action! He alters direction slightly, and the patrol, shifting throttle and rudder, keep close like a pack of hounds on the scent. He has seen, and they see soon, six scouts 3,000 feet below. Black crosses! It seems interminable till the eleven come within diving distance. The pilots nurse their engines, hard-minded and set, test their guns and watch their indicators. At last the leader sways sideways, as a signal that each should take his man, and suddenly drops ...

That was how SE.5 pilot Lieutenant Cecil Lewis, in his acclaimed book *Sagittarius Rising*, described the start of the battle that was to cost the life of Britain's ace of aces, Captain Albert Ball, on that evening of 7 May 1917. Ball, a flight commander with No. 56 Squadron, the holder of the Distinguished Service Order and two Bars, plus the Military Cross, had taken off a while earlier from Vert Galand to carry out an offensive patrol in the direction of Douai aerodrome, the base of *Jagdstaffel* 11, which was commanded by a German officer who was already legendary – his name was Manfred von Richthofen.

As the fight was joined it began to rain, cutting down the visibility. The section leaders of No. 56 Squadron, which had only arrived in France with its

SE.5 Scouts a month earlier, tried hard to hold their men together, but in the confusion of the dogfight the squadron became split up. Some of the pilots broke away and made for home; others, including Ball, headed for a pre-arranged rendezvous over Arras. There, Ball joined up with another flight commander named Crowe and the two continued their patrol, joined by a lone Spad.

Near Loos, Ball suddenly fired off a couple of signal flares and dived on a red-and-yellow Fokker Triplane, following it into a cloud. It was the last time that he was seen alive. Of the eleven SE.5s that had set out, only five returned to base.

The credit for Albert Ball's death was claimed by Lothar von Richthofen, Manfred's brother. The claim was false, and to this day mystery surrounds the RFC pilot's demise. He was either shot down by a machine gun mounted on a church steeple, or became disorientated in low cloud and went out of control. The Germans buried him near Lille, and dropped a message to that effect over No. 56 Squadron's aerodrome. A month later, it was announced that Ball had been posthumously awarded the Victoria Cross. His score of enemy aircraft destroyed at the time of his death was forty-seven. He was twenty-two years old.

Less than six months later an SE.5 pilot brought the career of German ace *Leutnant* Werner Voss to an untimely end. Voss was due to go on leave with his two brothers, and on 23 September they arrived at his aerodrome, intending to travel back to Germany together. Before departing, Voss decided to go out on an offensive patrol, flying a Fokker Triplane. This type had made its first appearance at the front early in September, and in the hands of an experienced pilot was a formidable fighting machine.

Soon after starting his patrol, Werner Voss shot down an Airco DH.4, heading back towards the front line after a sortie, but then he developed engine trouble and returned to base, exchanging his Triplane for another. At 18.00 hours, in poor visibility, he took off again accompanied by two Albatros Scouts, which still formed the main equipment of Jasta 11. Approaching the front line, they saw an air battle in progress between a variety of German and British aircraft, including the SE.5s of No. 60 Squadron. Voss immediately manoeuvred into position to attack one of these, which was flown by Lieutenant H.A. Hamersley and which had become separated from the rest.

Twenty minutes earlier, six SE.5s of 'B' Flight, No. 56 Squadron, had taken off from their airfield at Estreé Blanche. The flight was led by Captain James B. McCudden, who was accompanied by 2nd Lieutenants Gerald Bowman, Arthur Rhys-Davids, Keith Muspratt, Richard Maybery and R.T.C. Hoidge. The flight attacked an enemy two-seater, which was shot down by McCudden, and then re-formed and climbed to attack a formation of six Albatros Scouts, flying just below the cloud base. At that moment, McCudden spotted Hamersley's lone SE.5, pursued by Voss, somewhat lower down. Abandoning the Albatros formation, he went after the Triplane in a diving turn, followed by Arthur Rhys-Davids.

The pair closed rapidly on the German, one on either side, taking it in turns to fire in short bursts. Voss, with four more SE.5s coming down hard and already effectively boxed in, took the only course of action open to him. Using the Fokker's remarkable agility to the fullest advantage, he decided to fight his attackers by turning to face them, doubtless hoping that he could hold them at bay until reinforcements arrived. The manoeuvre took McCudden completely by surprise, as he confessed later:

> To my amazement he kicked on full rudder without bank, pulled his nose up slightly, gave me a burst while he was skidding sideways, and then kicked on opposite rudder before the results of this amazing stunt appeared to have any effect on the controllability of his machine.

With a burst of gunfire through his wing, the startled McCudden broke away sharply. At that moment, a red-nosed Albatros joined the battle. Its pilot, almost as skilful as Voss himself, took on the task of protecting Voss's tail, and with his assistance the German ace abandoned his purely defensive tactics and got in some damaging shots at the SEs that were trying to out-turn him. The battle went on for a full ten minutes, but the help the German pilots were counting on never arrived, and the outcome was inevitable. The combat report of Rhys-Davids describes the last frantic minutes of the fight:

> The red-nosed Albatros and the triplane fought magnificently. I got in several bursts at the triplane without apparent effect, and twice placed a new drum on my Lewis gun. Eventually I got east of and slightly above the triplane and made for it, getting in a whole Lewis drum and a corresponding number of rounds from my Vickers. He made no attempt to turn in and we were so close that I was certain that we would collide. He passed my starboard wing by inches and went down. I zoomed, and saw him next with his engine apparently out, gliding east. I dived again and got one shot out of my Vickers. I reloaded, keeping in the dive, and got in another good burst, the triplane effecting a slight starboard turn, still going down. I had now overshot him, but never saw him again.

McCudden, who had temporarily broken off the fight to change his ammunition drum, witnessed the Triplane's last moments. He noted that it seemed to stagger and then fly erratically for a time before going into a steep dive, streaming smoke, and exploded on the ground. A few moments later the red-nosed Albatros also went down in flames. Later, James McCudden wrote of Voss, 'His flying was wonderful, his courage magnificent, and in my opinion he was the bravest German airman whom it has been my privilege to fight.' But perhaps the feelings of the British pilots were best summed up by young Rhys-Davids himself, the man who had ended the career of the 'Hussar of Krefeld', as Voss was nicknamed. As his colleagues gathered around to congratulate him, he shook his head and

Lieutenant Arthur Rhys-Davids, who shot down the German ace Werner Voss. (IWM)

murmured, as he set his glass aside, 'Oh, if only I could have brought him down alive!'

The SE.5 squadrons did much to restore Allied air superiority during the confused air fighting that accompanied the German spring offensive in Flanders in March 1918. A patrol of No. 2 (Australian) Squadron on 22 March was perhaps typical of many experiences along the battlefront:

> Ten SE.5As set out to patrol St Quentin; two had to turn back with engine trouble, but the other eight encountered five enemy two-seaters escorted by a number of single-seaters. Lieutenant Forrest dived on a two-seater, which burst into flames, and Lieutenant McKenzie sent an Albatros down out of control. Turning north along the front, the Australians passed over Bourlon Wood, where they spotted five German triplanes below. Captain Phillips attacked the leader, who rolled over and went into a slow spin; the other triplanes scattered in the haze. Over Bullecourt more Albatros Scouts were engaged; Lieutenant Forrest shot down two out of control and Lieutenant Holden got a third.

On 1 April 1918 – the day that saw the amalgamation of the Royal Flying Corps and the Royal Naval Air Service to form the Royal Air Force – Captain G.E.H. McElroy, an Irish flight commander with No. 24 Squadron, attacked three enemy scouts in his SE.5A, closing to well within 100 yards of one before firing a burst of 100 rounds from both guns into it. Three days later, the same pilot unhesitatingly attacked seven enemy fighters which he spotted flying eastwards over the lines and shot one of them down from fifty yards' range. Then, on 7 April, McElroy attacked one of three enemy two-seaters, braving intense defensive fire to shoot it up from fifty yards; it nose-dived into the ground. Shortly afterwards, flying through broken cloud at 3,000 feet, he sighted three SEs being attacked by five Fokker Triplanes and closed in to fire twenty rounds into one of the Fokkers from point-blank range, sending it down to crash.

One of the SE.5A units engaged in the period of bitter air fighting was No. 74 Squadron, based at La Lovie and commanded by Major Edward Mannock, a man very different in outlook and temperament from most of his peers. At the age of thirty, Mannock was much older than most fighter pilots. He had two infirmities, one physical, the other psychological. The physical one was a very bad left eye; the psychological one was a chip on his shoulder, the result of a hard struggle for existence during his boyhood and youth.

Having bluffed his way through the medical examinations by memorizing eye charts, Mannock was accepted for flying training in 1916, and was fortunate to have as his instructor a man who was already experienced in combat – Captain James McCudden. He taught Mannock all the tricks of his new trade, and the two became firm friends. It was a partnership that only death would sever.

Early in 1917 Mannock joined No. 40 Squadron in France, and it was now that McCudden's teaching paid off. Mannock worked hard to improve his flying and shooting, and despite his bad eye became a better than average marksman. Unlike many of his colleagues, he approached the science of air fighting with extreme caution, preferring to skirt the fringes of his early air skirmishes rather than throw caution to the winds and dive into the middle of a fight. Some of his fellow pilots even began to hint that he might lack courage, but Mannock took no notice. He watched his more hot-headed critics go down in flames one after the other, and knew that he was right.

After two months, Mannock was satisfied with the tactics he had been striving to perfect, and now the change that came over him in action was dramatic. In the next three weeks he shot down six enemy aircraft, earning the Military Cross and rapid promotion to flight commander. Now that he could impart his skills to other pilots he really came into his own, forging a first-rate fighting team. His pilots had the utmost trust in him; he shepherded them carefully, never lost his head in action, and always ensured that the odds were right before committing himself to battle. He became a master of ambush, and before attacking an enemy he made certain that his pilots conformed to the golden rule: 'Start the attack from above, seldom on the same level, never from beneath.' He taught his men to attack from astern, if possible, hitting the enemy on the first diving pass. He also taught them the full range of aerobatics to build up confidence in handling their aircraft, at the same time stressing that aerobatics in a dogfight were pointless and dangerous. Tight turns, he said, were the only manoeuvres that paid real dividends in an air battle.

At the end of 1917, by which time he had been posted to No. 74 Squadron, Mannock's score had risen to fifty-six, surpassing McCudden. The latter levelled the score in February 1918 with the destruction of a Hanoveraner two-seater, but then he was sent back to England, where he was awarded the Victoria Cross. He was never to have an opportunity to gain further victories. After four months in England, McCudden was promoted and ordered back to France to take command of No. 60 Squadron. On 9 July 1918 he crossed the Channel in his SE.5A and landed at a French aerodrome to refuel before continuing to No. 60's airfield at Boffles. On take-off, his engine failed and McCudden disobeyed one of the cardinal rules of flying, a rule he had instilled over and over again into his students: if your engine fails on take-off, never turn back towards the airfield. He did so; his aircraft lost flying speed in the turn, stalled and went into a spin. Too low to recover, McCudden was killed in the crash.

With Mick Mannock in command, No. 74 Squadron arrived in France on 30 March 1918 and installed itself a few days later at La Lovie, near Poperinghe, which it shared with the Camels of No. 54 Squadron under Major R.S. Maxwell. Its first patrols were flown on 12 April, and on that day Mannock celebrated his return to action in fine style, as the official summary of the day's operations records: 'Capt E. Mannock, 74 Sqn, after one or two pilots of his patrol had engaged a hostile machine without result, fired a burst into it. It then crashed east of Carvin. He fired a long burst with both guns at 30 yards into another EA, which went down and crashed near the first machine.'

There was very heavy air fighting in May 1918, after the German spring offensive had been halted. One SE.5 pilot who distinguished himself during this period was Captain A.W. Beauchamp-Proctor of No. 84 Squadron, based at Bertangles. A South African, Beauchamp-Proctor was to end the war with fifty-four victories, making him the fifth-ranking British ace.

On 10 May, Beauchamp-Proctor stalked a two-seater which he had seen climbing for altitude as it approached the British lines and fired fifty rounds into it, killing the observer. He then closed in and opened fire again, at which the two-seater went into a vertical dive. The RAF pilot watched it fall through 4,000 feet until it was lost to sight in the haze, but another 84 Squadron pilot confirmed that it had crashed.

On 15 May, Beauchamp-Proctor took off on a pre-dawn sortie in an attempt to intercept enemy bombers that had been attacking Amiens. He failed to find them, so flew east in the hope of catching them over their airfield as they returned from their bombing mission. He had no difficulty in finding the enemy aerodrome, where landing flares had been lit. Throttling back, he glided down to 3,000 feet, then circled a few miles to the west to await events. A few minutes later a twin-engine aircraft, probably a Gotha, flew just over him and he turned to attack it, but its gunner was on the alert and opened fire. Proctor fired in turn, and the German gunner fell silent. Then Proctor's own guns jammed, and by the time he had cleared the stoppage the bomber was almost over its airfield.

Beauchamp-Proctor closed in again and renewed his fire, seeing the enemy aircraft discharge a red flare, which was answered from the ground. The next instant the airfield's defences opened up and the RAF pilot found himself flying through a storm of heavy machine gun fire and tracer shells. At 2,000 feet he was forced to break off the combat, having driven the enemy aircraft some distance away from the aerodrome. When he last saw the bomber it was in a dive, and although it was still under control it had almost certainly suffered heavy damage.

Another exponent of the SE.5A was Major Roderic Dallas of No. 40 Squadron, who lost no time in opening his May air fighting account, shooting down a Pfalz Scout on the morning of the 2nd. Later in the day he carried out a daring low-level attack on the enemy airfield at La Brayelle. After strafing the hangars, he turned and raced back over the aerodrome, dropping a pair of army boots in a parcel and a message which read, 'If you won't come up here and fight, herewith one pair of boots for work on the ground. Pilots – for the use of.'

Circling in the haze, he waited until a party of Germans had gathered to examine the package and then made another low-level run, firing 100 rounds of ammunition and dropping two 20 lb Cooper bombs. To round off a very satis-factory day's work, he caught an unwary Albatros Scout on its own and shot it down.

Dallas destroyed two more enemy aircraft in mid-May, and another on the 27th. It was his thirty-nineth and last victory, although according to some sources his true total was fifty-one. His personal SE.5 was well known to the enemy; instead of the drab khaki upper surfaces and cream underside that was the standard RAF colour scheme, he had it painted in a distinctive green and brown camouflage pattern similar to that which the RAF was to adopt many years later.

The SE.5A has always been a favourite subject for building as a replica. (Source unknown)

On 1 June 1918, Roderic Dallas failed to return from a lone patrol high over the front line. Later, the wreckage of his aircraft was found near the village of Lieven. According to a German account published later, he had dived on a Fokker Triplane, unaware that it was a decoy, and two others had pounced on him.

For the Allied squadrons, late May and early June 1918 was a period of consolidation. To make good the RAF's losses, fresh squadrons were sent out from England. One of them was No. 85, equipped with the SE.5A, which arrived at Petite Synthe on 25 May. Its commanding officer was Major William Avery (Billy) Bishop, whose score at that time stood at sixty enemy aircraft destroyed.

Billy Bishop reopened his scoring on 27 May, when he attacked an enemy two-seater over Houthulst Forest. He pursued it, firing as it turned east, and saw both sets of wings and the tail unit break off, the fragments crashing east of Passchendaele. On 30 May he destroyed two more two-seaters, and shot down an Albatros Scout later in the day. On 3 June, however, the authorities decided that Bishop was too valuable an asset as a leader to have his life continually at risk, and ordered him to return to England in a fortnight's time.

During that fortnight, Bishop destroyed a further twelve enemy aircraft, the first on 4 June. On 17 June, his last day in action but one, he destroyed three in the space of thirty minutes with the expenditure of only fifty-five rounds of ammunition. The next day was even more dramatic. Patrolling near Ypres, Bishop sighted and attacked three Pfalz Scouts, one of which he quickly sent down in flames. As the others turned to attack him, two more Pfalz dropped down from the clouds to join the action. For a few minutes the five machines circled, the Germans endeavouring to box in the lone SE.5. Then, as two of the Pfalz turned towards him, Bishop acted quickly. He dived between them and the two enemy aircraft, tightening their turns, collided with one another and went down in a cloud of wreckage. The other two at once broke off the combat and turned away. Bishop went after them, opening fire on one from 200 yards. His aim was good and the Pfalz went down, bursting into flames as it fell. The other escaped into a cloud.

On 19 June, 1918, Billy Bishop left France for good. In just over a year of air combat he had destroyed seventy-two enemy aircraft. Such were the men who flew the SE.5, the nimble fighter that has since been described as the 'Spitfire of World War One'.

CHAPTER THREE

The Bristol F.2B Fighter

The first Allied offensive of 1917 involved a major French attack on the Aisne while the British pinned down a large part of the enemy forces in the north, the main objective in their sector being the capture of Vimy Ridge. The offensive began on 17 March and ended on 4 April. The First and Third British Armies were supported by twenty-five RFC squadrons, about half of them equipped with single-seat fighters.

It was during this battle that a new British combat aircraft, the Bristol F.2A fighter, made its operational debut. Fifty F.2As were built. Powered by a 190 hp Rolls-Royce Falcon engine giving it a top speed of around 115 mph and armed with a centrally-mounted forward-firing Vickers gun and a single Lewis mounted in the rear cockpit, the first examples arrived in France with No. 48 Squadron towards the end of March.

The squadron had only six Bristols in operation at the time of its arrival at its new base, Bellevue, and they were rushed into action before their crews had time to get used to them or develop appropriate tactics. At first they were flown like earlier two-seaters, orientated around the observer's gun as the primary weapon, and losses were heavy. During their first patrol on 5 April 1917, six Bristols led by No. 48 Squadron's CO, Major W. Leefe Robinson VC (who had earlier distinguished himself by shooting down the Schütte-Lanz airship SL11 at Cuffley on 2 September 1916) encountered five Albatros D.IIs led by Manfred von Richthofen. The British pilots adopted the standard two-seater tactic of turning their backs on the enemy to allow their observers to bring their guns to bear. It was a serious mistake, and four of the six – including Leefe Robinson, who spent the rest of the war in a prison camp – were shot down.

Later, in an interview with a Berlin newspaper, Richthofen was openly contemptuous of the British machine, with the result that many German pilots came to regard the Bristol Fighter as easy game, with fatal consequences to themselves. When flown offensively, in the same way as a single-seat fighter, it proved to be a superb weapon and went on to log a formidable record of success in action. Several hundred Bristol Fighters were ordered in 1917, these being the F.2B version with a 220 hp Falcon II or 275 hp Falcon III engine, wide-span tailplane, modified lower wing section and an improved view from the front cockpit. The F.2B eventually served with six RFC squadrons – Nos 11, 20, 22, 48, 62 and 88 – on the Western Front, as well as with No. 67 (Australian) Squadron in Palestine, No. 139 Squadron in Italy, and with Nos 33, 36, 76 and 141 Squadrons on home defence duties in the United Kingdom. The pilot who perhaps did most to vindicate the Bristol Fighter was a Canadian, Lieutenant

Pilots and observers of No. 22 (Bristol Fighter) Squadron at Vert Galand, France, 1916. (IWM)

Andrew McKeever, who destroyed thirty enemy aircraft while flying F.2Bs, his various observers shooting down eleven more.

Even so, the British two-seaters were no match for the cream of Germany's fighter squadrons. On 12 March 1918, for example, the Richthofen *Geschwader* engaged nine Bristol Fighters of No. 62 Squadron, which was operating north of Arras as part of the 9th Wing, and destroyed four of them. No. 62 Squadron remained in the thick of the fighting during the German offensive of March–April 1918, and took part in some notable combats. On 21 April, during some particularly fierce air fighting, Second Lieutenant L.M. Thompson, the gunner in an aircraft flown by Lieutenant D.A. Savage, opened the score by shooting down an Albatros near Lille; soon afterwards the Bristol was attacked by two Pfalz and Thompson opened fire on one of them. It went into a vertical dive and broke up in the air, whereupon the other aircraft flew away. Captain T.L. Purdon and 2nd Lieutenant P.V.G. Chambers, part of the same patrol, fired 200 rounds between them into a Fokker Triplane and saw it go into a steep spiral dive. As it pulled out it was attacked by 2nd Lieutenant W.E. Staton, also of No. 62 Squadron, who saw it crash near Estaires.

One of the RAF's leading scorers in May 1918 was a Bristol Fighter pilot, Lieutenant A.C. Atkey of No. 22 Squadron, based at Serny. Atkey, who had previously flown Airco DH.4s with No. 18 Squadron and who had been awarded the Military Cross in April, was posted to No. 22 Squadron at the end of the month and teamed up with 2nd Lieutenant C.G. Gass as his observer. They proved to be a formidable team, as an air battle of 7 May showed.

That morning, Atkey and Gass were in company with another Bristol Fighter, patrolling in showery weather, when they ran into a formation of seven

Bristol F.2Bs of No. 141 Squadron, RAF Biggin Hill, late 1918. (via Philip Jarrett)

Albatros and Pfalz Scouts in the vicinity of Henin-Lietard. The two Bristols (the second aircraft was crewed by Lieutenants J.E. Gurdon and A.J.H. Thornton) immediately initiated an attack, but the odds proved to be much heavier than had been anticipated, for the original enemy formation was quickly reinforced by two others which brought the number of enemy aircraft involved to twenty. During a dogfight that lasted thirty minutes, Atkey and Gass shot down two enemy aircraft in flames and saw three more crash, while Gurdon and Thornton disposed of three more, two of them in flames. The remainder did not stay to fight. Of all battles, this one proved conclusively that the Bristol Fighter, in expert hands, could more than hold its own against a far superior enemy force.

On 9 May Atkey and Gass destroyed another enemy scout, and on a second patrol that day they carried out a single-handed attack on a formation of eight enemy machines. Atkey fired fifty rounds into one at close range; flames burst from its fuselage behind the pilot's seat and it went down to crash. Later in the week they drove three more enemy aircraft down out of control (a First World War term for what would be called a 'probable kill' in a later conflict), and on 19 May they shot down a two-seater near Douai. During the next few days they drove four more Germans down out of control, and rounded off the month with a spirited engagement on 25 May. In the words of the official record:

> A patrol of 22 Squadron, led by Captain A.C. Atkey and 2nd Lieutenant C.G. Gass, while escorting DH.4s of No. 18 Squadron, encountered a large formation of about forty EA (enemy aircraft). A fierce fight ensued, in the course of which so many EA were seen spinning and diving away that it was impossible to tell whether they were out of control or not. At the conclusion of the fight four EA were seen crashed on the ground, and in addition, one Albatros Scout, attacked by Lieutenant S.F.H. Thompson and Sgt R.M. Fletcher, was seen to go down in flames.

The Bristol Fighter once again proved its worth during the air fighting of September 1918. When a flight of No. 20 Squadron aircraft was attacked by Fokker D.VIIs on 6 September, one of the enemy aircraft passed directly in front of the Bristol flown by Captain H.P. Lale, who shot it down in flames, and at the same time a second Fokker was destroyed by his observer, 2nd Lieutenant H.L. Edwards. Meanwhile, Lieutenant A.C. Iaccaci – one of the Americans in the RAF – manoeuvred his Bristol so that his observer, Lieutenant A. Mills, could get in a series of effective bursts at more attackers. One broke up in mid-air and another went down to crash, exploding in flames on impact. A fifth D.VII was shot down by Sergeant A. Newland, the observer in another Bristol.

From 9 to 14 September flying was severely curtailed over the northern sectors of the front by gale force winds and heavy rainstorms, but after that the tempo quickly picked up again, and the last two weeks of the month saw heavy fighting. During one of the early patrols of 16 September, Lieutenant W.T. Martin and Sergeant M. Jones, flying a Bristol Fighter of No. 22 Squadron, attacked a formation of Fokker D.VIIs, one of which they shot down. They were

Bristol F.2B C4814 of No. 11 Squadron. (via Philip Jarrett)

then attacked in turn and had their aileron wires shot away; the Bristol side-slipped, almost out of control, through 2,000 feet. Sergeant Jones, realizing the peril of the situation, climbed out on to the bottom wing and stood there, clinging to a strut, until his weight righted the aircraft. Martin was able to land the aircraft in friendly territory, and Jones was later awarded the Distinguished Flying Medal.

Another Bristol Fighter crew, Captain E.S. Coler and 2nd Lieutenant E.J. Corbett of No. 11 Squadron, also had a lucky escape that day. While out on a reconnaissance they were attacked by a large number of Fokker D.VIIs, which shot away their aileron controls and put a bullet through one of their petrol tanks. Coler dived to 1,000 feet over Cambrai, still under attack, and two of the Fokkers overshot. Coler got behind one and shot it down; the other, which had turned quickly away and was not coming in for a stern attack, was shot down by Corbett. The Bristol staggered back across the lines at 150 feet and Coler, realizing that it was rapidly going out of control, used a combination of rudder, elevator and throttle to nurse it towards the ground in a slow sideslip. One set of wings struck first and absorbed most of the impact, the crew climbing from the wreck relatively unharmed.

It must have seemed to the Bristol Fighter crews, in the last fortnight of September, that they were bearing the brunt of the enemy's rediscovered aggression. On the 17th, Lieutenants Frank Jeffreys and F.W. Addison, out on reconnaissance in an aircraft of No. 88 Squadron, were attacked by six Fokker D.VIIs. Addison shot down the first one, and another, which for a few terrifying moments seemed bent on ramming the Bristol, suddenly fell away on its back with its starboard wing in tatters. The remaining Fokkers harried the Bristol

Many Bristol Fighters, like this example pictured at Cranwell, were used in a training role after the war. (Source unknown)

until it crossed the lines, one bullet grazing Addison's hand and putting his gun out of action. The aircraft landed with both its petrol tanks shot through.

On 20 September, Bristol Fighters of No. 20 Squadron, together with SE.5s of No. 84 Squadron, fought a half-hour battle with twenty Fokker D.VIIs over St Quentin. Throughout the battle the RAF aircraft were at a great disadvantage because of a very strong westerly wind, which drove them progressively deeper into enemy territory. The Bristols quickly got the measure of their opponents; Lieutenant F.G. Harlock dived on one and shot it down, while his observer, 2nd Lieutenant A.S. Draisey, disposed of another. A third Fokker was shot down by Lieutenant F.E. Boulton and Sergeant Mitchell, and a fourth by Lieutenant M. McCall and 2nd Lieutenant C. Boothroyd. While the fight was in progress, another Bristol, flown by Captain T.P. Middleton with Lieutenant A. Mills as his observer, arrived and joined in; they engaged four Fokkers, two of which they shot down. The battle was then joined by the SE.5s of No. 84 Squadron led by Captain C.F. Falkenberg, who announced his arrival by shooting down one Fokker and driving another off the tail of a Bristol Fighter. Six more Fokkers were engaged by 2nd Lieutenant W.J.B. Nel, also of No. 84 Squadron, who destroyed one and then escorted a damaged Bristol towards the lines. On the way home the pair were attacked by seven Fokkers and Nel was obliged to take refuge in a cloud; the Bristol Fighter never returned.

Meanwhile, the Bristol Fighter had played a considerable part in securing air superiority over Sinai, between the Suez Canal and Palestine, where General

Bristol F.2B J6789 served with No. 208 Squadron at Aboukir, Egypt, until at least 1926. It is seen here on detachment to Turkey in 1923. (Source unknown)

Sir Edmund Allenby was planning an offensive against the Turks. Allenby wanted the Turks to believe that the main attack would be directed against Gaza, whereas in fact Beersheba was the objective. His preparations were completed by 30 October 1917. On that day a German reconnaissance aircraft was shot down by a Bristol Fighter of No. 111 Squadron, operating from Kantara, and its crew captured. They had in their possession photographs and sketches showing the British positions and the line of the attack. Had they got back to base, this information would have enabled the Turks to meet the assault; as it was, they were taken completely by surprise and Beersheba fell with 2,000 prisoners. The Turks retreated in confusion, harassed by artillery fire and air attack, and Jerusalem was captured on 9 November.

No. 111 Squadron had exchanged its Bristol Fighters for the SE.5A by February 1918, but the F.2B continued to be flown by No. 1 (Australian) Squadron, which carried out much ground attack work during the Turkish retreat from Palestine in September 1918. Every possible line of the Turkish retreat had been carefully studied by air reconnaissance before the start of the latest British offensive, and by the morning of 20 September 1918 General Allenby knew that the Turkish Eighth Army on the right flank, near the sea, was pulling back in a state of confusion. He therefore threw the weight of his assault against it and by nightfall the retreat had become a rout. This disaster made the position of the Turkish Seventh Army completely untenable, all its lines of retreat except one having been cut by British armoured cars and cavalry.

Soon, the Seventh Army had joined the remnants of the Eighth in a panic-stricken rout, columns of men and material jamming the road that ran south of

Nablus to cross the Jordan at Jisr ed Damiye. For a considerable distance this road ran through a deep defile, the Wadi el Far'a, and shortly after dawn on 21 September, the crews of two patrolling Bristol Fighters reported that the Wadi was choked by a dense mass of Turkish troops and transport.

It was now that the RAF squadrons unleashed their full fury on the luckless Turks. For an hour, from 11.00 until noon, the Bristol Fighters of No. 1 (Australian) Squadron, the DH.9s of No. 144 and the SE.5As of Nos 111 and 145 roved back and forth over the wadi, carrying out eighty-eight bombing and eighty-four machine gun attacks in which they dropped nine and a quarter tons of bombs and expended 56,000 rounds of ammunition. The slaughter was frightful. When the last aircraft droned away, the wadi was clogged with dead Turkish troops, dead and dying horses and shattered transport. Some days later, when British forces inspected the scene, they counted 100 guns, fifty-five lorries, four staff cars, 912 wagons and twenty water carts. The dead were numbered in thousands and no one ever bothered to establish an exact total. The utter destruction of the Turkish forces in Sinai had been accomplished in sixty minutes for the loss of two aircraft, brought down by ground fire.

East of the Jordan, the Turkish Fourth Army was under severe pressure from irregular Arab forces under Prince Faisal, aided by Colonel T.E. Lawrence and supported now – in addition to a pair of RE.8s of 'X' Flight, No. 14 Squadron – by two Bristol Fighters and a DH.9. A German air squadron was operating in the area and the Arabs had suffered several bombing and strafing

F.2B F4587 served with No. 16 Squadron and then went to Handley Page as a trials aircraft. Later sold privately and registered G-AFHJ, it was destroyed in a bombing attack in the Second World War. (Source unknown)

Bristol Fighters over Iraq. (Bill Thackeray)

This F.2B, serviced by RAF apprentices, was used by the Halton Relay Racing Team in the 1920s. (Source unknown)

attacks, but the tables were soon turned when the Bristol Fighters shot down two German two-seaters and a Pfalz in a single air engagement. The air support had a profound effect on the Arabs' morale and they were soon co-operating fully with the British forces that were moving against the Fourth Army, which was now being attacked from the air by the squadrons which had blocked the Wadi el Far'a.

On 28 September, the Turkish Fourth Army surrendered and the forces of Allenby and Faisal marched together on Damascus on 1 October. At the end of October, Turkey sought an armistice, bringing the long struggle in the Middle East to an end.

In the immediate post-war years, Bristol Fighters served with No. 6 Squadron at Hinaidi in Mesopotamia, the present-day Iraq. At the time of the 1918 Armistice there were also two resident RAF squadrons, Nos 31 and 114, in India. Both were re-equipped with Bristol Fighters in 1919, and in June that year the RAF's strength in India was boosted by the arrival of three more squadrons, Nos 20 and 48 with Bristol fighters and No. 99 with DH.9As. Another squadron, No. 97, arrived in August with twelve DH.10s. All six squadrons were incorporated into an India Group, with its HQ at Raisina (later New Delhi).

The RAF did not retire its last F.2Bs until 1932. Total production was 5,308 aircraft, and the type also served with ten overseas air forces.

CHAPTER FOUR

The Airco (de Havilland) DH.4 and DH.9A

I f the SE.5 scout was the Spitfire of the First World War, the Airco DH.4 was without doubt the Mosquito. One of the most outstanding combat aircraft produced during the First World War, the DH.4 day bomber was built in large numbers, 1,449 aircraft being built in Britain and 4,846 in the USA, where many were powered by the excellent 400 hp Liberty L-12 engine. The prototype DH.4 flew in August 1916, and pilots who flew the type were unanimous in their praise of its fine handling qualities, wide speed range and a performance which made it almost immune from interception. The first DH.4s arrived in France with No. 55 Squadron in March 1917 and began operations against German targets in April. In addition to its primary bombing role, the aircraft was also used for photo-reconnaissance, long-range fighter sweeps and anti-submarine patrols. The DH.4 was also widely used by the Royal Naval Air Service (RNAS), and on 15 August 1918 an aircraft from RNAS Great Yarmouth, flown by Major Egbert Cadbury, shot down the Zeppelin L.70.

There was no doubt that the Germans were a long way ahead of anyone else, in terms of equipment and practical application, in the strategic bombing field at the beginning of 1918; but the British, once they had begun to develop the concept, were not slow in catching up, and the DH.4 played a leading part in its development. During the early weeks of 1918, the Air Staff in London had been giving considerable thought to the expansion of an RFC bombing force to undertake long-range attacks on industrial targets and communications inside Germany. Such a force already existed in embryo; in September 1917 the 41st Wing RFC, comprising three squadrons under the command of Lieutenant Colonel C.L.N. Newall, had been formed specifically to undertake attacks on German targets in response to the Gotha raids on the British mainland. Of the three units, No. 55 Squadron was equipped with Airco DH.4s for the day bombing role, while Nos 100 (FE.2b) and 16 (Handley Page O/100) Squadrons were reserved for night bombing.

The 41st Wing's first attack was carried out on 17 October 1917 by No. 55 Squadron against the large steelworks at Saarbrücken Burbach. Eleven DH.4s took off from Ochey and eight of them attacked the target, killing four people, injuring four and causing 17,500 marks' worth of damage. On 21 October the same squadron sent out twelve DH.4s to bomb factories and railway yards at Bous, on the Moselle north of Hangendingen and about sixty miles from the squadron's base. One aircraft turned back with engine trouble, but the remainder pressed on and bombed the objective from 15,000 feet. On the way home from the target the DH.4s were attacked by ten Albatros Scouts but managed to beat them off, claiming four enemy aircraft destroyed for the loss of one DH.4, whose pilot, Captain Daniel Owen, succeeded in landing behind the German lines despite being severely wounded in the left eye.

On 1 February the status of the 41st Wing was upgraded and it was re-designated VIII Brigade, Newall being promoted to the rank of brigadier general. At the same time, work began on getting three new night bomber and three day bomber airfields ready for operations. On 18/19 February No. 100 Squadron flew its longest-range mission so far, sending eleven FEs out to attack Trier, a round trip of 200 miles. Some of the aircraft flew so low over the town that the German anti-aircraft gunners were compelled to cease fire for fear of their shells causing more damage to Trier than the raiders' bombs. The next day it was the turn of No. 55 Squadron, which despatched ten DH.4s under Captain J.B. Fox to Mannheim, with Kaiserlautern as an alternative target. The mission got away to a bad start when one of the DH.4s got out of control in a cloud and went into a spin; the pilot recovered at 1,000 feet and returned to base, severely shaken and in an overstressed aircraft. A second aircraft lost contact with the rest of the formation and it also returned. Over no-man's land, the other DH.4s ran into a very strong and unexpected headwind that cut down their ground speed so much that it soon became obvious that they would not reach either of their selected targets. They therefore bombed Pirmasens, between Saarbrücken and Karlsruhe, which was the principal production centre of German army boots. All the attacking aircraft returned safely to Ochey, having encountered no opposition from either anti-aircraft fire or fighters.

One of the fiercest – and most one-sided – air battles involving a DH.4 took place on 1 April 1918, when five Fokker Triplanes attacked a No. 57 Squadron aircraft, flown by Captain F. McD. Turner, during a photographic sortie. Turner's observer, 2nd Lieutenant A. Leach, fired thirty rounds into one of the attackers at 100 yards, sending it down in flames, but things began to look hope-less when the remaining four were joined by ten more Triplanes and Albatros Scouts. Leach fired a complete drum into an Albatros, which was seen to roll over and break up in mid-air; astonishingly, for no friendly fighters appeared to be in the vicinity, the rest broke off the attack and flew away.

The RAF's day bomber squadrons, with the DH.4 units at the forefront, continued to attack the enemy relentlessly throughout the summer months of 1918, often having to fight their way through fierce opposition.

On 10 June, for example, Captain George Fox-Rule and Lieutenant E.H. Tredcroft of No. 49 Squadron, Fourneuil, were carrying out a low-level bombing attack in their DH.4 when they were jumped by five Albatros Scouts which cut off their line of escape. Fox-Rule promptly dived through the middle of the enemy formation and fired a long burst into the leader, which burst into flames and was seen to hit the ground. The DH.4 was then attacked by three more enemy fighters, which came in from astern. Tredcroft opened fire, sending one down out of control and forcing the others to break off. Fox-Rule brought his aircraft safely back, although its tailplane bracing wires had been shot through.

In another incident on the same day, Lieutenant C.W. Peckham and Sergeant J. Grant of No. 57 Squadron were carrying out a daylight bombing attack on an ammunition dump at Bapaume when they were attacked by eight Fokker Triplanes. Grant fired at the first one, which went down in flames. The others then positioned themselves west of the DH.4, forcing Peckham to fly north; one of them broke away and opened fire from beneath the bomber, but Peckham turned swiftly and dived on his attacker, firing eighty rounds into it from his front gun. It, too, went down in flames and the rest broke off the action, enabling the DH.4 to make its escape.

On 17 June, the crew of a No. 205 Squadron DH.4 from Bois de Roche had a very lucky escape when, during an attack on Chaulnes, the pilot – Captain Gamon – was hit in the head by shrapnel from an anti-aircraft burst, and fainted. More shrapnel struck the engine, severing the main fuel pipe, and a fire broke out. The DH.4 went out of control and spiralled down for 1,000 feet; the fire went out and the observer, Major Goble, managed to bring the aircraft under control. He released his bombs and turned towards the lines, the DH.4 gliding over them at 6,000 feet. At this point the pilot regained consciousness and took control again, just in time to take evasive action and shake off a Pfalz Scout which made several determined attacks on the aircraft. He landed safely a few minutes later.

It was a gunner of No. 205 Squadron – Airman 1st Class (later Sergeant) W.J. Middleton – who was awarded the first Distinguished Flying Medal. The Distinguished Flying Cross and Air Force Cross for officers, and the Distinguished Flying Medal and Air Force Medal for other ranks, were introduced on 3 June 1918; thirty-one DFCs had been awarded by the end of the month.

The Airco DH.9 was an initial disappointment, having a performance inferior to that of the DH.4, which it was supposed to replace. (Philip Jarrett)

The apparent class distinction of awarding different medals for equal acts of gallantry was following the precedent set by the Military Cross and Military Medal, and it is doubtful whether anyone thought much about it at the time; but it was to be nearly eighty years before the distinction was eliminated.

June 1918 saw the formation of the Independent Force RAF, commanded by Major-General Sir Hugh Trenchard. It was the first aerial force in the world to be formed for the purpose of conducting a strategic war against the enemy without reference to or subordination by either the Army or Navy, and was the ancestor of RAF Bomber Command. The Independent Force comprised the squadrons of the former VIII Brigade, from which it was formed. Some new units had been added to its strength in May; these were Nos 99 and 104 Squadrons, both fresh out from England and equipped with DH.9s. Derived from the DH.4, the DH.9 had first entered service with No. 103 Squadron at Old Sarum, Wiltshire, in December 1917, and had first gone into action with No. 6 Squadron in France the following March. Crews soon discovered that the DH.9 had a disappointing performance, mainly because its BHP engine and derivatives yielded only 230 hp instead of the anticipated 300 hp. With a full bomb load the DH.9 could barely climb to 15,000 feet, which was 7,000 feet lower than the ceiling of the DH.4, which it was supposed to replace. In addition, fuel consumption above 10,000 feet was appallingly high at fifteen gallons per hour, and engine failures were rife; of twelve DH.9s which set out to bomb the railway triangle at Metz-Sablon on 29 May, for example, six had been forced to turn back with engine trouble.

On 8 August, 1918 – a date later described by Ludendorff in his memoirs as 'the black day of the German Army' – the First French Army under General Debeney and General Rawlinson's Fourth British Army attacked on a fifteen-mile front east of Amiens. By three o'clock in the afternoon the Allied forces had made advances of up to seven miles and taken 7,000 prisoners. During the week preceding the offensive, the Allied air forces made numerous attacks on enemy airfields and lines of communication, suffering considerable losses in the process.

On the opening day of the offensive, many RAF units were assigned to ground attack work. Casualties among the low flying squadrons were particularly heavy, reaching 23 per cent. Many of the losses were sustained in attacks on bridges over the Somme, across which the Germans were retreating in considerable confusion; the tragedy was that not one of the bridges was hit. It was not until the afternoon of 9 August that a hit was at last registered on the bridge at Brie, by a DH.4 of No. 205 Squadron.

On 11 August, the pilot of a Pfalz Scout got a nasty shock when he attacked a No. 205 Sqn DH.4 crewed by Lieutenant W. Grossart and 2nd Lieutenant J.S. Leach, engaged on a medium level bombing raid. As the Pfalz completed its firing run and passed underneath the British aircraft, Leach dropped a 112 lb bomb on it. The missile smashed the Pfalz's wings and the enemy aircraft exploded on the ground.

The DH.4 squadrons were heavily involved in airfield attacks, usually following up low-level strafing by fighter aircraft with a bombing raid. The daylight attacks were attended by success, as these two extracts from the official RAF summary reveal:

August 13th. A raid was carried out by the 17th American Squadron on Varssenaere Aerodrome, in conjunction with squadrons of the 5th Group. After the first two squadrons had dropped their bombs from a low height, machines of the 17th American Squadron dived to within 200 feet of the ground and released their bombs, then proceeded to shoot at hangars and huts on the aerodrome, and a chateau on the NE corner of the aerodrome was also attacked with machine gun fire. The following damage was observed to be caused by this combined operation: a dump of petrol and oil was set on fire, which appeared to set fire to an ammunition dump; six Fokker biplanes were set on fire on the ground, and two destroyed by direct hits from bombs; one large Gotha hangar was set on fire and another one half demolished; a living hut was set on fire and several hangars were seen to be smouldering as a result of phosphorus bombs having fallen on them. In spite of most of the machines taking part being hit at one time or another, all returned safely, favourable ground targets being attacked on the way home. No. 211 Squadron (DH.4s) bombed the aerodrome after the low flying attack was over, and demolished the chateau previously referred to.

August 16th. A raid was carried out on Haubourdin Aerodrome by Nos 88 and 92 Squadrons RAF and Nos 2 and 4 Squadrons AFC. Sixty-five machines took part in all, dropping 136 25 lb and six 40 lb bombs and firing a large number of rounds from a height varying from 400 to 500 feet. Three large hangars containing machines were completely burnt, and two machines standing outside were set on fire. Several fires were also started in huts, and what is believed to be the officers' mess was blown up and burnt. Several other hangars, in addition to those burnt, received direct hits. The station at Haubourdin was also attacked with machine gun fire from a low height, causing confusion among the troops. Two staff cars were fired at, one of which upset in a ditch and another ran up a steep bank; the occupants were not observed to leave. A train was also shot at, which stopped. Considerable casualties were caused among the personnel at the aerodrome, who were seen rushing to take refuge in a hospital. All our machines returned.

On this day, No. 3 Squadron AFC photographed the whole of the Australian Corps' front, while No. 25 Squadron RAF (DH.4s) flew similar sorties in the adjoining sector. Almost the whole of this operation was carried out up to twenty miles behind the enemy lines and the observation aircraft were subjected to heavy attacks, but all returned safely.

The reason for all the reconnaissance activity became apparent when, on 22 August, the Allies renewed their offensive on the Somme. The first British attack, on a six-mile front between the Somme and the Ancre, was thwarted by a

Post-war, many DH.4s were converted to civilian use, like this one which ended up as a mail carrier in the USA. (American Airlines)

strong German counter-attack, but the next day the main attack in the battle for Bapaume began with an advance by the British Third and Fourth Armies, supported by about 100 tanks. The British advanced some two miles, and on the 24 August took the much-contested Thiepval Ridge and reached the outskirts of Bapaume. The principal objective was to take the high ground, and in this the British were successful. By 26 August their attack was spreading northwards along both banks of the River Scarpe, and twenty-four hours later the Anglo-French-American forces were advancing along the whole front. By the end of the month the Somme line had been decisively turned, twenty-three British divisions beating thirty-five German, taking 34,000 prisoners and capturing 270 guns.

One of the most gallant fights during this period occurred on 29 August, when Lieutenant J.M. Brown and 2nd Lieutenant H. Lawrence, returning from a bombing raid in their No. 98 Squadron DH.9, fell behind the rest of the formation through engine trouble and were attacked by twenty Fokker D.VIIs. Almost at once their elevator controls were shot away, but Brown managed to retain control and dived towards the west, under constant attack. Lawrence, although badly wounded, continued fighting and shot down a Fokker in flames, sending another down out of control soon afterwards. By this time all the DH.9's petrol tanks were shot through, the engine hit in several places, and most of the instruments smashed. Lawrence, taking the brunt of the enemy fire in the rear cockpit, now had ten bullets in him; despite severe pain and loss of blood he tried to keep on firing, but his guns jammed. Brown managed to evade the attacking aircraft by diving through a cloud and crash-landed near Mory. He later received the DFC, but there is no record of Lawrence receiving any award, nor indeed of what became of him; the inference is that he died of his very severe wounds.

The troubles experienced by the DH.9 squadrons persisted. At 7.30 am on 22 August, thirteen DH.9s of No. 104 Squadron set out from Azelot in two formations of six and seven aircraft to bomb the Badische Anilin factory at Mannheim (a key target, as it produced a high proportion of Germany's explosives). One aircraft in the rear flight turned back over the lines with engine trouble, and soon afterwards another was shot down by heavy anti-aircraft fire. Then the fire died away as eight enemy scouts appeared; they remained on the flanks of the formation, waiting to pick off stragglers and contenting themselves with exchanging a few shots at long range. Their chance came when the DH.9 flown by Lieutenant J. Valentine suffered engine failure; they pounced on him as he broke formation and glided down, but he survived intense attacks to make a forced landing behind the enemy lines. Over the Vosges mountains a third DH.9, piloted by Captain McKay, 'B' Flight commander, also had engine failure and had to come down, the crew being taken prisoner.

The remaining DH.9s approached Mannheim at 11,500 feet. As they started their bombing run they were attacked by fifteen Fokker and Pfalz Scouts, SSW D.IIIs and Halberstadt two-seaters. In the ensuing battle the RAF forma-

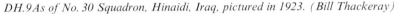

DH.9As of No. 30 Squadron, Hinaidi, Iraq, pictured in 1923. (Bill Thackeray)

tion was broken up and forced down to 6,000 feet, where two of the scattered bombers were quickly shot down. The five surviving aircraft managed to fight their way back to base, but it had been a black day for the squadron, which had lost seven out of twelve DH.9s and most of its best aircrew.

Yet the DH.9 was capable of giving an excellent account of itself. On 23 August, an aircraft of No. 49 Squadron, returning from a bombing raid and crewed by Lieutenant A.R. Spurling and Sergeant F.W. Bell, became separated from the rest of the formation in cloud. After flying west for some time, Spurling saw what he took to be a friendly airfield and prepared to land, but as he lost height he was suddenly attacked by a Fokker D.VII. Spurling then saw a formation of thirty more Fokkers directly below him and, with little other option, continued his dive through the middle of them, firing as he went. One of the Fokkers was hit and burst into flames; two more, taking violent evasive action, went into a spin and one of them was seen to crash. The DH.9 was then harried from astern by four Fokkers, one of which was shot down in flames by Sergeant Bell; a few moments later Bell also accounted for another which attempted a beam attack. The DH.9 was pursued by three more D.VIIs as it climbed hard towards the lines, but they did not attack. An enemy two-seater tried to intercept it as it headed for home, but a few well-aimed bursts from Bell drove it away. The fact that Spurling was awarded the DFC and Bell the DFM came as no surprise to their squadron colleagues.

Once the DH.9 was re-engined with the Packard Liberty motor it became an entirely different aircraft. RAF Squadrons in France began rearming with the new variant – designated DH.9A – in August 1918, and the type played an important part in the Allied bombing offensive until the end of the war. For many years afterwards, the DH.9A played a vital role in policing the outposts of the British Empire.

One that didn't work out – a DH.9A in a bad way after a forced landing. (Bill Thackeray)

CHAPTER FIVE

The Bristol Bulldog

Almost before the echoes of the First World War had died away, powerful lobbies in the Admiralty and the War Office began plotting the demise of the Royal Air Force as an independent organisation and in sub-ordinating British air power to the Army and Navy. That they failed to do so was mainly due to the determination of the Chief of the Air Staff, Sir Hugh Trenchard. By 1921 the strength of the RAF was at a very low ebb, with only twenty-four squadrons of all types at home and abroad (including a solitary fighter squadron in the United Kingdom), but in April 1922 a defence sub-committee recommended the force's expansion to 52 Squadrons, totalling some 500 aircraft – later increased to 600 – for home defence. The re-equipment pro-gramme had to start from scratch, and to fulfil the air defence role it was decided to standardise on the Sopwith Snipe, the fighter designed during the closing months of the First World War to replace the Camel.

The first squadron to equip fully with Snipes was No. 29, which re-formed at Duxford on 1 April 1923. By the end of the year the fighter strength available for the air defence of Great Britain stood at eleven squadrons, equipped pre-dominantly with Snipes. It was still a long way from the planned total of fifty-two squadrons. It was also clear that the Snipe, although invaluable as an interim aircraft, was quickly approaching obsolescence, and steps were taken to rearm the fighter squadrons with post-war designs at an early date. The first such design was the Gloster Grebe, a product of the Gloucestershire Aircraft Company (which changed its name to Gloster in 1926), whose chief designer, H.P. Folland, had previously worked for the Nieuport and General Aircraft Company, which had been set up in Britain late in 1916 to licence-build the fighter designs of the French company. In 1917 the British-based firm began to design its own fighters, the first of which was the Nighthawk. Although it never went into service with the RAF, the Nighthawk deserves its place in history as the first British fighter to be powered by a stationary radial engine instead of the more common rotary type. The Grebe prototype was originally ordered as a Nighthawk; it made its first public appearance at the RAF Air Pageant, Hendon, in June 1923 and entered RAF service with No. 111 Squadron in October that year, subsequently equipping five more RAF fighter squadrons. One of them, No. 25 Squadron, subsequently became famous for its spectacular aerobatic displays in the mid-1920s. Despite early problems with wing flutter, the Grebe was a highly manoeuvrable and robust little aircraft, and was the first British machine to survive a terminal velocity dive, reaching 240 mph. Grebes also took part in some interesting experiments, one of which involved the release of a pair of aircraft from beneath the airship R.33 in October 1926.

Although the Grebe replaced the Sopwith Snipe in some first-line RAF squadrons, the true successor to the Snipe was the Hawker Woodcock, the H.G. Hawker Engineering Company having re-established Sopwith's former aviation enterprises. The Hawker Company's early activities involved refurbishing Snipes and Camels for sale overseas. The first of its own designs, the Duiker parasol monoplane, was unsuccessful, but the Woodcock single-seat fighter was accepted after lengthy trials and was delivered to No. 3 Squadron in May 1925, becoming the first new British fighter to enter production after the end of the First World War. The Woodcock only equipped one other RAF squadron, No. 17, but a version of it known as the Danecock (or Dankok) served with the Danish Army and Naval Air Services until 1937. It was at this juncture that the Hawker design office accepted the services of Sydney Camm, who had previously worked for Martinsyde Aircraft Ltd. Later, Camm was to be responsible for one of the most famous fighters of all time, the Hawker Hurricane.

In common with other aircraft manufacturers of the 1920s, Hawker produced a series of aircraft prototypes that covered the whole spectrum of military and naval requirements at that time. Among them were the Hornbill fighter, which had mixed wood and metal construction and which reached a speed of 200 mph in 1926 with a 690 hp Rolls-Royce Condor engine, the Hawker Hawfinch, which set trends for several other biplane fighter designs; and the Heron, the first fighter to use the patent all-metal construction evolved by Sydney Camm and works director Fred Sigrist. From the Gloster stable, the Grebe was followed by the Gamecock, which first flew in February 1925 and equipped five RAF fighter squadrons, beginning with No. 23 Squadron in May 1925. The Gamecock's service life was relatively short-lived. This was partly because of an abnormally high accident rate; of ninety Gamecock Is that were built, twenty-two were lost in spinning or landing accidents.

The Snipe, Grebe, Woodcock and Gamecock were for the most part replaced in service by the Armstrong Whitworth Siskin IIIA. The first Siskin IIIs, in fact, were delivered to No. 41 Squadron at Northolt in May 1924, and a month later to No. 111 Squadron at Duxford. These were the only two units to use the early mark, but the Siskin IIIA, with a more powerful engine and a number of aerodynamic refinements, began to replace the Snipes of No. 1 Squadron and the Grebes of No. 56 from mid-1927. The type subsequently equipped nine RAF fighter squadrons, all in the United Kingdom.

The expansion of the Royal Air Force towards the planned target of fifty-two squadrons was dictated, apart from economic considerations, by the activities of the French. In the late 1920s, an emasculated Germany was not regarded as a serious threat, but the idea of France, a mere twenty-one miles away across the English Channel, possessing a larger and more effective air force than Britain's was unthinkable. The speed of formation of new RAF squadrons was therefore dictated by the need to match the French in air matters, and when the expansion of the French Air Force slowed down, so did that of the R.A.F. The original target date for the 52-squadron force was 1930, but by 1927 this had been put back to 1936, and in 1929 it was again postponed to 1938.

In September 1926 the Air Ministry issued a requirement for a new single-seat day and night fighter to be armed with two machine guns and powered by a radial air-cooled engine. The tender submitted by the Bristol Aeroplane Company was successful, and its prototype fighter, designated Bulldog I, flew for the first time on 17 May 1927. The new fighter was designed for the Mercury II engine, but as this powerplant was not immediately available a supercharged Jupiter VII was substituted, and it was with this engine that the prototype made its first flight. A few weeks later the aircraft was transferred to the Aeroplane and Armament Experimental Establishment at Martlesham Heath in Suffolk, where it proved superior to all other contemporary types tested there and received one of the most satisfactory test reports ever issued.

One modification recommended by the RAF was an increase in fin area, but as this was found to reduce the fighter's agility a satisfactory compromise was reached by retaining the original tail and slightly lengthening the fuselage. With these modifications the type re-emerged as the Bulldog Mk.II. The successful outcome of prototype trials early in 1928 led to an initial order for twenty-five machines in the following September to equip Nos 3 and 17 Squadrons. First deliveries were made in May 1929 to No. 3 Squadron at Upavon in Wiltshire, No. 17 Squadron receiving its full complement of machines a few months later.

When the Bulldog first entered service with the Royal Air Force, the latter's air and ground crews were without doubt the most professional and best trained in the world. Fighter pilots completed some 150 hours' flying training before they were awarded their wings and posted to an operational squadron, where – weather permitting – they would fly at least once a day, or more usually two or three times, carrying out a great deal of formation practice, cross-country flying, battle climbs and so on. After completing 200 hours' flying a fighter pilot would make his first night flights, which involved two or three circuits and landings. Night flying became more frequent after that, but not routine, and was accompanied by radiotelephony (R/T) practice. R/T equipment was progressively being fitted to all RAF fighter aircraft assigned to the Air Defence of Great Britain, and high priority was given to developing operational tactics with its aid.

Eight Bulldog IIs with supercharged engines were shipped to Australia in January 1930 to equip a fighter flight of the Royal Australian Air Force (RAAF), but the Bulldog was already attracting the attention of foreign governments. In September 1929, five Bulldogs with Jupiter VI engines licence-built by Gnôme-Rhône and Oerlikon gun gear were supplied to Latvia, and in the following month the Air Ministry ordered a further twenty-five machines for the RAF, the last four examples of which were Mk.IIAs with a slightly strengthened structure, wider undercarriage and larger tyres, and a redesigned oil system. Two Bulldog Mk.IIAs were shipped to the USA for trials with the US Navy, one example was assembled by Nakajima for comparison with their own Type 91 experimental fighter, another was imported by Mitsui Bussan and delivered to the Imperial Japanese Navy, and two Jupiter VIIF-powered were supplied to the Royal Siamese Air Force.

The Bulldog fighter squadrons vied with one another over matters of smartness. This aircraft of No. 17 Squadron displays its squadron markings on the upper wing. K1085 was destroyed in a mid-air collision with two others (J9587 and K1083) at Arundel Park on 30 September 1930. (RAF)

Early in 1930, four Jupiter VIIF-powered Bulldogs were ordered for evaluation by the Royal Swedish Air Force, and this was followed by a repeat order from Latvia for a further seven aircraft. At the same time, Estonia ordered twelve, and in October 1930 the Air Ministry decided to equip All RAF fighter squadrons with the Bulldog. The type eventually equipped ten RAF home defence squadrons, the main version being the Mk.IIA. With a top speed of 180 mph, the Bulldog was much faster than the fighters it replaced. By November 1934, when production was completed, 293 Bulldog IIs and IIAs had been delivered to the RAF, sixty of these being supplied as two-seaters.

In March 1934 the Finnish Air Force acquired seventeen Bulldog Mk.VI aircraft, and Sweden donated two Mk.IIs. Although obsolete by 1939, the Bristol Bulldog performed creditably in action with the Finnish Air Force against far superior Russian equipment during the so-called 'Winter War' of 1939–40. The first contact between Finnish Bulldogs and Russian aircraft occurred in the morning of 1 December, when two Bulldogs of LLv 26 were attacked by six Polikarpov I-16 fighters. In the ensuing melee the two Bulldogs became separated, leaving one pilot, Flight Sergeant Toivo Uuttu, to face the enemy alone. He scored some hits on an I-16, which subsequently crashed to become the first aerial victim of the Winter War, but Uuttu himself was also forced to make crash-landing, in which he was injured. Before the end of the month more Russian aircraft – two SB-2 bombers and an I-16 – were also shot down by the Bulldog pilots, and another SB-2 was destroyed in January, but

A Bristol Mercury-powered Bulldog IIA of the Royal Swedish Air Force. (Lars E. Lundin)

The Bulldog's contemporary was the Hawker Fury, seen here making a dummy attack on a Handley Page Heyford bomber. (RAF)

further combats during this brief conflict were inconclusive. One Bulldog was lost in action.

At least seven Bristol Bulldogs were also in service with the Spanish Republican Air Arm at the outbreak of the civil war in 1936, these being based at Lamiaco aerodrome. The fate of these machines is unknown.

In RAF service, the Bulldog was replaced by the Gloster Gauntlet from 1934, but the last examples were not withdrawn until 1937. The Bulldog's contemporary was the Hawker Fury, the epitome of British fighter biplane design and one of the most beautiful aircraft ever built. The first of 118 Fury Mk.Is entered service with No. 43 Squadron at Tangmere in May 1931, and the type also served with Nos 1 and 25 Squadrons. Further development of a version known as the High Speed Fury led to a production order for twenty-three Fury Mk.IIs, followed by another seventy-five, and the first of these entered service with No. 25 Squadron in December 1936, also serving with four more squadrons of what was, by then, RAF Fighter Command. Other fighter units in the early 1930s were equipped with the Hawker Demon, a fighter variant of the Hart light bomber; 244 Demons were built for the RAF in the United Kingdom, serving with six Regular and five Auxiliary Air Force squadrons.

CHAPTER SIX

The Short C Class Flying Boats and Sunderland

I n the mid-1930s, Imperial Airways mail flights to the Far East were under-taken in fierce competition with KLM, and in 1935, when the Dutch airline introduced fast Douglas DC-2s to replace its Fokkers, there was no doubt that the British were losing the battle. Many of the airfields used by Imperial Airways' landplanes on the Middle East-Singapore route were regularly un-serviceable because of heavy rain, and so the decision was made to re-equip Imperial Airways with flying boats to serve its long-range sectors.

Imperial Airways' aspirations centred on the four-engine 'C' Class flying boat, which was designed in 1935 by Short Brothers, the Rochester-based flying boat specialists, to meet the requirements of the Empire Air Mail Service. With Britain lagging behind the United States in flying boat development there was no time to be wasted, so Imperial Airways took a gamble and ordered twenty-eight aircraft straight off the drawing board at a total cost of £1.75 million. As things turned out, the gamble was to be justified.

The C-Class boats had a two-deck hull, the upper deck designed to house 3,000 lb of mail and the lower to accommodate twenty-four daytime passengers or nineteen 'sleepers'. The version intended for transatlantic operation, specifi-cally the service to Bermuda, was the S.30, the prototype of which, G-ADHL *Canopus*, flew for the first time on 4 July 1936. Nine S.30s were eventually built. The aircraft was powered by four 890 hp Bristol Perseus XIIC engines, giving it a maximum speed of 200 mph.

The other C Class variant, the S.23, although it was to prove very successful on the England–Australia mail service, did not have sufficient range for trans-atlantic operations, but in December 1936 one example of this type, G-ADUU *Cavalier*, was fitted with extra fuel tanks and then shipped to Bermuda, where, in May 1937, it began proving flights to New York alongside Pan American's Sikorsky S-42 Bermuda Clipper. Scheduled services began on 16 June, and by the end of November 405 passengers had been carried on the six-hour journey at a single fare of £20. Cavalier remained in service on the Bermuda–New York route until 21 January 1939, when severe engine icing forced it down in a heavy sea. The impact tore a hole in the hull and the aircraft sank in minutes, ten survivors being picked up by a tanker.

Another S.23, G-ADHM *Caledonia*, was used to survey the first leg of the proposed transatlantic route, flying from Hythe to the Azores via Lisbon on 5 July 1937. The next day she was joined on the same route by G-ADUV

Cambria and these two aircraft made several survey flights during August and September.

The first of the Short Empire boats, as the C Class aircraft were now generally known, designed for the Bermuda run was G-AFCT *Champion*, which flew for the first time on 28 September 1938. It was followed by four more, G-AFCU *Cabot*, G-AFCV *Caribou*, G-AFCW *Connemara* and G-AFCX *Clyde*. These aircraft were equipped with flight refuelling gear – trials having taken place earlier in the year, when *Cambria* was successfully refuelled in flight by an Armstrong Whitworth AW.23 – and in 1939 three Handley Page Harrow bombers were equipped as tankers, two being positioned at Hattie's Camp (later Gander) in Newfoundland and the third in Ireland at Rineanna, which was later to become Shannon Airport. The Short S.30s *Cabot* and *Caribou* both underwent refuelling trials in conjunction with these aircraft in May and July, as a preliminary to starting a scheduled transatlantic service from Southampton to New York via Foynes, Botwood and Montreal.

Meanwhile, the preceding months had witnessed considerable technological developments in the transatlantic commercial race. The boldest of these was British – the Short-Mayo composite aircraft. This was the brainchild of Major R.H. Mayo, Technical Adviser to Imperial Airways, and was a revolutionary attempt to solve the problem of increasing range and payload without sacrificing performance by mounting one aircraft pick-a-back on top of another, the lower aircraft carrying most of the fuel and providing the power for take-off and climb. Both components were designed and built by Short brothers under the designations S.20 and S.21, the latter – G-ADHK *Maia* – being similar in design to the Short C Class flying boat, although with modifications that included a broader hull beam and increased wing and vertical tail areas.

The second component, a much smaller four-engine twin-float seaplane, D-ADHJ *Mercury*, was attached to the larger aircraft by a trapeze-like structure mounted above the latter's wing centre section. The two aircraft were test-flown separately, *Maia* flying on 27 July 1937 and *Mercury* on 5 September, and the two flew as a composite on 20 January 1938. The first commercial flight was made on 21 July that year, *Mercury* separating from *Maia* over Foynes on the Shannon and heading for Montreal with a payload of 600 lb of newspapers, press photographs and newsreels. The flight took twenty hours and twenty minutes, the aircraft covering a distance of 2,930 miles. The pilot was Captain D.C.T. Bennett, who was later to command RAF Bomber Command's Pathfinder Force, and his radio operator (and Air Ministry observer) was A.J. Coster. The pilot of *Maia* was Captain A.S. Wilcockson, one of Imperial Airways' senior officers, who had also commanded the C Class boat *Caledonia* during its first Atlantic flights in July the previous year.

On 6 October 1938, *Maia* launched *Mercury* on a record-breaking non-stop flight to South Africa. With Don Bennett once again at the controls and Ian Harvey as his radio operator, the aircraft flew a straight-line distance of 5,997.5 miles in just over forty-two hours, landing on the Orange River near the Alexander Bay diamond mine settlement. It flew on to Cape Town after refuelling. Further non-stop flights, to Alexandria from Southampton carrying

Maia *and* Mercury *on Loch Foyle, Northern Ireland. (Short Brothers)*

Maia *and* Mercury *joined together.* Maia *was similar to the Short Class C Empire flying boat. (Short Brothers)*

Christmas mail, were made in December 1938, and the success of operations so far encouraged Imperial Airways to plan a regular transatlantic service in the summer of 1939. This however was frustrated by the approach of war and the preoccupation with flight refuelling trials, and the Short-Mayo Composite never flew commercially again. *Maia* was used for a time to carry passengers between Southampton and Foynes and was taken over by the British Overseas Airways Corporation, which replaced the older companies in April 1940; it was destroyed by German bombs in Poole Harbour, Dorset, on the night of 11 May, 1941. *Mercury* was allocated to No. 320 (Netherlands) Squadron of RAF Coastal Command in June 1940 and used as a trainer until it was withdrawn from service and broken up in August 1941, a sad fate for such a pioneering aircraft.

The first eastbound proving flight by an Empire Boat was made on 22 October 1936, when *Canopus* flew from Rochester to Alexandria via Caudebec, Bordeaux, Marseille and Rome. The return trip was started on the 30th, the aircraft flying via Athens, Mirabella and Brindisi. On 13 December, G-ADHM *Caledonia* set out for India with five and a half tons of Christmas mail on board, carrying a similar load on the return trip. On the homeward flight, the pilot, Captain Cumming, left Alexandria on 21 December and flew the 1,700 miles to Marseille non-stop in eleven and one-quarter hours. On the following day, he flew direct across France to land at Southampton after four and a half hours.

Regular flights from Marseille to Alexandria via Rome were started on 4 January 1937, using G-ADUW *Castor*, and on 12 January a through service was started between Alexandria and Southampton with G-ADUT *Centaurus*. G-ADUX *Cassiopeia* also joined the service on 26 January, and on 18 February G-ADHM *Caledonia* flew the whole 2,200-mile distance from Southampton to Alexandria non-stop in thirteen hours.

By the end of 1937 twenty-two Empire Boats were in service with Imperial Airways, and two more, VH-ABA *Carpentaria* and VH-ABB *Coolangatta* – were also supplied to Qantas for use on the Singapore–Brisbane sector. Early in the following year the Australians received a third aircraft, VH-ABC *Coogee*, which was transferred from the British register.

Although the Empire Boats brought a new dimension of speed and efficiency to the Far Eastern route, there were three unfortunate casualties in 1937, the first on 24 March when G-ADVA *Capricornus* (Captain Paterson) crashed in a snow-storm near Lyon. The aircraft was carrying the first through mail to Australia, but turned back when the pilot encountered bad weather over the Alps. Then, on 1 October, G-ADVC *Courtier* flew into the sea as the result of a misjudged landing at Phaleron Bay, Athens, three passengers being drowned when the hull split open; and finally, on 5 December, G-ADUZ *Cygnus* porpoised out of control at Brindisi when the pilot tried to take off with full flap and sank, drowning two passengers and injuring seven. The latter included Air Marshal Sir John Salmond, who had done much to pioneer long-range mail routes in the early 1920s and who was now a director of Imperial Airways.

Inevitably, the flying boats suffered less serious mishaps too. On 23 June 1937, for example, one of *Canopus*'s engines failed and the captain made an emergency landing in the Mediterranean. The aircraft taxied into Mirabella, the faulty engine was removed, the open engine nacelle was blanked off and the flying boat flew back to England on three engines.

In September 1937, G-AETX *Ceres* made a survey flight over a new route from Alexandria to Karachi, the aircraft flying via the Dead Sea, Habbaniyah and Sharjah, and a regular service was started the following month by G-AEUA *Calypso*. On this occasion, mail was flown from Southampton to Alexandria by G-AETY *Clio*, the journey being continued by *Calypso*, but on the return service G-AEUB *Camilla* made the entire through trip from Karachi to Southampton.

On 15 November 1937, G-AEUD *Cordelia* left Karachi to make a survey flight to Singapore, where she arrived six days later, and on 3 December G-ADUT *Centaurus* left Hythe to carry out a survey flight all the way through to New Zealand, completing the last leg from Sydney to Auckland on 27 December. This sector of the route was to be operated by Tasman Empire Airways Ltd, formed jointly by the British, Australian and New Zealand Governments, and three Empire Boats were allocated for this purpose. Originally ordered by Qantas as G-AFCY *Captain Cook*, G-AFCZ *Canterbury* and G-AFDA *Cumberland*, they were renamed *Aotearoa*, *Australia* and *Awarua* before delivery to New Zealand. In fact this did not take place until 1940, so in the meantime Imperial Airways retained the three aircraft for operations on the Southampton–Karachi route.

Meanwhile, in 1938, delivery of six Empire Boats to Qantas had been completed, and these were used on the Singapore–Darwin sector. One of them, VH-ABE *Coorong*, came to grief on 12 December, when she was driven ashore in a gale at Darwin. The engines and mail were salvaged, and the boat was later repaired. There had been a more serious casualty three weeks earlier, on 27 November, when G-AETW *Calpurnia* ran into an unexpected sandstorm and crashed in Lake Habbaniyah, killing two crew members and two passengers. The casualty figures might have been higher had it not been for the RAF, who mounted a rapid rescue operation and salvaged the Christmas mail carried by the aircraft.

On the Cairo–Cape Town route, the Imperial Airways workload was shared between Handley page HP.42s and Armstrong Whitworth Atalantas until 1937, when the first Empire Boats joined the service. In the summer of 1937, the Empire Boats started an air mail service to Durban, and at the same time one of them – G-ADUV *Cambria*, commanded by Captain Egglesfield – made a 20,000-mile survey of the African routes, the task being completed on 4 June.

Generally, there were fewer accidents on the African mail run than on the India–Australia route, although on 14 March 1939 *Corsair* was driven off track by strong winds and ran out of fuel, compelling her captain to make a forced landing on the River Dangu in the Belgian Congo, 150 miles south-west of Juba. There were no injuries and the mail was salvaged, but the hull was holed and the aircraft sank in shallow water. A repair crew of Imperial Airways and Short Brothers engineers flew to Juba, and after travelling as far as they could by road they literally hacked their way through the jungle to reach the stranded flying boat. Enlisting the help of local tribesmen, they managed to beach the aircraft and completed their repair work by the end of June, labouring in sweltering conditions and tormented constantly by mosquitoes and other savage insects.

By this time, the rainy season was at its height and the river was in spate. Nevertheless the pilot, Captain Kelly Rogers, decided to attempt a take-off, even though there was a dangerous bend in the river some way ahead. This proved to be his undoing, because as he swerved the aircraft to negotiate the bend it lost speed and he could not get it airborne in a safe distance. As he turned to taxi back, *Corsair* struck a submerged rock, which tore another hole in the hull, and she immediately flooded.

This time, the repair crew had to remove the engines and lash petrol drums to the flying boat to raise her, and repair work had to begin all over again. While it was in progress, teams of locally-recruited natives felled timber and built a dam to create an artificial lake. The work took months, and was completed just in time for the start of the new rains. At last, on 6 January 1940, Captain Rogers took off along a waterway fifty yards wide, only twelve yards more than *Corsair*'s wing span, and refuelled at Juba before flying on to Alexandria, where the aircraft was completely overhauled. The saga had lasted ten months from start to finish, and was commemorated in an unusual way. Today, by the banks of the River Dangu, there stands a little village known as Corsairville. The lake built by the engineers and the Africans is still there, and the village is served by the road they carved through the jungle to the site.

The Empire Boats had an eventful wartime career, flying much of the time on sectors of BOAC's 'Horseshoe Route' via East Africa and India to Australia. Two S.30s and two S.23Ms (the 'M' denoting Military) served with No. 119 Squadron RAF for a few months in 1941, operating from Pembroke Dock, and three were lost during the war. Thirteen boats survived, being refitted with Pegasus 22 engines, and continued to serve for a short period after the war, but all had been withdrawn by the end of 1947.

Three examples were also built of the larger S.26 'G' Class (G-AFCL *Golden Hind*, G-AFCJ *Golden Fleece* and G-AFCK *Golden Horn*. These aircraft were powered by four 1,380 hp Bristol Hercules VI engines and were ordered for non-stop services across the Atlantic, but instead they were impressed for RAF service as armed VIP transports. Two were lost during the war, but *Golden Hind* survived until 1954, when it was wrecked in harbour at Harty Ferry by a storm.

The design of the Short Sunderland, which eventually was to become one of the RAF's longest-serving operational aircraft, was based on that of the Short C Class. The maiden flight of the prototype took place on 16 October 1937, powered by four 950 hp Bristol Pegasus X radial engines. The first production Sunderland Mk.Is, powered by Pegasus XXII engines and with a revised nose and tail armament, were delivered to No. 230 Squadron in Singapore early in June 1938. The Sunderland Mk.II was fitted with Pegasus XVIII engines with two-stage superchargers, a twin-gun dorsal turret, an improved rear turret and ASV Mk.II radar. Production of the Sunderland Mk.II reached fifty-five aircraft, these equipping Nos 119, 201, 202, 204, 228 and 230 Squadrons. The fitting of extra equipment meant that the Mk.II had a much higher operating weight than the Mk.I, and a new planing hull bottom was designed, with a less pronounced forward step that gave better unstick characteristics. The hull was tested on a Mk.II, which in effect became the prototype of the next variant, the Mk.III, which was to be the major production model of the Sunderland.

The first Short-built Sunderland Mk.III flew on 15 December 1941 and the parent company eventually produced 286 Mk.IIIs, a further 170 being built by Blackburn Aircraft (The latter company had already built fifteen Mk.Is and five Mk.IIs). One of the principal exponents of the Sunderland as an antisubmarine weapon was No. 10 Squadron RAAF, which was based in Britain and which first experimented with a group of four 7.7 mm (0.303 inch) machine guns mounted on either side of the aircraft's bow, bringing the total armament to ten guns. The revised forward-firing armament meant that the Sunderland could lay down an effective fire on a surfaced U-boat as the aircraft made its run-in, and with ten guns the flying boat presented a dangerous target to enemy fighters, which learned to be wary of it at an early stage of the war. The Germans nick-named the Sunderland *Stachelschwein* (porcupine).

The Sunderland III equipped eleven RAF squadrons (including one Polish and one Free French), and was followed by the Sunderland IV, a larger and

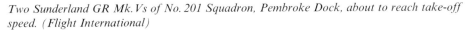

Two Sunderland GR Mk.Vs of No. 201 Squadron, Pembroke Dock, about to reach take-off speed. (Flight International)

Sunderland GR Mk. V of No. 5 (Maritime Reconnaissance) Squadron, Royal New Zealand Air Force, raises a cloud of spray near its base at Hobsonville. (RNZAF)

heavier development with 1,700 hp Bristol Hercules engines, eight 12.7 mm (0.50 inch) machine guns and two 20 mm cannon. In fact, only two prototypes and eight production aircraft were built and given the name Seaford, but after evaluation by Coastal and Transport Commands the Sunderland IV/Seaford was abandoned and the aircraft later converted for commercial use as the Short Solent. The last operational Sunderland, therefore, was the Mk.V, 100 of which were built by Shorts and fifty by Blackburn. The MK.V, powered by four 1,200 hp Pratt & Whitney R-1830-90 Twin Wasps and carrying the ASV Mk.VIc radar, made its appearance late in 1943 and continued to serve for many years after the Second World War, the last RAF Sunderland Vs retiring from No. 205 Squadron at Changi, Singapore, in 1959. Nineteen Sunderland Mk.Vs were exported to France's Aéronavale, retiring in 1960, and sixteen to the RNZAF, where they served until 1966. At the end of the Second World War Sunderlands equipped no fewer than twenty-eight RAF squadrons at home and overseas.

CHAPTER SEVEN

The Vickers Wellington

The Vickers Wellington was designed by Barnes Wallis, who was later to conceive the mines that destroyed the Ruhr Dams, to Specification B.9/32. Like its predecessor, the Vickers Wellesley, the aircraft featured geodetic construction, a system that enabled the Wellington to absorb a tremendous amount of battle damage, and still survive. In December 1933 Vickers was awarded a contract for the construction of a single prototype under the designation Type 271, this aircraft (K4049) flying on 15 June 1936. This aircraft was lost on 19 April 1937 when it broke up during an involuntary high-speed dive, the cause being determined as elevator imbalance. As a result, the production prototype Wellington Mk.I and subsequent aircraft were fitted with a revised fin, rudder and elevator adapted from a parallel project, the Vickers B.1/35, which would enter service later as the Warwick. The fuselage also underwent considerable modification, so that production Wellingtons, ordered to Specification 29/36, bore little resemblance to the ill-fated prototype. The first Mk.I, L4212, flew on 23 December 1937, powered by two Pegasus XX engines, and the first Bomber Command squadron to rearm, No. 9 Squadron, began receiving its aircraft in December 1938.

The most numerous early model of the Wellington was the Mk.IC, which had Pegasus XVIII engines and self-sealing fuel tanks, adopted after some particularly disastrous daylight raids in the Heligoland Bight area in the closing weeks of 1939. In all, 2,685 Wellington Mk.1C aircraft were built.

The Wellington squadrons were in the forefront of Bomber Command's offensive. On 4 September 1939, the day after war was declared, fourteen Wellingtons of Nos 9 and 149 Squadrons set out to attack warships lying off Brunsbüttel in the river Elbe. Three of the No. 9 Squadron aircraft bombed an unidentified warship with no apparent result and one jettisoned its bombs over the harbour, hitting a merchantman. Of the No. 149 Squadron aircraft, one claimed to have bombed the target area and the others jettisoned their bombs into the sea. Two aircraft of No. 9 Squadron failed to return. One was shot down by anti-aircraft fire and the other was destroyed by a Messerschmitt Bf 109 of II/JG 77, operating out of Nordholz and flown by *Unteroffizier* Alfred Held. It was the *Luftwaffe*'s first victory against the RAF.

On 3 December, twenty-four Wellingtons of Nos 38, 115 and 149 Squadrons, flying in tight formation through heavy flak, attacked the warships without success. The bombers were intercepted by Messerschmitt Bf 109s and Bf 110s, one of which was damaged, but all the Wellingtons returned safely to base.

This operation seemed to vindicate the theory that a tight bomber formation was sufficient defence against fighter attacks in daylight, and on

Vickers Wellingtons of No. 9 Squadron, 1939. The squadron crest depicts a bat, and the motto is Per Noctem Volamus *(By Night We Fly). (IWM)*

14 December twelve Wellingtons of No. 99 Squadron, led by Wing Commander J.F. Griffiths, took off from Newmarket to attack the cruisers *Nürnberg* and *Leipzig*, which had been torpedoed by a British submarine and were limping back damaged to the Jade estuary. The attack ended in disaster. The bombers were intercepted by the Bf 109s of II/JG 77 and five of them were shot down in a matter of minutes, a sixth crashing on landing at Newmarket.

Despite this reverse, another daylight attack on the German fleet was planned for 18 December. This time, twenty-four Wellingtons of Nos 9, 37 and 149 Squadrons, led by Wing Commander R. Kellet – a veteran of the 3 December raid – set out with orders to patrol the Schillig Roads, Wilhelms-haven and the Jade Estuary and to attack any warships, sighted. The bombers were detected by two experimental Freya radars on Heligoland and Wangerooge, which raised the alarm after some delay. The Wellingtons, now reduced to twenty-two in number – two having turned back with engine trouble – detoured round Heligoland and turned in towards Wilhelmshaven from the north. Soon afterwards, they were attacked by the Bf 109s of 10/JG 26 and JG 77, followed by the Bf 109s of ZG 76, and in the running fight that ensued twelve of the bombers were shot down. At the subsequent post-mortem, it was established that some of the bombers had caught fire very quickly after being hit, and as a result priority was given to the fitting of self-sealing fuel tanks to No. 3 Group's Wellington force. In the meantime, there were to be no further armed reconnaissances of the Heligoland Bight area. There was one other consequence. In the light of the 18 December disaster, Bomber Command's policy underwent a complete revision. From now on, the emphasis would be on the development

Some Wellingtons were fitted with degaussing gear, their mission to fly low over the sea and detonate magnetic mines. (IWM)

of night bombing techniques, and both Nos 3 and 5 Groups were ordered to take part in leaflet-dropping operations to give their crews night-flying experience.

In 1940 the Wellington squadrons saw action over Norway and the Low Countries, and during the Battle of France they attacked targets in Germany itself, notably marshalling yards and communications. Three squadrons also operated as part of the Western Desert Air Force, and in January 1941 Wellingtons operating from Malta raided Naples, the headquarters of the Italian

Armourers preparing to bomb-up a Wellington of No. 70 Squadron for a mission against Axis forces in the Western Desert, 1941. (IWM)

fleet, and badly damaged the battleship *Giulio Cesare*, with the result that both she and the *Vittorio Veneto* were withdrawn to Genoa in the north. This attack served to underline the importance of Malta as a strategic base.

Throughout 1941, RAF Bomber Command turned much of its effort to attacking the ports on the French Atlantic coast, which were being used as bases for U-boats and surface units. On 24 July 1941, a major daylight operation was mounted against the German battle cruiser *Gneisenau* and the heavy cruiser *Prinz Eugen*, lying in Brest harbour. *Gneisenau*'s sister ship, the *Scharnhorst*, had sailed for La Pallice only a day or two earlier to make room for the *Prinz Eugen*, which had escaped after the battleship *Bismarck* had been sunk, so the original force of 150 aircraft scheduled to take part in the attack was reduced. The plan called for Brest to be attacked by seventy-nine unescorted Vickers Wellington bombers, while diversionary sorties were to be flown by eighteen Handley Page Hampdens, escorted by three squadrons of Spitfires fitted with long range tanks, and by three Boeing Fortress Is, the latter bombing from 30,000 feet. As a further diversionary measure, the Cherbourg docks were to be attacked by thirty-six Bristol Blenheims, with a strong Spitfire escort. Meanwhile, the *Scharnhorst* at La Pallice was to be attacked by fifteen Handley Page Halifax four-engine heavy bombers. The Brest attack was a disaster. The raid was broken up by fierce and prolonged fighter opposition; ten Wellingtons and two Hampdens were shot down by fighters or flak, and the warships in the harbour were not hit.

Pilot Officer Jim Heyworth, a co-pilot in a Wellington of No. 12 Squadron, described the attack:

> We took off in the morning, not a cloud in the sky over England and France. We approached the estuary in a formation of three aircraft at 10,000 feet, a sitting duck for the ground defences. Flak shells were bursting all around, indicated by large puffs of smoke and streams of tracer. We released our bombs and turned to port to cross the north-west peninsula. We could see fighters approaching, and as second pilot the captain told me to go to the astrodome to direct our fire and tell him what evasive action to take.
>
> An Me109 approached from directly astern and fired cannon shells from about 500 yards, which was beyond the effective range of our rear guns. The German pilot continued to hold that range and I told the rear gunner to cease firing in the hope that the fighter would close the gap in an attempt to finish us off. It was unnerving to watch the tracers coming straight towards one's face, then swerving above, below or to one side at the last second.
>
> The firing stopped and the fighter closed in for the kill. I told the gunner 'Hold . . . hold . . .' then at about 200–300 yards range I shouted 'Fire, and keep your finger on the trigger!' He said the guns would overheat; my reply was 'Kill him, and to hell with the guns!'
>
> The Me109 continued to close in and drew level with us on the port side. As it slowly passed I could clearly see the pilot's head bent down and he was slumped forward in his straps, presumably dead. The

fighter banked and turned over, diving vertically from 10,000 feet, and disappeared at about 5,000 feet. We did not see it hit the ground, and therefore could only claim a 'probable'.

Our lives were saved by the rear gunner's courage, as he kept his nerve while holding his fire until the Me 109 was well within range. I was nineteen years old, and grew up very quickly that day ...

One of the most extraordinary acts of bravery to emerge from the Second World War involved Sergeant James Ward, the second pilot of a Wellington of No. 75 (New Zealand) Squadron, which was returning to its base at Mildenhall following an attack on Muster on 7 July, 1941. Ward's action that night earned him a Victoria Cross. The citation tells the story:

While flying over the Zuider Zee at 13,000 feet, the aircraft was attacked from beneath by a Messerschmitt 110, which secured hits with cannon shell and incendiary bullets. The rear gunner was wounded in the foot but delivered a burst of fire which sent the enemy fighter down, apparently out of control.

Fire then broke out near the starboard engine, and, fed by petrol from a split pipe, quickly gained an alarming hold and threatened to spread to the entire wing. The crew forced a hole in the fuselage and made strenuous efforts to reduce the fire with extinguishers and even the coffee in their vacuum flasks, but without success. They were then warned to be ready to abandon the aircraft.

As a last resort, Sergeant Ward volunteered to make an attempt to smother the fire with an engine cover which happened to be is use as a cushion. At first he proposed to discard his parachute, to reduce wind resistance, but was finally persuaded to take it. A rope from the dinghy was tied to him, though this was of little help and might have become a danger had he been blown off the aircraft. With the help of the navigator, he then climbed through the narrow astro-hatch and put on his parachute. The bomber was flying at reduced speed, but the wind pressure must have been sufficient to render the operation one of extreme difficulty.

Breaking the fabric to make hand and foot holds where necessary, and also taking advantage of existing holes in the fabric, Sergeant Ward succeeded in descending three feet to the wing and proceeding another three feet to a position behind the engine, despite the slip-stream from the airscrew, which nearly blew him off the wing. Lying in this precarious position, he smothered the fire in the wing fabric and tried to push the cover into the hole in the wing and on to the leaking pipe from which the fire came. As soon as he removed his hand, however, the terrific wind blew the cover out and when he tried again it was lost. Tired as he was, he was able with the navigator's assistance, to make successfully the perilous journey back into the aircraft. There was now no danger of the fire spreading from the petrol pipe as there was no fabric left nearby, and in due course burnt itself out.

When the aircraft was nearly home some petrol which had collected in the wing blazed up furiously but died down quite suddenly. A safe landing was then made despite the damage sustained by the aircraft. The flight home had been made possible by the gallant action of Sergeant Ward in extinguishing the fire on the wing, in circumstances of the greatest difficulty and at the risk of his life.

Sergeant Ward's VC was gazetted on 5 August, 1941. On 15 September, during his fifth mission as aircraft captain, Ward's Wellington was shot down over Germany. Only two crew members survived. Ward was not one of them.

By early 1942 the principal Wellington version in service with Bomber Command was the Mk.III (1,519 built), with two 1,500 hp Bristol Hercules engines replacing the much less reliable Pegasus, although four squadrons (Nos 142, 300, 301 and 305, the last three being Polish units) used the Mk.IV, which was powered by American Pratt & Whitney Twin Wasps. The Wellington III entered service with the experienced No. 9 Squadron on 22 June 1941, and was to be the backbone of Bomber Command's night offensive against Germany until such time as the Command's four-engine heavy bombers became available in numbers.

On the night of 30/31 May 1942, Wellingtons formed the backbone of the thousand-bomber force that attacked Cologne. Bomber Command sustained a loss of forty-one aircraft in the raid, of which twenty-nine were Wellingtons. Many more Wellingtons suffered serious damage but survived thanks to the strength of their geodetic structure, a tale that was repeated time and again during the bomber's career. It was demonstrated on one mission, flown in December 1942, under somewhat peculiar circumstances.

A few months earlier, in July 1942, the RAF's 'Y' Service, which monitored enemy communications, picked up indications that the German night fighters operating over Holland were using an airborne detection device referred to as Emil Emil, but its exact nature could not be ascertained. In an attempt to gather more information, a special duties unit, No. 1474 Flight, was formed, and its Wellingtons, equipped with radio detection gear, began operations over northwest Europe. Seventeen sorties were flown without result; then, on the night of 3/4 December, 1942, the wireless operator of an eighteenth Wellington picked up weak signals at 04.30 hours, possibly from German AI radar. The signal strength increased rapidly, and the crew knew that an enemy fighter was locked on to them.

A few moments later, the Wellington was heavily attacked by a Junkers Ju 88. The captain of the British aircraft, Pilot Officer Paulton, took evasive action and his rear gunner returned the fire. The specialist radio operator, Pilot Officer Jordan, was badly wounded by the night fighter's first burst of fire; he nevertheless went on transmitting information about the enemy radar signals back to base for some minutes before he collapsed. The Ju 88 finally broke off the attack when Paulton took the Wellington down in a long dive from 14,000 to 500 feet. The bomber was severely damaged. Both throttles were jammed, its gun turrets were out of action and most of its instruments had been smashed by shell splinters. As the aircraft limped homewards the second specialist wireless operator, Flight Sergeant Bigoray, continued to transmit data, although he was wounded in both legs. The Wellington ditched 200 yards off the British coast and the crew was rescued. For their part in what turned out to be a mission of vital importance, Pilot Officer Jordan received the DSO, the pilot was awarded the DFC and Flight Sergeant Bigoray the DFM.

The Wellington played a leading part in the early campaigns in North Africa. No. 70 Squadron began operations from Kabrit, Egypt, in mid-September 1940, a few weeks after Italy entered the war on the side of Germany, and was soon reinforced by two more Wellington squadrons, Nos 37 and 38. These units frequently detached aircraft to Malta, and towards the end of 1940 the Wellingtons on the island were formed into a single squadron, No. 148, which carried out attacks on targets in Italy and North Africa at every opportunity. The Wellingtons were eventually driven away by the intensity of enemy air attacks on Malta, but the Mk.IIs of No. 104 Squadron deployed to the island from Driffield in the UK from October 1941 and were replaced in the autumn of 1942 by the torpedo-carrying Mk.VIIIs and Xs of Nos 38 and 221 Squadrons.

Coastal Command also found its uses for the versatile Wellington. The first general reconnaissance version of the aircraft, which made its appearance in the spring of 1942, was the GR.III, 271 being converted from standard Mk.IC airframes. The aircraft were fitted with ASV Mk.II radar and adapted to carry torpedoes. Fifty-eight more GR.IIIs were equipped as anti-submarine aircraft,

Photographed on Malta, this Wellington appears to be a C Mk.XVI transport variant. Its nose turret has been deleted. (A. Blackwell)

Operations from Malta were hazardous in the extreme, as this crumpled wreck of a Wellington in its blast pen testifies. (A. Blackwell)

being fitted with a powerful Leigh Light searchlight to illuminate U-boats travelling on the surface, which they often did at night in transit to and from their Biscay bases. The Leigh Light was a 24-inch naval carbon search light developed by Squadron Leader Humphrey Leigh and modified to fit into the Wellington's retractable belly gun turret. The device was intended to illuminate the target following the initial ASV approach. The first Leigh Light attack was made on the night of 3/4 June 1942 by a Wellington of No. 172 Squadron operating from Chivenor in Devon. On this occasion the U-boat escaped, but on the night of 5/6 July another Wellington of the same squadron made a successful Leigh Light attack on the U-502, which sank in the Bay of Biscay. As a point of interest, the pilot of the Wellington was an American, Pilot Officer Howell, who had joined the RAF before the United States entered the war.

The last bomber version of the Wellington was the Mk.X, of which 3,803 were built, accounting for more than 30 per cent of all Wellington production. Its career with Bomber Command was brief, but it was used in the Far East until the end of the war. Coastal Command's next version was the GR.Mk.XI, which was the first of four purpose-built variants; the GR.XI and GR.XIII were specifically intended for the torpedo-bomber role, while the GR.XII and GR.XIV were dedicated anti-submarine aircraft. Other Wellingtons were converted as transports and trainers, and a special variant designated DWI was fitted with a large electro-magnetic ring to trigger off enemy magnetic mines.

Preliminary work on a high-altitude version of the Wellington had started in 1938, with two prototypes – one to be powered by Bristol Hercules engines

A Wellington T.18 wireless and navigation trainer. An SCR720 radar scanner is fitted in the bulbous nose. (Source unknown)

and the other by Rolls-Royce Merlins – being ordered in May 1939. The Hercules-powered variant, known as the Mk.V, flew for the first time in September 1940. The aircraft was decidedly ugly, the crew of three being accommodated in a long cylindrical pressurised cabin built into the upper nose area, which was faired flush with the top surfaces of the fuselage. The pilot was provided with an elliptical bubble canopy slightly offset to port, in line with the propellers. Cabin pressure was initially set at approximately 10,000 feet; the anticipated operational altitude was 36,000 feet.

Only three Wellington Mk.Vs (R3298, R3229 and W5797) were built, all converted from Mk.IC aircraft, and the flight test programme revealed many problems, from severe icing of the canopy to oil freezing. The Hercules engines did not live up to expectations at high altitude, and development of the Mk.V was terminated in favour of the Mk.VI, which was intended from the outset to use the two-stage supercharged Merlin 60.

One of the more important roles assigned to the Wellington during the Second World War was as a test-bed for the early British turbojet engines, then under development for the Gloster Meteor jet fighter.

The Wellington was built in greater numbers than any other British bomber, production of all variants running to 11,461 aircraft. Today, two Wellingtons are preserved on display in British museums. One is Wellington Mk.1a N2980, at the Brooklands Museum, and the other is T.10 MF628, which is in the Royal Air Force Museum at Hendon.

CHAPTER EIGHT

The Hawker Hurricane

By the time the Gloster Gauntlet, the last of the RAF's open-cockpit fighter biplanes, entered squadron service in 1935, radical changes in fighter design were already being implemented as a result of the development of new monoplane types, powered by the new Rolls-Royce Merlin engine and given an unprecedented armament of eight Colt-Browning 0.303-inch machine guns. The fact that this armament was adopted was a consequence of a vigorous campaign conducted by Squadron leader Ralph Sorley of Flying Operations 1 (FO1) in the Air Ministry, who wrote later:

> The choice lay between the 0.303 gun, the 0.50 gun and a new 20 mm Hispano gun which was attracting the attention of the French, and in fact of other countries in Europe who could obtain knowledge of it from them. During 1934 this gun was experimental and details of its performance were hard to establish. On the other hand, designs of better 0.303 guns than the Vickers had been tested over the preceding years with them result that the American Browning from the Colt Automatic Weapon Corporation appeared to offer the best possibilities from the point of view of rate of fire.
>
> Our own development of guns of this calibre had been thorough but slow, since we were in the throes of economizing, and considerable stocks of old Vickers guns still remained from the First War. The acceptance of a new gun in the numbers likely to be required was a heavy financial and manufacturing commitment. The 0.50-inch on the other hand had developed little, and although it possessed a better hitting power the rate of fire was slow and it was a heavy item, together with its ammunition, in respect of installed weight. The controversy was something of a nightmare during 1933–34. It was a choice on which the whole concept of the fighter would depend, but a trial staged on the ground with eight 0.303s was sufficiently convincing and satisfying to enable them to carry the day.

It was just as well, for otherwise the new generation of RAF monoplane fighters might have gone to war with a wholly inadequate armament of four machine guns. One type, in fact, did so; but it was a biplane, the Gloster Gladiator, which entered service in February 1937 and which went on to give gallant service during the early months of the war in both Europe and North Africa.

The first of Britain's new monoplane fighters was the Hawker Hurricane, powered by the Rolls-Royce Merlin engine and given an armament of eight

*K5083, the prototype Hurricane, pictured on one of its early test flights in the hands of C.W.S.
'George' Bulman. (BAe)*

0.303-inch Colt-Browning machine guns. Developed from the Hawker Fury
biplane (it was originally known as the Fury Monoplane) under the design
leadership of Sydney Camm to meet Air Ministry Specification F.36/34, the
prototype flew on 6 November 1935. An order for 600 machines eventually
materialised in June 1936, and the first of these flew on 12 October 1937, an
initial batch being delivered to No. 111 Squadron at Northolt in November. At a
later date the Merlin II was replaced by the Merlin III, driving a three-blade
Rotol or de Havilland propeller. In 1938 the first deliveries were made to foreign
customers (Portugal, Yugoslavia, Persia and Belgium); Hurricanes were also
exported to Romania and Turkey. Eventual production of the Hurricane Mk.I,
shared between the Hawker and Gloster factories in the UK and the Canadian
Car and Foundry Company of Montreal, amounted to 3,954.

RAF Hurricanes were in action in France from the very beginning of the
period known as the 'Phoney War', engaging enemy reconnaissance aircraft that
were flying almost daily over France. When the fighting began in earnest, the few
Hurricane squadrons in France were in the thick of it, and the rugged qualities

of the aircraft soon earned the admiration of its pilots. One of them was Flying Officer (later Wing Commander) Jack Rose, who later described his experience:

On 14 May No. 32 Squadron was asked to provide four pilots and aircraft to reinforce 3 Squadron, then stationed at Merville near Armentières in northern France. No. 3 Squadron had suffered very heavy casualties during the preceding few days and so in addition to the pilots and aircraft from No. 32 Squadron they were strengthened by a flight from No. 601. With three other volunteers from 32 Squadron, I flew the same day to Merville. We were led by a Fairey Battle as we had no maps of France; I imagine that the crew of the Battle must have been equipped with the right maps but they seemed to spend a long time flying around France before we landed, for we were very short of fuel when we pitched up at Merville.

My aircraft, like those of my three companions, was a Hurricane Mk.I fitted with a Merlin II engine and a two-speed airscrew. Soon after our arrival in France, the CO of our new squadron was reported killed and so Walter Churchill, one of the flight commanders, took over. He was later killed while commanding the fighter aircraft based on Malta. Churchill proved to be a very keen tactician and a great morale booster: a first-class squadron commander.

My three companions from 32 Squadron and I soon learned that the aircraft we had joined in France had all been equipped with armour plate behind and beneath the pilot's seat; as our own aircraft were not similarly protected I think we were perhaps forgiven if our morale was marginally less receptive to the boosting process than it might have been. A further snag was that we had arrived without the appropriate crystals in our four-channel VHF sets and spares were not available locally until damaged aircraft could be cannibalised. The result was that, at times over the next few days, we were not in contact by radio either with our new colleagues of 3 squadron when airborne, or with such ground control as there was, or both.

During this period I became more and more impressed by the robust qualities of the Hurricane. I think that some of the emergency repairs that were carried out by the maintenance crews during those few days in France would have made Sydney Camm's hair stand on end, but they worked. On 19 May, after a few hectic days, I was flying one of a formation of six Hurricanes which had been ordered to patrol between Tournai and Oudenarde, about midway between Lille and Brussels, where we had been told to expect German bombers by ground control. We soon spotted twelve or so Heinkel 111s flying in close formation roughly level with us at 12,000 feet, and after a quick check of the sky for enemy fighters we attacked the German aircraft from astern.

I was positioned to attack the Heinkel on the port flank of the enemy formation and closed very rapidly, firing for a few seconds up to

HM King George VI inspecting RAF units in France, 1939. The Hurricanes belong to No. 85 Squadron. (IWM)

very close range, and as I was about to break away the Heinkel's port engine erupted oil which covered my windscreen, almost completely blocking off my forward vision and making the reflector sight useless. I had a quick look round above and behind and, seeing what I took to be an enemy-free sky, I throttled back, gained a little height to reduce speed and pulled back the cockpit hood. I pulled a handkerchief from my right trouser pocket but I couldn't reach far enough to wipe the front of the windscreen clear without releasing my seat harness, so I had to do that and then set about cleaning the windscreen.

As I was doing a speed of somewhere between stalling and cruising, my seat harness undone, more or less standing on the rudder stirrups and half out of the aircraft, concentrating on clearing the windscreen and with no armour plate behind, I suddenly saw tracer fly past and felt strikes on the Hurricane. I was being attacked from the rear by a 109 which had not been in sight a few seconds earlier – probably no German fighter pilots has ever had a more inviting target. At my low speed, immediate evasive action resulted in a spin, and from my point of view this was probably the best thing that could have happened. As I was spinning down I left a long trail of glycol and petrol which must have satisfied my German opponent that he need not waste any further rounds on me.

I switched off the engine as soon as I became aware of the glycol and petrol spewing out, but carried on with the spin until the immediate danger of a second attack seemed over. After I had checked the spin and adjusted the Hurricane to a glide I had to decide whether to leave the aircraft in a hurry or try a landing without engine. Then, slightly to the west and 6,000–7,000 feet below, I spotted the airfield of Seclin, just south of Lille. The aircraft was still discharging fuel and glycol but it had not caught fire. The fire risk was now greatly reduced as the engine temperature had fallen very considerably, so I decided on a wheels-down landing at Seclin. After a long zigzag glide approach, still with the tell-tale stream behind, I used the hand pump to lock the undercarriage down and lowered the flaps in the last few seconds before touching down.

Under all the circumstances it was a reasonably good landing and the aircraft's run after touchdown left me near the northern boundary of the airfield, some distance from the Lysanders of No. 4 Army Co-op Squadron which was then based at Seclin. I doubt if I have ever left an aircraft as quickly or as thankfully as when my Hurricane stopped rolling. When I checked the damage it seemed almost impossible that so many hits could have been registered without one bullet passing down the centre of the fuselage and through the back of my unprotected seat. A shell from the 109 had torn a gaping hole in the radiator just below me, while another had removed much of the starboard aileron. Bullets had pierced both port and starboard main petrol tanks in several places and there were a number of holes in the fuselage and wings elsewhere.

The exploits of the Hurricane and its pilots in the Battle of Britain became legendary, even though the aircraft itself was always in the shadow of its contemporary, the more glamorous Spitfire. One of its leading exponents was Flight Lieutenant (later Group Captain) Frank Carey, a veteran of the Battle of France. During that battle Carey destroyed four enemy aircraft, together with two probables, before being wounded on 14 May. On his return to England he was posted to No. 43 Squadron as a flight commander, and destroyed a Bf 109 over the Channel on 19 June. During July Carey added two more aircraft – a Bf 109 and a Bf 110 – to his score. Then, on 12 and 13 August, the first two days of heavy *Luftwaffe* attacks on the RAF airfields in the south of England, Carey claimed two Junkers 88s, and on the 16 August he was involved in a fierce air battle over the south coast. His combat report describes the action:

I was leading 'A' Flight behind the leader of the squadron, having taken off at 12.45 hours to patrol Selsey Bill at 11,000 feet when I gave Tally Ho on sighting waves of Ju 87s. The leader ordered the squadron to attack one formation of Ju 87s from the front and immediately on closing the leader of the enemy aircraft was hit by Squadron Leader and crew baled out.

Hurricanes of No. 601 Squadron in echelon formation. This type of formation was unwieldy and placed RAF fighter pilots at a disadvantage. (Flight International)

I pulled my flight over to the left to attack the right hand formation as we met them. Almost as soon as I opened fire, the enemy aircraft's crew baled out and the machine crashed into the sea, just off Selsey Bill. I turned to continue my attack from the rear as enemy aircraft were completely broken up by frontal attack and several other waves behind me turned back to sea immediately although we had not attacked them. I picked out one Ju 87 and fired two two-second bursts at him and the enemy aircraft burst into flames on the port wing-root. I did not wait to see it crash as I turned to attack another. After one burst at the third enemy aircraft, two large pieces of metal broke off the port wing and the enemy aircraft seemed to stop abruptly and go into a dive, but I did not see the machine crash as two other Ju 87s were turning on to my tail. I eventually picked on a fourth, but after firing two bursts and causing the engine to issue black smoke, the enemy aircraft turned out to sea and I ran out of ammunition. I noticed firing behind me and turned to see a pair of Me 109s behind me, one firing and the other guarding his tail. After a few evasive actions the enemy aircraft broke off and I returned to land and refuel and rearm at 13.40 hours.

Between 1 July and 31 October 1940, the period that roughly encompasses the Battle of Britain, the RAF lost 565 Hurricanes and 361 Spitfires. Fighter Command began the battle with twenty-seven squadrons of Hurricanes, against nineteen squadrons of Spitfires, so bearing that in mind, the margin between the losses suffered by each type was not very wide.

Fine shot of a Hurricane Mk. IIc as it rolls over the English countryside. The aircraft is fitted with a tropical filter. (BAe)

A cannon-armed Hurricane IIc of No. 1 Squadron, which frequently operated in the night intruder role. (Flight International)

On 11 June 1940 Hurricane P3269 flew with a 1,185 hp supercharged Merlin XX engine, serving as prototype for the Hurricane Mk.II, and as more Mk.IIs reached the squadrons many Mk.Is were sent to the Middle East. Early Mk.IIs, which retained the eight-gun armament, were designated Mk.IIAs; with twelve machine guns the designation became Mk.IIB, while the Mk.IIC had a wing armament of four 20 mm Hispano cannon. The Mk.IID was a special anti-tank version, armed with two underwing 40 mm Vickers 'S' guns and two 0.303 Brownings in the wings. Both IIBs and IICs were fitted with cameras and used for reconnaissance as the Mk.PR.IIB and Mk.PR.IIC. In 1942, Hurricane Is and IIAs operated in Singapore, the Netherlands East Indies, Ceylon and Burma, and it was during the Burma Campaign that the Hurricane really came into its own as a tactical support aircraft, armed with a pair of 500 lb bombs.

The Hurricane also performed remarkably well in fending off Japanese air attacks on target in India, as one of its pilots, Flying Officer (later Wing Commander) Gordon Conway recalled:

> On 24 March 1943 we flew our war-weary Hurricane IIBs to Allahabad and returned with new Mk.IICs. At last we had Hurricanes with four 20 mm cannon and VHF radio! The last few days of March 1943 brought a raid a day, during which 135 and 79 Squadrons

intercepted thirty-three bombers at 125,000 feet without fighter escort. The escort had lost their bombers under a cloud layer, and while we had a series of inconclusive scraps at 30,000 feet over base with the fighters, the squadrons down south destroyed eleven of the unescorted bombers.

The fighting in April followed this pattern, starting with more raids against our airfields. Our squadron was involved each time. On the first raid we had visual contact with the fighters and bombers, but we were still climbing when they bombed from 27,000 feet. In the afternoon, on a second scramble, my aircraft was still having its guns checked and was not ready in time for the scramble ... I later got off alone and joined up with a flight of 67 Squadron at 21,000 feet, just as half a dozen Oscars jumped them. I saw a big red spinner coming up fast behind, called the break and was peppered in my starboard wing and aileron; I can still recall the surprisingly loud bang as he hit me. I flicked to starboard as the Oscar dived underneath, hit my attacker in the fuselage and tail and claimed my first 'damaged'.

Our armourers used to clean our cannon throughout the day, taking one aircraft at a time. Mine were being worked on when the wing scrambled against an incoming raid. Despite hasty replacement of covers and panels I was again left behind and climbed up alone under control without making contact with the wing. As I reached 28,000 feet by myself I saw twenty-one enemy fighters coming from my left; they were sweeping at the same height over their bombers, which were in the act of bombing base. The fighters were in two groups, twelve in front and another nine slightly behind and above. I intended a head-on attack as the most suitable under the circumstances, but because of the high closing speed it developed into a classic opposite quarter attack, ending with me in the middle of the two formations, astern of some but with other aircraft visible in my rear-view mirror. I believe that discretion is the better part of valour, so I half-rolled into a tight aileron turn right down to the sea, going so fast that my bullet-proof windscreen cracked. The Japs must have been as startled as I was, for within a few minutes they were bounced by several of our chaps and hit. We lost one pilot, but in this two-day period claimed six probables and a further eleven damaged. Our new cannons were clearly paying dividends ...

On the 22nd they hit us with twenty-five bombers at 20,000 feet, escorted by fifteen plus Oscars. Both 67 and ourselves intercepted; 67 claimed two destroyed, two probables and one damaged, while we claimed five destroyed, four probables and three damaged ... I got into the fighter screen and claimed one destroyed and another probable. A week later the Japs repeated this raid, using fifteen-plus bombers at 18,000 feet, with twenty plus fighters at 22,000 feet. Joe Edwards was leading, and as he dived on the top fighters, another fighter from a different flight turned on to his tail in front of my sight. I gave this

Oscar a long burst of cannon, closing from astern, and he literally fell apart. He seemed to stop in mid-air, his port wheel came down followed by his flaps, and with pieces flying off all around he flicked and spun vertically into the sea, just by the airfield. We claimed five, one and two, while 67 claimed three probables and one damaged. So ended a good month in which our only casualties were two pilots, both of whom escaped with slight injuries . . . In six months we (Nos 136 and 67 Squadrons) had destroyed fourteen enemy aircraft, probably destroyed ten and damaged eighteen for the loss of four pilots. Down south, 79 Squadron had destroyed seventeen enemy aircraft; 135 Squadron had claimed over twenty, but at the great cost of thirteen of their own pilots . . .

The final British production model of the Hurricane, the Mk.IV, was a ground attack type, armed principally with eight 60 lb rocket projectiles and fitted with a 1,620 hp Merlin 24 or 27 engine. Alternative payloads included two 250 lb or 500 lb bombs, or two Vickers 'S' guns. The Hurricane Mk.V was designed to take the higher-powered Merlin 27 or 32 engine, but only two were built.

In 1941 the Hurricane was adopted by the Royal Navy for fleet protection duties, the first Sea Hurricane Mk.IAs being deployed on escort carriers in 1941.

Hurricane Mk.IV BP173 with rocket rails and a single 60 lb rocket projectile under the port wing. (BAe)

A Hurricane of the Merchant Ship Fighter Unit blasts off from a launching ramp mounted on the bow of a CAM (Catapult Aircraft Merchantman). (IWM)

One major user of the Hurricane was the Soviet Union, the first batch to be delivered comprising twenty-four Mk.IIBs turned over to the Soviet Navy's 72nd Fighter Air Regiment by No. 141 Wing RAF, which operated in North Russia in the late summer of 1941. One Hurricane variant shipped to Russia during 1943 was the Mk.IID, with 40 mm Vickers 'S' guns. Sixty were delivered from RAF stocks in the Middle East and were followed by thirty Hurricane IVs with similar armament. Tank-busting Hurricanes were used to good effect in the battles of Kuban and Kursk in 1943. Altogether, 2,952 Hurricanes – over 20 per cent of the total number built in the UK – were delivered to the USSR.

Some Hurricanes were issued to the 3rd Fighter Regiment of the Soviet Baltic Fleet, operating in the Leningrad sector, the Russian pilots, used to the much lighter Yaks and LaGGs, viewing it with mixed feelings.

'I thought that the name "Hurricane" hardly matched the technical qualities of the machine,' wrote Lieutenant Viktor Kaberov, 'The armament on it was now good – two 20 mm cannons and two heavy calibre machine guns. One burst and pieces would fly off any aircraft. The armour plating (taken from our

LaGG) was fine. Such protection was like a stone wall. The horizon indicator was also a wonderful instrument. It was easy to fly in the clouds with it. The radio worked perfectly, like a domestic telephone: neither noise nor crackle. But the speed, the speed ... No, this aircraft was far from being a Hurricane. It was slow to gain height and was not good in a dive. As for vertical manoeuvrability – not good at all!'

Shortcomings or not, it was aircraft like the Hurricane that helped the Soviet fighter pilots to hold their own against the *Luftwaffe* in the dark days of 1942.

Overall Hurricane production in the UK was 13,080 by Hawker, Gloster and Austin Motors; another 1,451 Mks X, XI, XII and XIIA, fitted with various armament combinations and Packard-built Rolls-Royce Merlins, were produced by the Canadian Car and Foundry Co.

The last Hurricane allocated to the Royal Air Force was Mk.IIC LF363, which was delivered to the RAF in January 1944 and which served successively with Nos 63, 309 Polish (Ziemia Czerwienska) and 26 Squadrons, No. 65 OTU, Middle Wallop and Waterbeach Station Flights, No. 61 Group Communications Flight at Kenley, and the Battle of Britain Memorial Flight. Badly damaged in a crash-landing in 1991, it was rebuilt, and in the 2006 display season it appeared in the colour scheme of Hurricane Mk.1 P3878 'YB-W', the aircraft of Flying Officer Harold Bird-Wilson of No. 17 Squadron during the Battle of Britain.

Also based with the Battle of Britain Memorial Flight at RAF Coningsby is PZ865, the last Hurricane ever built. Completed in August 1944 and appropriately named The Last of the Many, this aircraft never entered RAF service. Instead, it was bought by Hawker Aircraft Ltd off the final Ministry of Aircraft Production contract and, after the war, placed on the civil register as G-AMAU, resplendent in Royal Blue and Gold. It featured in several air races and, together with LF363 and a number of Portuguese Hurricanes, in films such as *Angels One Five*. Its working life went on for a long time, for in 1959–60 it was used as a chase plane during target towing trials on a batch of Sea Fury conversions ordered by the Germans, and during the Hawker P.1127's early flight trials. Reverting to its original camouflage scheme in 1960, PZ865 was later donated to the BBMF by Hawker Siddeley Ltd, and in 2007 it was painted to represent Hurricane IIc BE581, 'Night Reaper', the aircraft flown by the Czech fighter ace Flight Lieutenant Karel Kuttelwascher DFC* during night intruder operations from Tangmere in 1942 with the RAF's No. 1(F) Squadron.

Only a handful of the 14,533 Hurricanes built in the United Kingdom and Canada before the end of the Second World War survive. Apart from the aircraft mentioned above, the largest collection is, not unnaturally, in Britain. The Battle of Britain Museum at Hendon has two Hurricane Mk.1s, P2617 and P3175; the former served with No. 607 Squadron in France during 1940 and with No. 9 FTS in the summer of 1941. The other aircraft, P3175, is in a badly damaged condition, and was serving with No. 257 Squadron when it was shot down by a Bf 110 over North Weald in August 1940.

Another Hurricane Mk.I, L1592, is in the Science Museum at South Kensington; this machine served with Nos 56 and 615 Squadrons in the Battle of Britain and force-landed near Croydon in August 1940. The Shuttleworth Museum at Old Warden has a Sea Hurricane Mk.IB, Z7015, while Biggin Hill, a name synonymous with the Battle of Britain, has a Hurricane Mk.IIC, 5405M, formerly LF738 of No. 41 OUT and 5 MU. Together with a Spitfire, it stands guard outside the RAF Memorial Chapel.

At Bentley Priory, HQ No. 11 Group – which was HQ Fighter Command during the Battle of Britain – there is a Hurricane Mk.IID, LE751 (5466M) 'FB:B', a composite aircraft rebuilt with parts of Z3687 and PG593; the original served with No. 27 OTU and No. 1681 Bomber Defence Training Flight.

Other Hurricanes survive as museum pieces around the world, and there are many replicas on display, hard to distinguish from the real thing. One museum piece, in particular, provides an interesting postscript to the Hurricane story. In March 1940, the Air Ministry had authorised the release to Finland, then in the closing stages of the bitter Winter War with the Soviet Union, of twelve Hawker Hurricane Mk.Is from stocks held by Nos 19 and 20 MUs at St Athan and Aston Down. The Hurricanes set out for Finland via northern Scotland and Norway, but one of them crashed in bad weather at Stavanger, injuring its pilot, Martii Laitinen. A replacement aircraft was later delivered by sea. By the time the Hurricanes arrived an armistice had been concluded between Russia and Finland.

In June 1941, when hostilities resumed between the Soviet Union and Finland in what became known as the 'Continuation War', the squadron

Hurricane Mk.IIc HV608, in Turkish Air Force markings, seen at a maintenance unit in Egypt prior to its delivery flight. (BAe)

operating the Hurricanes was assigned to the defence of Helsinki and the fighters saw some action against Soviet bomber and reconnaissance aircraft. However, the Hurricane was not particularly popular with the Finnish pilots, who preferred the Brewster 239 and the Curtiss Hawk 75A, and early in 1942 the Hurricanes were replaced by captured Polikarpov I-153s, which arrived in Finland via Germany and were used in the tactical reconnaissance role. The surviving Hurricanes were used as operational trainers until 1944, when the Russian onslaught brought about the collapse of Finland and the Finns were forced to co-operate with the Soviet forces in driving their erstwhile allies, the Germans, from their homeland.

So it was that the Hawker Hurricane, the aircraft that performed every imaginable task that could be undertaken by a single-engine fighter in the Second World War, also had the dubious distinction of fighting on both sides.

CHAPTER NINE

The Supermarine Spitfire

In 1929 the Schneider Trophy was won outright for Britain by a Supermarine S.6 racing floatplane, powered by a Rolls-Royce 'R' engine of 1,900 hp. The success of this engine was a powerful factor in persuading the Directorate of Technical Development that Rolls-Royce had established a firm lead in the design of high-performance liquid-cooled power plants, and in 1934 their PV.12 was approved for installation in a new monoplane fighter then being developed by the Hawker Aircraft Company, the Fury Monoplane – later to be called the Hurricane. Similarly, it was the PV.12 that was chosen to power Supermarine's monoplane fighter design, based on the S.6 racer – the aircraft that was to become the incomparable Spitfire.

The legendary Supermarine Spitfire was designed by a team under the direction of Reginald Mitchell. The design was so evidently superior to the original Air Ministry Specification to which it had been submitted, F.5/34, that a new one, F.37/34, was drafted to cover the production of a prototype. This aircraft, K5054, made its first flight on 5 March 1936 and, like the Hawker Hurricane, with which it was to share so much fame, was powered by a Rolls-Royce Merlin 'C' engine. A contract for the production of 310 Spitfires was issued by the Air Ministry in June 1936, at the same time as the Hurricane contract, and the first examples were delivered to No. 19 Squadron at Duxford in August 1938. Eight other squadrons had equipped with Spitfires by September 1939, and two Auxiliary Air Force units, Nos 603 and 609, were undergoing operational training.

It was in the hands of these two squadrons, both located in Scotland, that the Spitfire first saw combat in the early weeks of the war, as enemy bombers attempted to attack British naval facilities, but it was over Dunkirk in May 1940 that it had its first real test in action. A few weeks later, the Germans launched the preliminary phase of their air offensive against England, beginning with attacks on convoys in the English Channel. The main phase, *Adler Angriff* (Eagle Attack) was launched on 13 August 1940, and the first days of the attack soon revealed the strengths and weaknesses of both sides.

One aspect already appreciated by RAF fighter pilots was the wisdom of arming their Spitfires and Hurricanes with eight machine guns instead of four, as had originally been intended. At first, the idea was that the eight guns would throw out a large bullet pattern, rather like the pellets from a shotgun cartridge, so that the average pilot would stand some chance of striking the enemy, but experience showed that this was a waste of hitting power and eventually the guns were harmonized so that their bullets converged 250 yards in front of the fighter's nose and then spread out again to a width of a few yards within a

An early production Spitfire Mk.I of No. 19 Squadron, RAF Duxford. (IWM)

The Spitfire's narrow-track undercarriage made it difficult to handle on the ground in certain conditions. This is an aircraft of No. 72 Squadron, RAF Acklington.

distance of 500 yards. In the few seconds available in which to destroy or disable an enemy aircraft, the concentration of eight guns firing 8,000 rounds per minute (or 400 per three-second burst, representing a weight of metal of about 10 lb) was frequently enough to knock a fatal hole in the wings, fuselage, tail or engine, assuming that vital cockpit area was not hit.

Production of the Spitfire Mk.I, which was powered by a 1,030 hp Merlin II or III engine, eventually reached 1,566 aircraft. It was this variant that saw the most combat in the Battle of Britain, the Mk.II with the 1,175 hp Merlin XII engine being issued to the squadrons of Fighter Command in September 1940. Mk.II production, including the Mk.IIB, which mounted two 20 mm cannon and four 7.7 mm (0.303 inch) machine guns in place of the standard eight 0.303s, totalled 920 aircraft. During the battle, from 1 July to 31 October 1940, 361 of the 747 Spitfires delivered to Fighter Command were destroyed, not all in combat.

With the Battle of Britain won and Hitler's planned invasion of England postponed indefinitely, RAF Fighter Command began to go over to the offensive. On 9 January 1941, in brilliant sunshine and perfect visibility, five fighter squadrons penetrated thirty miles into France. There was no sign of movement on the snow-covered airfields they flew over; not a single Messerschmitt took to the air to engage them. Offensive sweeps, usually in concert with small-scale bombing raids, were carried out whenever the weather permitted during the early weeks of 1941, and *Luftwaffe* opposition gradually increased. It was clear that the Germans, following the policy adopted by the RAF before the Battle of Britain, were reluctant to commit their fighter defences in strength.

By March 1941, fighter sweeps over the continent were becoming organized affairs, with the Spitfire and Hurricane squadrons operating at wing strength. A Fighter Command wing consisted of three squadrons, each of twelve aircraft. There were Spitfire wings at Biggin Hill, Hornchurch and Tangmere, mixed Spitfire and Hurricane wings at Duxford, Middle Wallop and Wittering, and Hurricane wings at Kenley, Northolt and North Weald. The Hurricane wings would soon be rearmed with Spitfires; these were Mk.Vs, which had begun to enter service in March 1941. Converted from Mk.I airframes, the Mk.V was to be the major Spitfire production version, with 6,479 examples completed. The majority of Spitfire Mk.Vs were armed with two 20 mm cannon and four machine guns, affording a greater chance of success against armour plating. The Mk.V was powered by a Rolls-Royce Merlin 45 engine, developing 1,415 hp at 19,000 feet (5,800 m) against the 1,150 hp of the Merlin XII fitted in the Mk.II.

The Spitfire Mk.V, however, failed to provide the overall superiority Fighter Command needed so badly. At high altitude, where many combats took place, it was found to be inferior to the Bf 109F on most counts, and several squadrons equipped with the Mk.V took a severe mauling during that summer, especially after the Focke-Wulf Fw 190 made its appearance. As the Fw 190 was encountered more frequently it became apparent that it outclassed the Spitfire Mk.V in all aspects except radius of turn.

The type of operation flown by the Spitfire squadrons of Fighter Command is admirably summarised by the War Diary of No. 118 Squadron, which early in

1943 was based at Coltishall in Norfolk with Spitfire VBs. Much of its activity involved shipping reconnaissance and bomber escorts to the Low Countries. No. 118 generally operated in concert with No. 167 Squadron, which also had Spitfire VBs and which was based at Ludham, a few miles near the coast of East Anglia. No. 118 Squadron shared Coltishall with No. 68 Squadron, which operated Beaufighters:

> 29.1.43. Misery (the Squadron Intelligence Officer) was on a forty-eight and of course things happened: there were four flights by twenty-seven aircraft in fine weather. In the morning there was drogue towing, air-to-air and air-to-sea firing, camera gun practice, camera tests and in the afternoon a sweep over Ijmuiden.
>
> In the afternoon the squadron made rendezvous with 167 and twelve Venturas over Mundesley, and flew at sea level to within a few miles of the Dutch coast, then climbed to 9,000 feet over Ijmuiden. As we crossed the coast four Fw 190s were seen breaking cloud below at 2,000 feet. Our allotted task was to give top cover to the bombers which, instead of bombing immediately, went inland for ten minutes then turned round and bombed from east to west on an outward heading. Squadron Leader Wooton decided not to go down for the 190s until the bombers had carried out their task, or while they were still in danger of being attacked.
>
> While the bombers and escorts were making their incursion the 190s climbed up and were joined by others, but before they could attack the bombers they were engaged by 118 Squadron. In the resultant dog-fight, of which no one seemed to have a very clear picture, Sergeant Lack destroyed an Fw 190 which he followed down to sea level and set on fire; it was eventually seen to crash into the sea by Hallingworth.
>
> Hallingworth was attacked and his aircraft hit, and he in turn claimed a 190 damaged. The CO, who engaged the leading Fw 190, also claimed one damaged, the enemy aircraft breaking away after being hit by cannon fire and going down followed by Sergeant Buglass, who lost sight of it. Shepherd went to Hallingworth's rescue when he was being attacked, and was himself fired at head-on by two Fw 190s. Flight Sergeant Cross is missing from this engagement; no one saw what happened to him, but as he was a flying number two to Shepherd it is believed that he must have been hit during the double attack on his section leader. The squadron got split up during the engagement, seven aircraft coming back together with the other four in two pairs, one in company with the Venturas and 167 Squadron.
>
> No one saw Cross crash. He was a very nice, quiet Canadian and will be very much missed, particularly by his friend, Flight Sergeant Croall. The weather was seven-tenths at 1,000 feet over the target. The day's work brings our squadron total to fourteen enemy aircraft destroyed, six probably destroyed and thirteen damaged.

Increasing numbers of Spitfires were deployed to North Africa from 1942. This is a photo-reconnaissance Mk.IV, ER939, pictured in Tunisia. (IWM)

Despite its inadequacies, it was the Spitfire Mk.V that played a key part in defending the strategically vital island of Malta in 1942, where its principal fighter opponents were the Messerschmitt Bf 109F and the Macchi C.202. The original defence was in the hands of three Gloster Sea Gladiators, then Hurricanes, but in March 1942 the island's defences were reinforced by the arrival of fifteen Spitfires, flown off the carrier HMS *Eagle* at enormous risk. They arrived at a time when only thirty serviceable Hurricanes were left. On 20 April 1942, forty-seven more Spitfires reached the island after flying from the aircraft carrier USS *Wasp*. Their arrival, however, had been detected by the Germans, and within hours their airfields were under attack. By the end of the next day, after further heavy raids, only eighteen of the original forty-seven Spitfires were still airworthy.

On 9 May the USS *Wasp* returned, together with HMS *Eagle*, and between them the carriers flew off sixty-four more Spitfires, which went into action almost immediately. The following day saw a major air battle over the island when the *Luftwaffe* made a determined effort to sink the minelayer HMS *Welshman*, which had docked in Valletta harbour, laden with supplies and ammunition. Between them the island's Spitfires and Hurricanes flew 124 sorties that day, destroying fifteen enemy aircraft. Three Spitfires were lost, but two of the pilots survived. Seventeen more Spitfires arrived later in May and deliveries of fighter aircraft continued throughout the summer months of 1942; HMS *Eagle* alone delivered 182 Spitfires before she was sunk by a U-boat on 11 July.

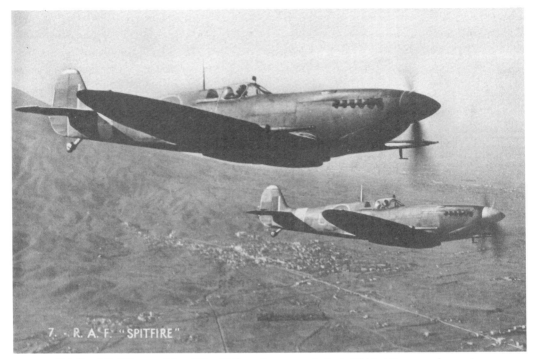

Spitfire Mk.IXs, possibly of No. 43 Squadron, over Italy in 1944. (Source unknown)

Most of the ferry work was undertaken by HMS *Furious*, which flew off thirty-seven Spitfires on the day HMS *Eagle* went down, followed by twenty-seven more on 7 August. Several RAF pilots distinguished themselves in the summer of 1942; one of them was Canadian-born Pilot Officer George F. Buerling, who gained twenty-seven victories while flying Spitfires over the island. He survived the war only to be killed while ferrying an aircraft to Israel in 1948.

The Spitfire Mk.V also played its part in the Pacific air war, forming a component of the air defences of northern Australia. In 1942, after Japanese carrier aircraft had first attacked Darwin, three squadrons of Spitfires had been shipped to Australia at the urgent request of the Australian government. The three squadrons – Nos 452 and 457 RAAF and No. 54 RAF – were formed into No. 1 Fighter Wing, RAAF, under the command of Squadron Leader Clive Caldwell, a highly skilled and experienced fighter pilot who had already gained twenty victories in the Middle East. The Spitfire variant that was sent to Australia was the 'tropicalised' Mk.Vc. In a turning fight, and in the climb, it was outclassed by the Mitsubishi Zero. The Fighter Wing's losses were initially heavy as a consequence, but Caldwell continued to develop the wing's tactics, ignoring the growing storm of criticism about the celebrated Spitfire's lack of success, and one day in July 1943 his efforts paid dividends. On that day, No. 54 Squadron was scrambled to intercept a raid on Darwin by forty-seven bombers and their fighter escorts. Only seven Spitfires reached the attackers, but they shot down seven bombers and two Zeros for no loss. Then, on 20 August, three Japanese reconnaissance aircraft appeared over Darwin, heralding another raid; the Spitfires shot down all three of them. The Japanese sent another; it was shot down by Clive Caldwell, his twenty-eighth and last victory. The Japanese sent yet another, this time under strong fighter escort. No. 54 Squadron was scrambled to intercept, and the Zeros fell on the Spitfires as they climbed, shooting down three of them. But the Spitfires in turn destroyed one Zero and damaged two more so badly that it is almost certain they came down somewhere in the Timor Sea. Soon afterwards, the Japanese daylight raids on Darwin ceased and the enemy switched to sporadic night attacks which were to continue, with little effect, until early in 1944. Caldwell's Spitfires had achieved their objective.

Early in 1943 it was still the Spitfire that formed the bulk of RAF Fighter Command's offensive and defensive day forces. To counter the activities of high-flying German reconnaissance aircraft the Spitfire Mk. VI was produced, with a long, tapered wing and a pressurized cockpit; the aircraft was assigned to one flight of the RAF's home defence squadrons. The Mk. VII, also with a pressurized cockpit, was powered by a Rolls-Royce Merlin 60 engine, a two-stage, two-speed, inter-cooled powerplant which was to take development of the Merlin to its ultimate. The answer to the problems experienced with the Spitfire Mk. V was to marry a Mk. V airframe with a Merlin 61 engine. The resulting combination was the Spitfire Mk. IX, which for a stop-gap aircraft turned out to be a resounding success. Deliveries to the RAF began in June 1942 and 5,665 were built, more than any other mark except the Mk. V.

From the spring of 1943, the fighter wings of No. 11 Group equipped with the Spitfire Mk. IX were assigned to escort missions with the US Eighth Army Air Force, which had begun deep-penetration missions into Germany in March. The Spitfires' limited range meant that escort could only be provided for part of the way, leaving the bombers to continue unescorted into Germany, and the *Luftwaffe* soon shattered the myth that large formations of heavy bombers, without fighter escort and relying entirely on their defensive armament, could operate deep inside enemy territory without sustaining serious losses. Wing Commander J.E. 'Johnnie' Johnson, commanding a formation of Spitfires heading out into the Low Countries to escort the returning bombers, described the aftermath of one terrible encounter on 14 October 1943, a day on which the US VIIIth Bomber Command lost seventy-seven heavy bombers:

> It was a clear afternoon, and we first saw their contrails many miles away, as well as the thinner darting contrails of the enemy fighters above and on either flank. As we closed the gap we could see that they had taken a terrible mauling, for there were gaping holes in their precise formations. Some Fortresses were gradually losing height, and a few stragglers, lagging well behind, were struggling to get home on three engines. We swept well behind the stragglers and drove off a few 109s and 110s, but the great air battle was over, and what a fight it must have been, because more than half the bombers we nursed across

the North Sea were shot up. One or two ditched in the sea, and many others, carrying dead and badly injured crew members, had to make crash-landings. How we longed for more drop tanks, so that some of the many hundreds of Spitfires based in Britain could play their part in the great battles over Germany ...

Of the other marks of Spitfire, the Mk.III was an experimental 'one-off' aircraft, while the Mk.IV (229 built) was a photo-reconnaissance version. It was actually produced after the Mk.V. The Spitfire Mk.X and XII were also un-armed photographic reconnaissance variants. One could write volumes about the PR Spitfire pilots and their exploits; theirs was a lonely, dangerous and sometimes excruciatingly painful task. One of them was Wing Commander (later Air Marshal Sir) Alfred Ball, who flew PR Spitfires over Europe and North Africa:

> In Tunisia at the end of 1942 we did a lot of front-line mapping for the First Army. It was very costly and on one occasion we lost four aircraft in three days from a squadron of nine. The difficulty was the great concentration of Fw 190s and Me 109Gs and standing patrols in the battle area; our own fighters were having a bad time just then (December 1942 and January 1943). In this case our problem was solved by the replacement of our Mk.IV Spitfires by Mk.XIs whilst our fighter squadrons got Mk.IXs.
>
> Let me outline an experience in a Spitfire Mk.IV at 24,000 feet (a bad height for the Spitfire but ideal for the Fw 190) near Tunis. I was just completing some forty-five minutes of front line photography when I spotted four Fw 190s some three to four miles away and about 1,000 feet below going in the opposite direction. They turned towards me shortly after I saw them and I opened up to full throttle and dived slightly to gain speed as quickly as possible. Within a very few minutes, however, they were on to me and the first of eight attacks took place. My only chance lay in out-turning them. In the event I was hit by the very first burst of fire – having left my turn (maximum possible) a fraction too late – but although the aircraft was hit in a number of interesting places, the damage was not catastrophic. This one-sided combat went on for five to ten minutes until the Focke-Wulfs broke off, either out of ammunition or short of fuel.

The Spitfire Mk.XII, powered by a 1,735 hp Rolls-Royce Griffon engine, was developed specifically to counter low-level attacks by Focke-Wulf 190s on the south coast of England. It first went into service with No. 41 Squadron in February 1943. Only 100 Mk.XII Spitfires were built, but they were followed by the more numerous Mk.XIV. The latter, based on a Mk.VIII airframe, was the first Griffon-engined Spitfire variant to go into large-scale production, and the first examples were issued to No. 322 (The Netherlands) and No. 610 Squadrons in March and April 1944. The Spitfire Mk.XVI, which entered service in 1944, was a ground-attack version similar to the Mk.IX, but with a Packard-built

Men of No. 3210 RAF Servicing Commando giving a Spitfire a rapid turnaround at Tilly sur Mer, near Arromanches, in June 1944. (Source unknown)

Merlin 266 engine. The Spitfire Mk.XVIII was a fighter-reconnaissance variant, just beginning to enter service at the end of the Second World War, as was the PR Mk.XIX. The last variants of the Spitfire, produced until 1947, were the Mks 21, 22 and 24. They bore very little resemblance to the prototype Mk.I of a decade earlier. Total production of the Spitfire was 20,351 plus 2,334 examples of the naval version, the Seafire.

The Seafire was a consequence of the fact that, between the two world wars, the Royal Navy's carrier-borne aircraft evolved at a much slower pace than did their land-based counterparts. With the outbreak of the Second World War the RN found a partial solution to the problem of its outdated fighters by adapting land-based aircraft like the Hawker Hurricane for carrier operations, and in late 1941 it was decided to adapt the Spitfire in similar fashion under the name of Seafire. The main variants were the Seafire Mk.IB (166 conversions from Spitfire VB airframes); Mk.IIC (372 intended for low- and medium-altitude air combat and air reconnaissance); thirty Mk.III (Hybrid) aircraft with fixed wings, followed by 1,220 examples of the definitive Seafire Mk.III with folding wings; and the Seafire Mks XV, XVII, 45, 46 and 47, these being Griffon-engined variants. The Seafire saw much action in the Mediterranean in the summer of 1943 and in the Pacific in 1945. The Seafire 47, operating from HMS *Triumph*, took part in air strikes against terrorists in Malaya and against North Korean forces in the early weeks of the Korean War.

Because of its flimsy undercarriage, the Seafire was far from ideal for aircraft carrier operations. This Mk.XV, PR494, was one of a batch built by Cunliffe-Owen. (Source unknown)

The Israeli Air Force used Spitfires during the War of Independence in 1948–49. These are LF.16Es of No. 101 Squadron, pictured at Hatzor in the Negev. (Source unknown)

The Supermarine Spiteful, first flown in 1944, was a redesign of the Spitfire Mk.XIV, featuring a laminar flow wing. Seventeen examples were completed, but the type did not enter service. The Supermarine Seafang was the naval equivalent of the Spiteful, and flew in prototype form. It was abandoned in favour of the turbojet-powered Supermarine Attacker. With these aircraft, the Spitfire line came to an end.

Today, there are approximately forty-four Spitfires still in an airworthy condition around the world, together with a few Seafires. Many more are retained in museums or as 'gate guardians' at airfields such as the famous wartime fighter station of Biggin Hill in Kent.

CHAPTER TEN

The Bristol Beaufighter

I n October 1938, the Bristol Aeroplane Company submitted a proposal for a twin-engine night fighter, heavily armed with a mixture of cannon and machine guns and equipped with AI radar, to the RAF Air Staff. The proposal was based on the design of the Beaufort torpedo-bomber, which had just made its first flight, and was initially called the Beaufort Fighter. The Air Staff's reaction was enthusiastic and prompt; Specification F.17/39 was written around the proposal and an order placed for 300 Beaufighters, as the aircraft would be named.

The first of four Beaufighter prototypes (R2052) flew for the first time on 17 July 1939, powered by two Bristol Hercules I-SM engines (forerunners of the Hercules III). By mid-1940 Bristol had received a second contract, for 918 Beaufighters. Two variants were now to be produced, the Mk.I with Hercules III engines and the Mk.II with Rolls-Royce Merlins, the Hercules being in short supply. The Beaufighter I was cleared for delivery to the RAF on 26 July 1940, and after evaluation by the Fighter Interception Unit, and deliveries to operational squadrons began in September. The aircraft was beset by more than the usual crop of teething troubles in its early operational career. In November and December 1940, Beaufighters and radar-equipped Blenheims flew over 600 sorties, made seventy-one radar contacts, and succeeded in destroying only four enemy aircraft.

Delays in the production of AI Mk.IV radar equipment prevented the full complement of five Beaufighter units (Nos 25, 29, 219, 600 and 604 Squadrons) from becoming operational until the spring of 1941, but despite early teething troubles those that were operational enjoyed some success. The first AI-assisted Beaufighter kill was claimed on the night of 19/20 November 1940, when Flight Lieutenant John Cunningham and Sergeant Phillipson of No. 604 Squadron were credited with the destruction of a Junkers 88, and by the time all five Beaufighter squadrons reached operational status their efficiency was greatly enhanced by the commissioning of six GCI (Ground Controlled Interception) radar stations on the south and east coasts of England. These could provide fairly wide coverage, and controllers could bring the fighter to within three miles of the target aircraft, at which point the AI Mk.IV radar took over. The first GCI-controlled interception was made by John Cunningham on 12 January 1941, but was unsuccessful because the Beaufighter's guns jammed. Then, on 10 May 1941 – the last major *Luftwaffe* attack on London – GCI-controlled Beaufighters destroyed fourteen German bombers, the highest loss sustained by the *Luftwaffe* on any one night since the Blitz began. Thirteen more Beaufighter squadrons were assigned to the night defence of Great Britain in 1941–42, and many of the RAF's night fighter aces scored their early kills while flying the heavy twin-engined fighter. Total Mk.I production was 914 aircraft, while 450 Mk.IIs were built.

Men like John Cunningham of No. 604 Squadron began to carve out reputations for themselves as bomber destroyers. Cunningham, known by the nickname of 'Cat's Eyes' bestowed on him by the popular press, and which he thoroughly detested, was to destroy no fewer than eight enemy bombers at night in April 1941, having been led expertly to his targets by his AI operator, Sergeant Jimmy Rawnsley. He was to end the war with a score of twenty enemy aircraft destroyed, two probably destroyed and seven damaged, most of them at night (The 'Cat's Eyes' nickname, of course, was designed to divert attention from the AI radar, which was still highly secret and about which the public as yet knew nothing).

At the end of 1941 nine squadrons of Beaufighters were assigned to the night defence of Britain, one having formed during the summer and three having converted from Defiants. The squadrons were No. 25 at Wittering (Northamptonshire), No. 29 at West Malling (Kent), No. 68 at High Ercall (Shropshire), No. 141 at Drem (East Lothian), No. 219 at Tangmere (Sussex), No. 255 at Coltishall (Norfolk), No. 307 at Exeter (Devon), No. 60 at Predannack (Cornwall) and No. 604 at Middle Wallop (Hampshire).

From bases in south-west England and Northern Ireland, Beaufighters attacked German maritime reconnaissance aircraft. Photographed from a Beaufighter, a Blohm und Voss Bv 138 goes down in flames. (IWM)

In December 1941 No. 89 Squadron deployed to Abu Sueir, Egypt, with Beaufighter Mk.Is, and in May 1941 No. 46 Squadron began re-forming as a night fighter unit at Idku, initially using some of 89 Squadron's aircraft. These two squadrons remained responsible for the night defence of the Canal Zone, and for protection of coastal shipping, throughout 1942, providing occasional detachments to Malta and, in 1943, carrying out intruder patrols over the Greek islands and Sicily. No. 89 Squadron left for Ceylon in October 1943, while No. 46 Squadron continued to provide air defence detachments around the eastern Mediterranean. In December 1942, meanwhile, another RAF Beaufighter night fighter squadron, No. 153, had arrived in North Africa; based at Maison Blanche in Algeria, its task was to protect the North African ports following the Allied invasion of November 1942 (Operation Torch). In March 1943 No. 108 Squadron, which had been operating in the night bombing role from various locations in North Africa, re-formed as a night fighter unit at Shandur with Beaufighter VIs (the Mk.VI being a variant fitted with Hercules VI engines) flying night patrols over Egypt and Libya before moving to Malta in June. Early in 1943 four USAAF night fighter units also arrived in North Africa; these were the 414th, 415th, 416th and 417th FS, whose crews had trained with RAF units in the UK. All four were armed with the Beaufighter VIF; they subsequently moved to Sicily and Italy, and were the only night fighter units operating with the US Twelfth Air Force.

No. 108 Squadron, in the meantime, soldiered on with its ageing Beaufighters, and the arrival of its first Mosquitoes in February 1944 was greeted with euphoria. It was short-lived; the new Mosquitoes were flown by crews drawn from 256 Squadron, and No. 108 continued to fly Beaufighters until 5 April, when it flew its first Mosquito patrol.

By the beginning of 1943, in the UK, the RAF's night fighter squadrons were turning increasingly from defence to offence. The de Havilland Mosquito's long range and heavy armament of four 20 mm cannon made it highly suitable for the night intruder role, as well as for local night air defence. The intruder Mosquitoes (and Beaufighters), although stripped of their AI for operations over enemy territory, were fitted with a device named Serrate which, developed by the Telecommunications Research Establishment as a result of information on enemy night-fighting radars brought back by special countermeasures aircraft, enabled the British fighters to home in to the enemy's airborne radar transmissions. It had a range of about 50 miles, and was first used operationally in June 1943 by No. 141 Squadron, which scored 23 kills in three months with its help.

No. 141 Squadron's commander was Wing Commander J.R.D. 'Bob' Braham, whose combat report describes a night action off the Dutch island of Ameland on the night of 17/18 August 1943. Braham was flying a Beaufighter Mk.VI, and his navigator was Flight Lieutenant H. Jacobs:

> We took off from Coltishall at 2200 hours on intruder patrol to Stade.
> We flew to a point north of Schiermonnikoog and then turned NE at
> 2254. We continued on course for about five minutes when we sighted

one Me 110 flying east and jinking. We turned and followed him towards the coast, closing in on the aircraft until we were at 300 yards range, 20 degrees starboard astern and a little below. Fire was opened with a two-second burst from all guns and strikes were seen all over the enemy aircraft. Smoke came from the port engine and the Me 110 dived to port. We gave him another two-second burst from 250 yards and he caught fire and dived into the sea, burning on the water.

Immediately afterwards we saw a second Me 110 (which had been chasing us) a little above and turning gently to starboard on an easterly course. We gave a one-second burst of cannon and machine gun at 50 yards in a gentle turn. The enemy aircraft appeared to blow up and we had to pull up and turn to port to avoid ramming it. At that point we saw one man bale out and his parachute open, and the enemy aircraft dived vertically into the sea in flames ... we landed at Wittering at 0145.

Bob Braham, a pre-war regular RAF officer, had been involved in the development of night fighting techniques since the beginning of the war, and he destroyed his first victim – a Dornier 17 – while flying a Blenheim of No. 29 Squadron on 24 August 1940. By July 1941 he had four kills to his credit, all at night, and he increased this score to six by the end of the year. During this period, his observer was Sergeant Gregory, who was later commissioned. After a rest from operations (during which, incidentally, they destroyed a Dornier 217 in a Beaufighter 'borrowed' while on a visit to their old squadron) they rejoined No. 29 Squadron in July 1942, and in just a few weeks they destroyed three enemy bombers and damaged three more. In October 1942 the Braham-Gregory team shot down a Junkers 88 and a Dornier 217. In the following month, Braham was promoted and given command of No. 141 Squadron, beginning night intruder operations with its Beaufighters in June 1943. On his first such mission, on 14 June, he shot down a Messerschmitt 110, and by the end of September he had brought his score to twenty enemy aircraft destroyed, nineteen of them at night. He was now level with John Cunningham, but his second operational tour was at an end and it was not until February 1944 that he was again permitted to fly operationally, and then only on a limited basis, as Wing Commander (Night Operations) at HQ No. 2 Group. In the meantime, No. 141 Squadron, together with Nos 169 and 239, which flew Mosquitoes, had been transferred from Fighter Command to No. 100 (Countermeasures) Group, the task of the three squadrons being bomber support.

In March 1944 No. 100 Group's fighter force was joined by No. 515 Squadron, operating Beaufighters and later Mosquito VIs. This unit, however, was not equipped with Serrate. During this period, changing his tactics, Braham made six low-level daylight intruder sorties into occupied Europe in March and April 1944, and on five of these trips he destroyed seven enemy aircraft. On the first sortie on 5 March (he was now flying a Mosquito, borrowed from No. 305 Squadron at Lasham) he shot down a Heinkel 177, the biggest aircraft he had so far destroyed. His run of luck came to an end on 25 June 1944, when, flying a

Rocket-armed Beaufighter Mk.VIc of No. 236 Squadron, RAF North Coates. (RAF)

No. 21 Squadron Mosquito, he was hit by flak and had to make a forced landing on a sandbar near Ringkobing, Denmark. He spent the rest of the war in prison camp, as did his Australian navigator, Flight Lieutenant Don Walsh. Braham's score at the time of his capture was twenty-nine confirmed kills, making him the leading RAF night fighter pilot. He was also the first RAF pilot ever to be awarded three DSOs and three DFCs.

As well as bringing a new dimension to the science of night fighting, the heavily-armed Beaufighter also showed itself to be an excellent ground attack and anti-shipping aircraft. The Beaufighter Mk.IC, 300 of which were produced, was a long range fighter variant for RAF Coastal Command. Operated initially by Nos 252 and 272 Squadrons in Malta and North Africa, it was used success-fully as a strike aircraft against enemy shipping, and – modified locally to carry two 113 kg (250 lb) or 227 kg (500 lb) bombs under the fuselage – it was used equally as effectively as a ground attack aircraft in the Western Desert. It was supplanted by the Mk.VI (the Mks III, IV and V being experimental aircraft); Mk.VIs for Fighter Command were designated Mk.VIF (879 aircraft), and those for Coastal Command Mk.VIC (693 aircraft). Sixty Mk.VIs on the pro-duction line were completed as Interim Torpedo Fighters, but two new variants for Coastal Command soon appeared. These were the TF Mk.X torpedo bomber, known as the Torbeau, and the Mk.XIC, which was not equipped to carry torpedoes. Both were fitted with 1,770 hp Hercules XVII engines and had a dorsal cupola containing a rearward-firing 0.303-inch machine gun.

The SE.5A in replica form. *(Source Unknown)*

The SE.5A was a very agile aircraft. *(Source Unknown)*

The SE.5A, seen here flying in replica form. *(Source Unknown)*

The SE.5A. *(Source Unknown)*

The Shuttleworth Collection's Bristol Fighter D8096 is a popular attraction at air shows. *(Source Unknown)*

The Airco DH.4, seen here approaching to land with engine idling, has been dubbed the 'Mosquito' of World War I. *(Phillip Jarrett)*

Bristol Bulldog MkII of No 3 Squadron RAF. *(Source Unknown)*

A Bulldog resplendent in the markings of No 56 Squadron RAF. *(Thomas Fishburn)*

Wellington Mk III VR-Q of No 419 Squadron RCAF, based at RAF Middleton St George. *(Source Unknown)*

A Sea Hurricane of No 807 Squadron, Fleet Air Arm, in formation with two Seafires.
(Source Unknown)

Entry to the Spitfire's cockpit was made easier by an access door in the fuselage side.
(Source Unknown)

The Spitfire's long nose made the aircraft difficult to taxy, the pilot's view being severly restricted. *(Source Unknown)*

Lancaster B.Mk.I in the markings of No 207 Squadron, in which it replaced the dangerous Manchester bomber. *(Source Unknown)*

Evocative shot of the Battle of Britain Memorial Flight's Lancaster, PA474. *(BBMF)*

Canberra B.58 of the South African Air Force. *(BAe)*

Canberra PR.7 WH801 of No 31 Squadron, Laarbruch, at low level over Germany. This aircraft was eventually converted to a T.22 for the Royal Navy. *(BAe)*

Viscount 806 G-BLOA was formely G-AOYJ before being converted for freight duties and re-registered in 1983. *(G. Ditchfield Collection)*

Viscount V.813 G-OHOT was later owned by British World Airways and was written off in a crash near Birmingham on 25 February 1994. *(G. Ditchfield Collection)*

Hunters of No 1 Tactical Weapons Unit, RAF Chivenor, Devon. *(BAe)*

Comet 4C XS235 put in many years of service with the Aeroplane and Armament Experimental Establishment, Boscombe Down. *(Crown Copyright)*

Hunter F.6 XG190 at the end of a line-up of No 92 Squadron's aerobatic team, the Blue Diamonds. *(BAe)*

A Valiant of No 138 Squadron photographed from another aircraft at RAF Luqa, Malta, during the Suez operations in October 1956. The squdron commander, Wing Commander Rupert Oakley, is the figure in the flying suit. *(Bill Meadows)*

Lightning F.1A of No 92 Squadron, armed with Firestreak AAMs. *(BAe)*

XR219 on a test flight from Warton, Lancashire. *(BAe)*

Amoung the users of the AV-8A was the Spanish Navy, one of whose aircraft is seen here. *(BAe)*

Sea Harrier FRS.1s of Nos 800, 801 and 899 Naval Air Squadrons. (*BAe*)

A Sea Harrier launches from the 'ski-jump' of HMS *Hermes* during the Falklands campaign. (*BAe*)

RAF Coastal Command's first Beaufighter squadron was No. 252, which was armed with Mk.Is and based at Aldergrove in Northern Ireland from April 1941. Its task was to intercept the enemy's Focke-Wulf Fw 200 long-range reconnaissance aircraft, which co-ordinated U-boat attacks, as they headed out from their bases at Brest and Lorient to search for Allied Atlantic convoys to the west of Ireland and attack merchant shipping. No. 252's aircraft formed an effective barrier between the Focke-Wulfs and the convoys in the Western Approaches.

In September 1942, a serious threat to British patrol aircraft in the Bay of Biscay area appeared in the shape of a *Staffel* of Junkers Ju 88C-6 long-range fighters, soon to be followed by three more. In October the Ju 88s destroyed sixteen aircraft, but an effective counter-measure was already in place. Two squadrons of Beaufighter VIs, Nos 235 and 248, had deployed to Chivenor in Devon and Talbenny in Pembrokeshire, and the Germans soon felt their presence. The Coastal Command operations record for September 1942 described one very effective action that took place on 17 September:

At 1755 hours eight Beaufighters of 235 Squadron on interceptor patrol were flying at 200 feet in loose formation in the Bay of Biscay, when a Focke-Wulf 200 was sighted. It was flying one mile to starboard on a reciprocal course over an armed 300-ton trawler. The three leading Beaufighters (E, P, N) attacked the FW on the port side, while O/235 dived from 2,000 feet to make a head-on attack, and the remainder attacked from the starboard quarter. The attack tactics given out at briefing were carried out perfectly by all aircrews. The trawler immediately opened fire and shot down C/235 into the sea. Beaufighter J/235 attacked the FW again from the port quarter, and E/235 delivered a third attack from starboard, broke away and attacked again from the port beam. The FW now burst into flames and dived into the sea with a series of explosions. A dinghy was released and seen in the sea half-inflated, with one man trying to climb in and three floating in the water. The Beaufighters re-formed and resumed their patrol at 1810 hours.

Ten minutes later the seven Beaufighters were flying in various positions, with six miles between the first and last aircraft, when three Ju 88s were seen ahead, circling at 1,000 feet above a fishing vessel with a French flag. The Beaufighters climbed to 1,000 feet and attacked simultaneously from various directions. One Ju was hit in the port engine and tail, and dived nose down into the sea. N, O and E attacked a second Ju; flames appeared in the cockpit and a large piece of cowling flew off. This Ju also dived into the sea, enveloped in flames. Meanwhile, A/235 followed the third Ju and attacked, but it took evasive action and disappeared in a cloud. A/235 flew through the cloud and re-sighted the Ju, delivering a second attack, but lost it again in cloud. When the Beaufighters left the scene of the action the tails of two Ju 88s were still projecting from the water.

In the latter half of 1942, with plans for the invasion of German-occupied Europe already being laid, the importance of attacks on enemy shipping within range of aircraft based in the British Isles reached a new level. Coastal Command's three UK-based squadrons of Bristol Beaufort torpedo-bombers had registered notable successes, but they suffered from a slow reaction time. What Coastal Command needed was a force of aircraft fast enough to intercept enemy shipping whenever and wherever it was reported in the North Sea and Channel areas, and powerful enough to inflict crippling damage upon it.

The answer lay in the formation of strike wings equipped with Beaufighters. The first was formed at RAF North Coates, Lincolnshire, in November 1942 and consisted of No. 143 Squadron, with Beaufighter Mk.IIs, No. 236 with Beaufighter Mk.Is and No. 254 Squadron with torpedo-carrying Mk.VIs. The strike wing flew its first operation on 20 November against a convoy off Rotterdam, and results were discouraging; one large merchant vessel and two escorts were hit, but the attacking aircraft became split up in bad weather and arrived over the target in ones and twos, falling victim to patrolling Fw 190s. Three Beaufighters were shot down, and four more were so badly damaged that they had to be written off.

After this episode the strike wing was withdrawn from operations for further training; it returned to action in the following spring, and this time produced excellent results. On 18 April, nine Torbeaus of No. 254 Squadron, together with six Beaufighters each from Nos 143 and 236 Squadrons, escorted by Spitfires and Mustangs, virtually destroyed an enemy convoy in Dutch waters and all the attacking aircraft returned safely to base. The idea was therefore proven to be basically sound, and in the summer of 1943 a second Coastal Command strike wing was formed. This comprised No. 455 Squadron RAAF and No. 489 Squadron RNZAF, both operating Torbeaus from RAF Leuchars.

By April 1943, rocket projectile rails had been fitted to the Beaufighters of No. 236 Squadron at North Coates, and work had begun on those of No. 143 Squadron. As RP training continued, so did shipping attacks by the North Coates Wing's torpedo and anti-flak Beaufighters, and on 29 April the wing sank three vessels for the loss of one Beaufighter of No. 143 Squadron.

The strike wing suffered a serious reverse on 1 May, when 31 aircraft set out to hunt the cruiser *Nürnberg* and three destroyers off south-west Norway. The mission was beyond fighter escort range and the Beaufighters were badly hit by Messerschmitt 109s and Focke-Wulf 190s, No. 254 Squadron losing three Torbeaus and No. 143 Squadron two anti-flak Beaufighters. The whole wing was forced to jettison its torpedoes and rockets as the aircraft took evasive action.

The next attack, on 17 May, was accompanied by a strong fighter escort, and the Beaufighters sank the German freighter *Kyphissia* (2,964 tons), the minesweeper M414 (775 tons) and the flak ship Vp 1110 off the island of Texel.

Meanwhile, a detachment of No. 236 Squadron had been sent to Predannack, in Cornwall, and it was from here that a Beaufighter attacked and sank the German submarine U418 on 1 June 1943. The submarine was in the Bay of Biscay, heading for Brest, when it was sighted by Flying Officer Mark Bateman, who was accompanied by a naval specialist, Lieutenant Commander

A Beaufighter of the Balkan Air Force launching a rocket attack on a target in Yugoslavia. (IWM)

F.J. Brookes, RN. All four RPs hit the U418, which went to the bottom with the loss of all hands.

In March 1944 a two-squadron strike wing became operational at Leuchars, in Fife, the squadrons being No. 455 (Australian) and 489 (New Zealand). Their stay was brief, for in the following month both squadrons flew down to Norfolk to form the Langham Strike Wing as part of No. 16 Group.

Their hunting ground was mainly the area off the Dutch coast, and sometimes the Langam Wing joined up with the North Coates Wing to form a strike force of up to fifty Beaufighters.

September 1944 saw the formation of two more strike wings, both in northeast Scotland. At Banff, in Grampian, there was a mixed strike wing, comprising the Beaufighters of Nos 144 and 404 Squadrons and the Mosquitoes of No. 235 Squadron. The Banff Strike Wing was commanded by Wing Commander Max Aitken. In October the Beaufighter squadrons moved to Dallachy to form a strike wing comprising Nos 144, 404, 405 and 489 Squadrons. The Dallachy Strike Wing had a relatively short operational career, but it saw a huge amount of action, its Beaufighters ranging along the rugged coast of Norway to make devastating attacks on enemy shipping. Losses were heavy; on one occasion, on 9 February 1945 – a day that became known as Black Friday – nine out of thirty-one Beaufighters failed to return from a strike, six of them from No. 404 Squadron.

Production of the Beaufighter TF Mk.X, which was the most important British anti-shipping aircraft from 1944 to the end of the war, totalled 2,205 aircraft, while 163 aircraft were completed to Mk.XIC standard. The Beaufighter TF Mk.X was also built in Australia as the TF Mk.21 (364 examples), the RAAF and RNZAF using it to good effect in the South-West Pacific. British production of the Beaufighter (all variants) was 5,562.

In the immediate postwar years the Beaufighter was used by the Portuguese Air Force, as well as the air forces of Turkey and the Dominican Republic. A few examples were also used, and only for a short time, by the Israeli Air Force.

Known surviving Beaufighter examples in 2007 were as follows: The National Museum of the United States Air Force in Dayton, Ohio has completed the restoration of a rare Beaufighter Mk.I. The aircraft is displayed as the USAAF Beaufighter flown by Captain Harold Augspurger, commander of the 415th Night Fighter Squadron, who shot down an He 111 carrying German staff officers in September 1944. The Beaufighter went on display on 18 October 2006.

The Royal Air Force Museum at Hendon, London, has a Beaufighter TF Mk.X on display along with a Bristol Hercules engine.

The Canada Aviation Museum presently is storing Beaufighter TF Mk.X RAF RD867 for future restoration. The museum aircraft is a semi-complete RAF restoration with no engines, cowlings or internal components, received in exchange for a Bristol Bolingbroke on 10 September 1969.

A privately owned Beaufighter is currently undergoing a lengthy restoration in the UK. Its owner hopes eventually to restore it to flying condition.

CHAPTER ELEVEN

The de Havilland Mosquito

I n the years between the two world wars, the de Havilland Aircraft Company was preoccupied almost exclusively with the development of civil aircraft, notably the 'Moth' series of touring and training biplanes, the DH.84 Dragon and DH.86 Dragon Rapide airliners. The firm was also responsible for designing one of the most famous aircraft of this era, the DH.88 Comet, an elegant twin-engine machine specially built to take part in the 1934 London–Melbourne air race. The Comet won the race, completing the journey in seventy hours fifty-four minutes and eighteen seconds flying time.

Apart from its performance, one of the most interesting things about the DH.88 was its all-wood stressed-skin construction, which resulted in an extremely strong thin-section cantilever wing. A similar method of construction was used in the subsequent de Havilland DH.91 Albatross civil transport, one of the most beautiful aircraft ever built, whose fuselage was a plywood–balsa–plywood sandwich, moulded to a sleek double curvature under pressure. Originally designed to meet an Air Ministry requirement for a transatlantic mail-plane, the prototype Albatross flew for the first time on 20 May 1937.

In November 1936, the Air Ministry issued Specification P.13/36, calling for a 'twin-engine medium bomber for world-wide use', and in 1938, de Havilland submitted a proposal, which involved an aircraft with an all-wooden structure to economize on metal and to tap the reservoir of carpenters and woodworkers that formed a large part of Britain's working population. The Air Ministry showed no interest, and even suggested that de Havilland would be better employed in building wings for other bombers. Specification P.13/36 eventually resulted in the Avro Manchester and the Handley Page HP.55, later to be fitted with four engines and become the Halifax.

In September 1939, shortly after the outbreak of war, de Havilland again submitted his latest bomber design, which had now crystallized in the twin-Merlin DH98, to the Air Ministry. Its estimated performance was nothing short of phenomenal; with a crew of two, it would be capable of carrying two 500 lb or six 250 lb bombs for 1,500 miles at a cruising speed of 320 mph. It was estimated that maximum speed would be in the order of 405 mph.

On 12 December 1939 the decision was taken to order a single prototype of the unarmed DH98 under a new specification, B.1/40. This called for an aircraft capable of carrying a 1,000 lb bomb load, with a range of 1,500 miles and a top speed of 397 mph. It was to be fitted with radio equipment, a camera, and self-sealing fuel tanks.

With the prototype order secured, design work was accelerated. For reasons of security and safety from air attack, this phase unfolded at Salisbury Hall, an historic, moated country manor house near the village of London Colney, Hertfordshire, a few miles to the south-west of de Havilland's main airfield at Hatfield. On 1 March 1940, de Havilland received a contract for the construction of fifty examples of the B.1/40 bomber-reconnaissance aircraft. Then, in April, the Germans invaded Norway, bringing an abrupt end to the so-called 'Phoney War' period, and on 10 May they attacked France and the Low Countries in a lightning campaign that lasted only a matter of weeks. At this point the B.1/40 programme nearly ground to a halt, as the demands of war meant that de Havilland was prevented from purchasing the materials it needed to keep it going. Only after much urgent representation by the company was B.1/40 reinstated, and then only on the understanding that the work would not interfere with tasks which were considered more vital, such as the production of Tiger Moth and Airspeed Oxford trainers and the repair of Hawker Hurricanes and Merlin engines.

While the Battle of Britain raged in the summer of 1940 the DH98 prototype was taking shape in a building disguised as a barn, and it was only now that those concerned with the DH98's design and construction could fully appreciate what a magnificent and innovative aircraft de Havilland had produced. The oval-section fuselage was built in two halves, with the joint along the vertical centre plane (like the fuselage of a model aircraft built from a plastic kit). The fuselage, reminiscent of the DH88 Comet's, was a sandwich made from an outer layer of ply, a middle layer of balsa wood, and an inner layer of ply. Over the rear part of the fuselage, where the smaller diameter necessitated greater torsional rigidity, the plywood skin was wrapped diagonally; elsewhere the grain ran longitudinally and transversely, so saving wood. After the skin had been glued together, each fuselage half was placed in a jig and tightly secured by metal clamps from end to end.

The wing, built in one piece, was an all-wood structure comprising two box spars with laminated spruce flanges and ply webs, spruce and ply compression ribs, spanwise spruce stringers and a ply skin, double on the upper surface. A false leading edge, made up of nose rib formers and a D-skin, was attached to the front spar. The whole wing was screwed, glued and pinned and finally covered with Mandapolam over the plywood. The centre portion of the wing carried the radiators and engine mountings. Eight fuel tanks were installed inside the wing and there were two more in the fuselage. The hydraulically-operated flaps were also of wooden construction and were installed between the ailerons and engine nacelles, and between the nacelles and fuselage.

On 3 November the DH98 was dismantled and taken by road to Hatfield, where it was reassembled in a small blast-proof building. On 19 November it emerged to carry out engine runs, and on the 24th it carried out taxiing trials, during which test pilot Geoffrey de Havilland Jr. made a short hop. The following day, with Geoffrey de Havilland in the pilot's seat and John Walker, DH's engine installation designer, as flight observer, the DH98 prototype, resplendent in a chrome yellow colour scheme on which RAF roundels were superimposed, made a thirty-minute maiden flight.

Mosquito B.Mk.IV bombers of No. 105 Squadron, RAF Marham. (The Aeroplane)

On 19 February 1941, the DH98 prototype, W4050, now with upper surfaces camouflaged dark green and brown, was flown to the Aeroplane and Armament Experimental Establishment (A&AEE) at Boscombe Down, Wiltshire, for service trials. The trials showed the DH.98 handled well at all speeds and altitudes and had a high rate of climb. Its maximum speed was above the estimate at 386 mph, which made it 30 mph faster than the fastest known German fighter and 100 mph faster than any comparable bomber.

On 11 January 1941, de Havillands had been instructed to build a photo-reconnaissance prototype, and that they were to complete the remaining machines of the original as nineteen PR aircraft and twenty-eight fighters. Later, the programme was amended to include ten production bombers. The bomber prototype, W4057 – originally laid down as a PR aircraft – was delivered to Boscombe Down on 27 September 1941, and was followed by the first of the production bombers, W4064, on 18 October.

The initial photo-reconnaissance Mosquito, which was fitted with Merlin 21 engines, was the PR.Mk.I, based on the prototype, W4050. The first PR aircraft to enter RAF service was in fact the second Mosquito prototype, W4051, which was delivered to No. 1 Photographic Reconnaissance Unit at RAF Benson, Oxfordshire, on 13 July 1941, and was followed by nine production aircraft, W4053 to W4062. All were fitted with three vertical and one oblique cameras. Five aircraft had been delivered to No. 1 PRU by the middle of September 1941.

Four long-range PR.1s with additional fuel tankage were also delivered, two being tropicalised and deployed to Malta and Egypt in January 1942. Five PR.Is were lost on operations.

Other photo-reconnaissance variants were the PR.Mk.IV, a day and night reconnaissance aircraft which first flew in April 1942, 28 being converted from the B.IV Series 2; the PR.Mk.VIII , based on the PR.IV but with two-stage Merlins; the PR.Mk.IX, a photo-reconnaissance version for service in all theatres; the PR.Mk.XVI, with two-stage Merlins and a pressure cabin; the PR.Mk.32 high-altitude photo-reconnaissance aircraft with two-stage Merlins, pressure cabin; and specially lightened and extended wingtips; and the PR.Mk.34/34A very long-range reconnaissance aircraft with two-stage Merlins and extra fuel in a belly tank. All armour was removed to increase operational altitude. The Mosquito PR.40 and PR.41 were reconnaissance versions built in Australia.

The first operational PR Mosquito sortie – a reconnaissance of Bordeaux, Brest and La Pallice harbours by W4055 LY-T – was flown by Squadron Leader Rupert Clerke on the morning of 17 July 1941. The mission was flown at an average altitude of 24,000 feet, the Mosquito flying over Paris before returning to base and successfully evading interception by three Messerschmitt Bf 109s en route. Keeping a constant watch on the French Atlantic ports, where the German battle cruisers *Scharnhorst* and *Gneisenau* and the heavy cruiser *Prinz Eugen* were based in 1941, was a routine task for the PR Mosquitoes, as was the surveillance of Norwegian harbours, which in early 1942 sheltered other major German surface units, including the battleship *Tirpitz*. The Mosquitoes also ranged far and wide over the continent of Europe, the German rocket research establishment at Peenemünde being among their targets. Together with PR Spitfires, they provided photo-mapping coverage of the French coastline that enabled Allied planners to build up a complete intelligence picture prior to the D-Day landings, and provided pre-strike and post-strike photographs of Allied targets throughout Europe, including the V-1 flying bomb sites that were being constructed in the Pas de Calais. Their contribution to the eventual Allied victory was immense.

The third prototype Mosquito, W4052, was flown from the outset as a night fighter, with a 'solid' nose housing AI.Mk.IV radar and an armament of four 20 mm cannon and four 0.303-inch machine guns. In this form it was designated NF.Mk.II. The AI radar was of the external aerial type with the familiar 'bow and arrow' nose antenna, the cockpit display having separate azimuth and elevation tubes. The NF.II prototype, W4052, flew for the first time on 15 May 1941 and the first Mosquito fighter squadron, No. 157, formed at Debden in Essex on 13 December 1941, its first aircraft, a dual-control Mk.II, arriving at Debden's satellite airfield, Castle Camps, on 26 January 1942. Seventeen Mk.IIs were delivered to Maintenance Units for the fitting of AI Mk.V (which was supposed to be an improvement on the Mk.IV, but which was not), and by mid-April No. 157 Squadron had nineteen NF.Mk.IIs on its inventory, three of them without radar. By this time No. 151 Squadron at Wittering had also begun to rearm with the NF.Mk.II, with sixteen aircraft on strength at the end of April.

Mosquito F.II and NF.II production (the F.II being the fighter variant without AI radar) came to 494 aircraft. Twenty-five F.IIs, fitted with extra tanks, were issued to No. 23 Squadron in July 1942, the unit deploying to Malta in December for long-range intruder operations over Sicily, Italy and North Africa. Numerous Mosquito night fighter variants were produced, culminating in the NF.30 series. First flown in March 1944, the latter was a development of the NF.XIX with two-stage Merlins and equipped with AI.Mk.X. The NF.Mk.36 was a night fighter with later types of Merlin engines and upgraded AI radar; 163 were built, remaining in RAF service until 1953 The NF.Mk.38 was an upgrade of the NF.36; it was not used by first-line RAF squadrons, and most of those built were sold to Yugoslavia.

It was not until the end of June 1942 that the Mosquito night fighters scored their first confirmed victories. On the night of 24/25 June, aircraft of No. 151 Squadron accounted for two Do 217E4s, shooting down a Dornier of 2/KG40 into the North Sea and another into the Wash. The first two Mosquito night fighter squadrons, Nos 157 and 151, were followed in the course of 1942 by Nos 264, 85, 25 and 410 Squadrons, so that Mosquito night fighter coverage could now be provided from the south coast to the Scottish border. During Operation Steinbock, the so-called 'Little Blitz' of January to May 1944, which was conducted by all available German bombers on the Western Front, Mosquitoes equipped with AI.Mk.VIII radar destroyed 129 bombers out of the 329 lost by the *Luftwaffe* in that five-month period.

In June 1944, the home-based night fighter squadrons were suddenly pitched into a defensive battle against the first of Hitler's 'revenge weapons' – the V-1 flying bomb. The Mosquitoes opened their score against the V-1s on the night of 15/16 June, when a Mosquito VI of No. 605 Squadron from Manston (Flight Lieutenant J.G. Musgrave and Flight Sergeant Sanewell) exploded one over the Channel. Four Mosquito squadrons – Nos 96, 219, 409 and 418 – were assigned exclusively to anti-flying bomb operations, known as Diver patrols, and were joined later in June by Nos 85, 157 and 456. Other squadrons operated against the V-1s on a part-time basis, as priority was given to patrolling the Normandy beachhead. Between them, the seven full-time anti-Diver Mosquito squadrons claimed 471 flying bombs, while the part-timers claimed 152 to give a combined total of 623, or about one-third of the RAF's total claim against the V-1s.

The Mosquito squadrons began to take losses in the later phases of the campaign against the V-1. In September 1944, with their bases in the Pas de Calais overrun by the Allied advance, the enemy began flying bomb attacks on London and other UK targets, such as Portsmouth and Southampton, with V-1s air-launched from Heinkel He 111s of KG 53. Later in September air launches were made against east coast targets from positions off the Dutch coast. Catching the Heinkel launchers was very difficult, for they flew slowly at low level, and several Mosquitoes were lost to return fire, or because they stalled at low speed while trying to intercept. In an attempt to improve interception rates, a radar picket ship, the frigate HMS *Caicos*, and a specially equipped radar Wellington of the Fighter Interception Unit were used to direct the Mosquitoes, which patrolled over the sea at about 4,000 feet between Britain and Holland. These operations continued until 14 January 1945, by which time KG 53 had lost seventy-seven aircraft, forty-one of them on operations.

The Mosquito's long range and heavy armament of four 20 mm cannon made it highly suitable for the night intruder role, as well as for local night air defence. The intruder Mosquitoes (and Beaufighters), although stripped of their AI for operations over enemy territory, were fitted with a device named Serrate which, developed by the Telecommunications Research Establishment as a result of information on enemy night-fighting radars brought back by special countermeasures aircraft, enabled the British fighters to home in to the enemy's airborne radar transmissions. It had a range of about fifty miles and was first used operationally in June 1943 by No. 141 Squadron, which scored twenty-three kills in three months with its help.

Towards the end of 1943 three Mosquito squadrons, Nos 141, 169 and 239, were transferred from Fighter Command to No. 100 (Countermeasures) Group, their task being bomber support. The Mosquito crews of Nos 169 and 239 Squadrons had no experience of Serrate operations; moreover, the Mosquito Mk.II aircraft with which they were initially armed were worn out and their operations had to be severely curtailed so that they could be re-engined with new Rolls-Royce Merlin 22s on a rotational basis. During their first three months of operations the three squadrons combined claimed only thirty-one enemy aircraft destroyed or damaged. In March 1944 No. 100 Group's fighter force was joined by No. 515 Squadron, operating Beaufighters and later Mosquito VIs.

The first bomber version of the Mosquito was the B.IV Series I, nine of which were converted from PR.Mk.I airframes. These were followed by the much more numerous Mk.IV Series II, 273 of which were built. The first production aircraft flew in March 1942 and entered service with No. 105 Squadron, Marham, in May 1942. The aircraft had provision for wing drop tanks, and carried a bomb load of 2,000 lb. Some aircraft were later converted for special operations with the 'Highball' anti-shipping weapon. In Bomber Command fifty-four B.Mk.IVs were modified with bulged bomb bays to carry a single 4,000 lb HC bomb on the recommendation of No. 8 (Pathfinder) Group, these being equipped with OBOE navigational and bombing aids and serving in the Light Night Striking Force. The final bomber variant was the B.35, which served post-war in 2nd Tactical Air Force and with Nos 109 and 139 (target marking) squadrons until replaced by Canberras in 1952–3. Some were converted to TT.35 target tugs and PR.35 reconnaissance aircraft.

The Mosquito bomber squadrons opened their account in the early morning of 31 May, when four aircraft of No. 105 Squadron, led by Squadron Leader A.R. Oakeshott, made a daylight attack on Cologne, devastated by the first thousand-bomber raid the night before, while a fifth was despatched in the late afternoon to make a low-level reconnaissance flight over the city. One of the Mosquitoes was shot down by flak and crashed in the North Sea. A return visit to Cologne on 1 June resulted in the loss of another aircraft.

On 30 January 1943, the two original bomber squadrons, Nos 105 and 139, now at RAF Marham in Norfolk, combined to carry out an attack that had

BOAC used a number of Mosquitoes on a courier service between Scotland and neutral Sweden. Inset shows the cramped accommodation for the passenger in the bomb bay. (IWM)

enormous propaganda value. The target was Berlin, the first time that the German capital had been visited by the RAF in daylight. On this day, a military parade was to be held to mark the tenth anniversary of Hitler's Wehrmacht. In addition, a radio broadcast to the German people was to be made at 11.00 hours by *Luftwaffe* C-in-C Hermann Göring, followed by a second broadcast at 16.00 hours by Propaganda Minister Josef Goebbels. The first attack was made by three Mosquitoes of No. 105 Squadron, led by Squadron Leader R.W. Reynolds and Pilot Officer E.B. Sismore (navigator). They bombed at precisely 11.00 hours, interrupting Göring's speech. In the afternoon, three aircraft of No. 139 Squadron, led by Squadron Leader D.F.W. Darling, also headed for Berlin, but they were intercepted by enemy fighters and Darling was shot down. The other two made their attack on schedule about five minutes before Goebbels made his speech, and both returned safely to base.

On 1 June 1943, Nos 105 and 139 Squadrons were assigned to No. 8 (Pathfinder) Group, joining another Mosquito squadron, No. 109. In December 1942 this unit had pioneered the use of the blind bombing and target marking system known as Oboe, in which two ground stations transmitted pulses to an aircraft, which then received them and re-transmitted them. By measuring the time taken for each pulse to go out and return, the distance of the aircraft from the ground stations could be accurately measured. If the distance of the target from station A was known, the aircraft could be guided along the arc of a circle whose radius equalled this distance. The bomb release point was calculated and determined by station B, which 'instructed' the aircraft to release its bombs when the objective was reached. This meant that targets could be attacked through cloud.

The Mosquito strength of No. 8 Group eventually reached a total of eleven squadrons, the others being Nos 128, 142, 162, 163, 571, 608, 627 and 692. The Mosquito element was divided into two categories; the target markers, spearheaded by the Oboe-equipped units, and the Light Night Striking Force (LNSF), for which No. 139 Squadron, equipped first with the G-H and later the H2S target location and bombing systems, acted as marker squadron. The LNSF squadrons were armed with the Mosquito B.IV Special, an adaptation of the B.IV Series 2 with a bulged bomb bay to accommodate a 4,000 lb (1,812 kg) bomb, a weapon which had a devastating effect on built-up areas. This earned it the nickname of 'Blockbuster', a word much used nowadays to describe huge box office successes, the origin of which is all but forgotten. The 8 Group squadrons, mainly the target-markers, also used the high-flying Mosquito B.IX, which had an operational ceiling of about 31,000 feet (9,500 m), and the B.XVI, which was designed from the start to carry a 4,000 lb (1,812 kg) bomb and which had a pressurized cabin. The B.XVI flew its first operational sorties on the night of 10/11 February 1944, when aircraft of No. 139 Squadron attacked Berlin. In all, No. 8 Group's Mosquito squadrons flew 26,255 operational sorties during the Second World War; 108 aircraft failed to return and eighty-eight more were written off as a result of battle damage. In the closing months of the Battle of Germany their losses were reduced to one per 2,000 sorties; but things might have changed dramatically if the war had continued. On the night of 30/31 March, 1945, four Mosquitoes were destroyed on the approaches to Berlin by a single German night fighter; it was a Messerschmitt Me 262 jet, equipped with Lichtenstein SN-2AI radar.

The Mosquito FB.Mk.VI fighter-bomber, of which 2,718 were built during and after the war, was the major production version of the Mosquito. The first Mk.VI was a converted Mk.II (HJ662), and this flew for the first time in February 1943. The standard NF.II gun armament was retained, and the aircraft could carry two 250 or 500 lb bombs in the rear of the bomb bay, with two additional bombs or auxiliary fuel tanks beneath the outer wing sections. In the late spring of 1943, Mk.VI (HJ719) carried out trials with rocket projectiles (RPs). These proved very successful, and RAF Coastal Command began equipping some of its strike wings with Mk.VI Mosquitoes armed with eight 60 lb RPs under each wing. The Mosquito Mk.VI entered service with No. 418 Squadron in the spring of 1943 and subsequently armed several squadrons of No. 2 Group, replacing such aircraft as the Lockheed Ventura. These squadrons carried out some daring low-level precision attacks during the last year of the war, including the raid on Amiens prison in February 1944 and attacks on *Gestapo* headquarters buildings in Norway and the Low Countries.

Two months after the attack on Amiens prison, in what an Air Ministry bulletin described as 'probably the most brilliant feat of low-level precision bombing of the war', the Mosquitoes attacked the *Gestapo* headquarters at The Hague, the nerve centre of German operations against the resistance movements in the Low Countries. The *Gestapo* HQ was a 90 feet (27 m) high five-storey building tightly wedged among others in the Schevengsche Weg, and was strongly defended by light anti-aircraft weapons. The task of destroying the building was assigned to No. 613 Squadron, commanded by Wing Commander Bob Bateson. A scale model of the *Gestapo* HQ was built, perfect in every detail, right down to the thickness and composition of the walls. Alongside the planners, scientists worked hard to develop a new bomb, a mixture of incendiary and high explosive, that would have a maximum destructive effect on the *Gestapo*'s stored files and records.

Bateson picked his crews carefully, and put them to the test during several weeks of intensive training. The raid was scheduled for 11 April 1944, Bateson leading six Mosquitoes from Lasham, Hampshire. As they approached The Hague the Mosquitoes split up into pairs. Flight Lieutenant Peter Cobley, following in line astern behind Bateson, saw his leader's pair of bombs drop away and literally skip through the front door of the HQ. Cobley dropped his own bombs in turn, pulling up sharply over the roof of the building. The other four aircraft made their attacks at short intervals, all their bombs hitting the target, which was completely destroyed with very little collateral damage.

On 31 October 1944, another *Gestapo* HQ, this time at Aarhus in Denmark, was attacked by twenty-five Mosquitoes of No. 140 Wing, led by Wing Commander Bob Reynolds. The mission was flown from Thorney Island, the Mosquitoes carrying a total of thirty-five 500 lb (227 kg) delayed-action bombs. Fighter escort was provided by eight Mustangs. The *Gestapo* HQ was located in two adjoining buildings that had previously formed part of the University of Aarhus; once again, the Mosquito crews were faced with the problem of making an effective attack while causing minimum damage to civilian property. They did so brilliantly, leaving the headquarters shattered and ablaze. More than 200 *Gestapo* officials were killed in the attack, and all the files on the Dutch resistance movement were destroyed in the fire. One Mosquito actually struck the roof of the building, losing its tail wheel and half its port tailplane. Despite the damage; it flew home – a testimony to the aircraft's ruggedness.

Although the Bristol Beaufighter remained RAF Coastal Command's principal anti-shipping strike aircraft in the last two years of the war, three Mosquito FB.VI squadrons – Nos 143, 235 and 333 (Norwegian) – joined the Command's order of battle late in 1944, forming a strike wing based at Banff in Scotland. Another squadron, No. 248 at Portreath, Cornwall, was armed with Mosquito VIs and VIIIs, the latter mounting a 57 mm cannon, from January 1944, the VIIs escorting the VIIIs on their anti-shipping strikes in the Bay of Biscay.

In June 1943, a variant of the Mosquito was proposed to meet Specification S.11/43, calling for a torpedo-reconnaissance fighter/fighter-bomber. This emerged as the TR.33, a deck-landing version of the Mk.VI, with upward-

Israel used a number of Mosquitoes in the 1950s. They saw operational service in the 1956 Arab–Israeli war. (Stephen Peltz)

folding wings, an arrester hook, four-blade propellers oleo-pneumatic landing gear, American ASH radar in a thimble nose, JATO gear, four 20 mm cannon and provision for an under-belly 2,000 lb Mk.XV or XVII torpedo, or alternatively a bomb or mine. Mosquito FB.VIs LR359 and LR387 became the TR.33 prototypes, the first carrying out deck landing trials on HMS *Indefatigable* in March 1944. Two more aircraft, TS444 and TS449, undertook handling trials, these being followed by fifty production aircraft; forty-seven more were cancelled later. The only squadron to equip fully with the TR.33 was No. 811 at Ford, Sussex, in 1946; it relinquished them a year later. In 1954-55 fourteen TR.33s were taken out of storage, de-navalised, and sold to Israel.

The Mosquito's deployment to the Far East was delayed, the main reason being the need to alter the glue used on the aircraft's construction from a casein to a formaldehyde type, which was more resistant to the humid conditions of the tropics and to insects. The first ground-attack squadrons to arm with the FB.VI, in February and July 1944 respectively, were Nos 45 and 82, and these began operations in September and October with attacks on Japanese communications in Burma. Three more FB.VI squadrons, Nos 47, 84 and 110, joined South-East Asia Command's order of battle before the end of hostilities.

Between 1943 and the end of the war, Mosquitos were used as transport aircraft on a regular route over the North Sea between Leuchars in Scotland and Stockholm. Because Sweden was neutral, the aircraft carried civilian markings and were operated by Norwegian officers, who were nominally 'civilian employees' of BOAC. They carried small, high value cargos such as precision ball bearings and machine-tool steel. Occasionally, important passengers were carried in an improvised cabin in the bomb bay, one notable passenger being the physicist Niels Bohr, who was evacuated from Stockholm in 1943 in an unarmed Mosquito sent by the RAF.

Total Mosquito production reached 7,781 aircraft, 6,710 of which were built during the war years. Canadian Mosquito production, which ran to 1,134 aircraft, powered by Packard-built Merlins, included the Mk.XX and Mk.25 bombers, Mk.26 fighter-bomber and Mk.22 and Mk.27 trainers. Forty Canadian-built reconnaissance Mosquitoes were supplied to the USAAF as the F.8. The Mosquito was, without doubt, one of the most versatile and successful aircraft of the Second World War, seeing service throughout the world as a day and night fighter, fighter-bomber, high altitude bomber, pathfinder, anti-shipping strike aircraft, reconnaissance aircraft and trainer.

There are believed to be around thirty preserved examples of the Mosquito at various locations, including the Royal Air Force Museum at Hendon. The type's wooden construction makes restoration difficult. In 2006, the original

Too late to see service in the Second World War, the Mosquito's successor was the de Havilland Hornet, one of the finest piston-engine aircraft ever built. (Hawker Siddeley)

Mosquito prototype, W4050, was undergoing complete restoration in the de Havilland Aircraft Heritage Centre in Hertfordshire, UK. A restored example is currently on display in the Second World War gallery at the National Museum of the United States Air Force. This Mosquito is a British-built B Mk.35 manufactured in 1946, later converted for target-towing, and is similar to the PR Mk.XVIs used by the AAF. Having been flown to the Museum in February 1985, suffering several breakdowns along the way and taking many months to arrive, this aircraft has now been restored to a Mk.XVI configuration and painted to represent a weather reconnaissance aircraft of the 653rd Bomb Squadron, 25th Bomb Group, based in England in 1944–45. Another Mosquito is currently under restoration in a hangar at the RAAF Museum at Point Cook, Victoria, Australia.

CHAPTER TWELVE

The Avro Lancaster

O ne of the most famous bomber aircraft of all time, the Avro Lancaster was developed from the Avro Manchester, a design that suffered from the unreliability of its two Rolls-Royce Vulture engines. The 24-cylinder Vulture – a marriage of two Rolls Royce Peregrine engines joined together, one inverted on top of the other, driving a single crankshaft and served by a complex lubricating system – had proved a disaster and had eventually been abandoned. The engines had a tendency to overheat uncontrollably, and although initial over-heating problems were overcome, a major problem arose in the design of the connecting-rods. In the Vulture, Rolls-Royce had departed from Royce's own design of two con-rods using the same throw of the crankshaft, with the result that an abnormal stress was placed on one con-rod of each pair, which led to failures of the bolts holding its bearing together. The con-rod then failed and penetrated the crank-case, leading both to engine failure and inextinguishable engine fires.

There was a design scheme to overcome this design error, but the engine was doomed anyway, for two reasons: first, because the Manchester could not fly safely on one engine at the Vulture's rated power; and second, because the Vulture did not have the development potential to accommodate the ongoing increase in the aircraft's operational weight.

After the loss of the prototype Manchester, a crucial meeting was held with Avro's Managing Director, Roy Dobson, at which Air Chief Marshal Sir Wilfrid Freeman, the senior RAF officer in the Ministry of Aircraft production, and Air Vice Marshal Arthur Tedder, Director General of Research and Development in the Air Ministry, expressed their anxieties as to whether the Vulture-powered Manchester would prove a satisfactory aircraft. What happened next was recalled by Lord Tedder in his memoirs:

> On the desk in Dobson's office there was a nice model of the Manchester. Before we got any farther on the subject, Dobson asked Freeman a direct question: 'I am told you have plenty of Merlins coming in. Is this right?' to which Freeman answered 'Yes'. 'Then what about this?' said Dobson, taking one of the wings off and adding an extra wing and an extra engine on one side and then repeating the process on the other side. 'How's that?' he asked. 'That' was the Lancaster – an afterthought that became one of the most successful and effective bombers of the war.

Morale, understandably, was not at its best in the Manchester squadrons. Luckily, the Manchester's service career was relatively brief. While production of the Manchester was in progress, one airframe, BT308, was designated a 'four-engine Manchester' and fitted with four Rolls-Royce Merlin XX engines. It first flew on 9 January 1941 with triple fins and without ventral or dorsal turrets, and was the prototype of the Avro Lancaster, which, unlike its undistinguished predecessor, would become a legend. It first flew on 9 January 1941 with triple fins and without ventral or dorsal turrets (A ventral turret was to have been a feature of the Lancaster, but was eliminated to provide extra bomb-bay space). Before the full test programme was initiated, the aircraft was fitted with twin fins on a tailplane spanning 33 feet, which improved flight characteristics considerably.

The first Lancaster, BT308, was delivered to No. 44 (Rhodesia) Squadron at Waddington, Lincolnshire in September 1941 for familiarisation, and by January 1942 the squadron had begun to replace its Handley Page Hampdens with the type. First operational sortie with Lancasters was on 3 March 1942, when four aircraft laid mines in the Heligoland Bight.

The second squadron to be equipped with Lancasters was No. 97, and in April 1942, in company with No. 44 it carried out a low-level daylight raid on the MAN factory at Augsburg, Bavaria, which was manufacturing U-boat diesel engines. Seven out of the twelve Lancasters involved were lost. Squadron Leader J.D. Nettleton, one of 44's flight commanders, was awarded the VC.

As an insurance against possible interruption in supplies of Merlins, it was decided to equip some Lancasters with four 1,650 hp Bristol Hercules 6 (or 16) radials in place of the Merlin XX, these aircraft becoming the Lancaster Mk.II, 300 of which were built. Little modification was made during its life to the basic Lancaster airframe, a testimonial to its sturdiness and reliability, and so very little extra work was necessary when the Mk.III with Packard-built Merlin engines superseded the Mk.1 on the production lines. Deployment of the Lancaster III enabled Bomber Command to use first the 8,000 lb bomb, then the 12,000 lb Tallboy, and finally the 22,000 lb Grand Slam, recessed in the doorless bomb bay. Several Mks I and II were used for experimental work, particularly as engine test-beds. One of the Mk.I experimental aircraft, ED817, had its fuselage underside modified to accommodate development rounds of the special mine used in the famous raid by No. 617 Squadron on the Ruhr dams in May 1943. The last Lancaster raid of the war was made against an SS barracks at Berchtesgaden on 25 April 1945. During the war Lancasters flew 156,192 sorties, dropping 608,612 tons of bombs. Losses in action were 3,431 aircraft, a further 246 being destroyed in operational accidents. At its peak strength in August 1944 no fewer than forty-two Bomber Command squadrons were armed with the Lancaster.

One of the more spectacular attacks in which the Lancaster played a prominent part was the attack on the German secret weapons research establishment at Peenemünde, on the Baltic coast, on the night of 17/18 August 1943. Of the 596 heavy bombers involved, 324 were Lancasters, 218 Halifaxes and 54 Stirlings. The mission, which was code-named Operation Hydra, involved the precision bombing of a series of selected buildings grouped around three principal aiming points – the scientists' and workers' living quarters, the factory

The Lancaster Mk. II was fitted with the Bristol Hercules radial engine as a safeguard against possible shortages of the Merlin. Only 300 were built. (Source unknown)

producing V-2 rockets and the experimental station. It was a difficult task, as the buildings were widely dispersed along the narrow coastal strip.

The operation was directed by Group Captain J.H. Searby of No. 83 Squadron, Pathfinder Force, who remained over the target throughout the attack, passing instructions over the R/T to the main bomber force. It was the first time that the 'Master Bomber' technique was applied to a major attack. During the raid a new type of marker bomb was used; this was a 250-pounder crammed with impregnated cotton wool, which ignited at 3,000 feet and burned with a brilliant crimson flame for about ten minutes. It was easily recognisable, and the Germans found it extremely difficult to devise an effective decoy.

The conditions were good, with bright moonlight, and Searby was able to control the raid successfully from start to finish, although there was one unfortunate incident when the initial marking and bombing fell on a labour camp for forced workers situated a mile and a half south of the first aiming point, but Searby quickly brought the situation under control. Thanks to a handful of Mosquitoes, which dropped masses of flares over Berlin, the German fighter controllers were led to believe that the capital was the target, and as a result 148 fighters patrolled overhead for the best part of an hour without sighting a single enemy aircraft. A total of 560 aircraft attacked the target, dropping 1,800 tons of bombs, most of which were high explosive. Approximately 180 Germans were killed in the attack, nearly all in the workers' accommodation area, and 500–600 foreigners, mostly Poles, were killed in the workers' camp, where they were housed in flimsy wooden barracks without the benefit of air-raid shelters.

Despite the deception over Berlin, Bomber Command lost forty aircraft that night, many of them falling victim to the so-called *Wilde Sau* (Wild Boar) tactics adopted by the *Luftwaffe*, in which fighters cruised at high altitude and looked for their bomber targets silhouetted against the fires below. Twenty-three of the missing aircraft were Lancasters.

Apart from the celebrated and much-publicised attack on the Möhne, Eder and Sorpe dams, Lancasters were involved in a number of other operations that captured the public's imagination, some of them involving No. 617 Squadron and its 'earthquake' bombs. Precision was the keyword in 617 Squadron's missions, especially in one of the squadron's more unusual operations, carried out in the early hours of 6 June 1944 as D-Day dawned and an invasion fleet of over 3,000 vessels headed for their objectives on the coast of Normandy. Eight of the squadron's Lancasters flew a series of eight-mile legs over the Channel, each aircraft dropping twelve bundles of 'Window' (foil strips cut to the wavelength of the enemy radar) per minute from a height of 3,000 feet. Code-named Operation Taxable, this mission was a ruse designed to make the enemy think that the Allied invasion force was about to land north of Le Havre, the Window bundles producing echoes similar to those of a large number of surface vessels on the German radar screens.

Three nights later, 617 Squadron went into action with a formidable new weapon. Known as Tallboy, it was a 12,000 lb bomb designed by Barnes Wallis, architect of the mines which the squadron had used to breach the Möhne and Eder dams. It was a remarkable weapon, having both the explosive power of a high-capacity blast bomb and the penetrating power of an armour-piercing bomb without sacrificing explosive filling for thickness of casing. Its secret lay in its perfect streamlining, which gave it a terminal velocity of 3,600 feet per second – faster than the speed of sound.

Its use required a high degree of accuracy, because in order to achieve maximum penetration it had to be dropped from a height of 8,000 feet or more. No. 617 Squadron's Lancasters were therefore fitted with new Mk.IIA bomb sights, which enabled their highly trained crews to place the bombs within eighty yards of the target from an altitude of 20,000 feet. This margin of error was quite acceptable, for the exploding Tallboy displaced a million cubic feet of earth and formed a crater that took 5,000 tons of soil to fill. The Lancasters' bomb bays were also modified to accommodate the lengthy bombs.

Armed with Tallboys, nineteen Lancasters of 617 Squadron set out on the night of 8/9 June 1944 to destroy the Saumur railway tunnel in southern France, a vital point on the main rail artery through which the Germans were bringing in reinforcements from the south-west to the Normandy front. Ahead of 617, four Lancasters of No. 83 Squadron were to drop flares over the target so that the master bomber, Wing Commander Leonard Cheshire, could mark the south-west entrance to the tunnel with red spot flares, after which they were to bomb the railway bridge at the tunnel's other entrance with ordinary thousand-pounders.

Although some of 83 Squadron's flares went wide because of poor H2S indications, they provided sufficient light for Cheshire to sweep in and place his red spot markers within forty yards of the tunnel entrance. The bomb-aimers in 617's Lancasters, flying at 10,000 feet just under the cloud base, located them without difficulty and released their Tallboys, expecting to see spectacular results. They were disappointed: all they saw was a series of red pinpricks as the 6-ton bombs bored into the ground around the markers, and it was not until reconnaissance aircraft returned with photographs the following day that they realised the awesome devastation they had caused.

Seventeen Tallboys had fallen around the tunnel mouth, penetrating deep into the ground and causing enormous craters. An eighteenth had fallen on the railway bridge at the other end of the tunnel. It was the nineteenth bomb, however, that had caused the greatest damage, ripping through the hillside that towered over the tunnel mouth and exploding in the tunnel itself, bringing down something like 10,000 tons of earth. The tunnel was still blocked two months later, when the area was occupied by American forces.

During the weeks that followed, No. 617 Squadron's Tallboy-equipped Lancasters wrought more destruction on more 'hard' targets, notably the U-boat pens at Brest, Lorient, St Nazaire and La Pallice and the E-boat bases at Le Havre and Boulogne, all of which were protected by thick concrete. They struck at the V-1 flying bomb sites at Siracourt, Watten, Wizernes and Mimoyeques. The latter attacks were carried out in daylight, with Cheshire marking the objectives in a newly-acquired P-51 Mustang fighter, and despite heavy flak succeeded in wrecking most of them.

On the night of 23 September 1944 the squadron returned to Germany, when eleven Lancasters led by Wing Commander J.B. Tait – who had taken over as commanding officer from Leonard Cheshire – took off from Woodhall Spa to attack the Dortmund–Ems Canal aqueduct near Münster. Their task was to breach the banks of the canal, whose water level was higher than the level of the surrounding countryside, and drain it. The canal, which carried a large amount of industrial traffic, had been the object of bomber command's attentions on several previous occasions, but had always survived more or less intact. Now, No. 617 Squadron was going to try to knock it out once and for all, and just to make sure 125 Lancasters carrying ordinary bomb-loads were to attack in as well. The target was marked by five Mosquitoes, and despite unfavourable weather conditions, with seven-tenths cloud at between 8,000 and 9,000 feet, the attack was a complete success. The canal was breached and a six-and-a-half mile stretch was

Group Captain Leonard Cheshire, VC. (IWM)

completely drained. After that, Bomber Command breached the canal just as often as the Germans repaired it.

No. 617 Squadron was really warming up to its Tallboy operations now, and on 7 October it used the bombs in another dams raid, although one in no way as spectacular as the famous mission of May 1943. This time the target was the Kembs dam, which lay on the upper Rhine north of Basle. The Germans had intended to release the enormous volume of water contained by the dam to block the allied advance across the upper Rhine, but 617 Squadron did the job for them. Seventeen Lancasters, once again led by Wing Commander Tait, braved a massive anti-aircraft barrage to lay their Tallboys on the dam, shattering its wall and releasing the pent-up waters. By the time the Allied ground forces reached the area, the floods had subsided. The success, however, was bought at the cost of two Lancasters, one of which exploded over the target with its Tallboy still on board.

During the second week of November No. 617 Squadron carried out a mission which, in its own way, was to attract as much publicity as the famous attack on the Ruhr dams. The target was the German battleship *Tirpitz*, anchored in Tromsø fjord, Norway. The heavily-armed, 45,000-ton *Tirpitz* had presented a serious threat to the Allied North Atlantic convoys for two years, although damage inflicted on her in air and submarine attacks had prevented her from making any forays into the Atlantic so far.

No. 617, together with No. 9 Squadron –whose Lancasters had also been modified to carry Tallboys – had already made two attempts to sink her. On the first occasion, they had flown to the Russian airfield of Yagodnik, on the Archangel peninsula, which was considerably closer to any British airfield to Kaafjord, where the battleship was them anchored. Five days later, twenty-one Lancasters had set out from Yagodnik to attack the *Tirpitz* at a new anchorage in Altafjord. The weather had been very good, but the Germans laid a massive smokescreen over the fjord as the bombers approached, and by the time they reached their release point the battleship was completely obscured. However, the bomb-aimers had taken the *Tirpitz*'s flak, which could be seen rising through the smoke in glowing streams, as their aiming-point, and some were confident that hits had been obtained.

In fact, one Tallboy had exploded on her bow, wrecking it almost completely from the stem to the forward gun turret. Her main engines were also damaged, and it was estimated that even if she could make her way to a fully-equipped shipyard, it would be nine months at least before she could be made fully seaworthy again. The Germans therefore decided to move her to Tromsø, where her heavy armament might be used to help repel some future Allied landing.

The British Admiralty had no way of knowing that the *Tirpitz* no longer represented a threat to the convoys. She was still afloat, and so in their eyes she was still a menace. The two squadrons were once again briefed to attack her, and since Tromsø was 200 miles closer to the British Isles than the battleship's previous anchorages, it was decided to mount the raid from Lossiemouth in northern Scotland. On the morning of 29 October eighteen Lancasters of 617

Squadron, led by Wing Commander Tait, and eighteen of No. 9 Squadron under Wing Commander J.M. Bazin, took off in pouring rain and set course for Norway. The mission involved a round trip of 2,250 miles, so to compensate for the weight of the Tallboys and the extra fuel that had to be carried the Lancasters were stripped of every bit of equipment that was not considered absolutely necessary, including mid-upper gun turrets.

The bombers reached the target area at 0900 hours and the crews had a clear view of their intended victim as they began their run-in. Then, at the very last moment, dense cloud drifted in from the sea and the bomb-aimers were forced to drop their Tallboys through scanty gaps in the undercast. Only one near miss was recorded. One Lancaster was damaged by flak and made a forced landing in Sweden; the rest all returned safely to base.

Bad weather delayed the third attempt for twelve days. Then, on 11 November, thirty Lancasters once more took off from Lossiemouth in the darkness before dawn, crossing the black crags of the Norwegian coast at sunrise and turning north towards their target. The morning was brilliantly clear, and the battleship was clearly visible from a distance of twenty miles, her black silhouette resembling a spider nestling in the middle of a web of anti-submarine booms. This time the protective smokescreen came too late, and the Lancasters rode through waves of flak to drop their bombs. Wing Commander Tait's Tallboy was the first to go down, and as he turned away after release he saw bombs exploding all around the *Tirpitz*, obliterating her outline with rolling clouds of smoke and cascades of water. A moment later, a great plume of steam shot up through the darker clouds as a magazine exploded.

The *Tirpitz* was finished. As the Lancasters turned for home, she capsized in the shallow waters of the fjord. More than a thousand members of her crew died, many of them trapped inside her upturned hull. The destruction of the *Tirpitz* was perhaps the highlight of Bomber Command's Tallboy operations, even though it was only a small part of the whole. Between June 1944 and the end of the European war, 854 of the 6-ton bombs were dropped in targets in Germany and the Occupied Territories.

The Tallboy, in fact, was a scaled-down version of an even larger bomb, the 22,000 lb monster known as Grand Slam, which was also designed by Barnes Wallis. Following the success of Tallboy, plans for the development of Grand Slam were pushed ahead and the first live bomb was dropped experimentally on the Ashley Walk bombing range in the New Forest on 13 March 1945. It blasted a crater 30 feet deep and 124 feet across.

Once again, No. 617 Squadron was chosen to pioneer the 10-ton bomb's operational debut. On 14 March 1945 one of the bombs was carried by a Lancaster flown by Squadron Leader C.C. Calder to the Bielefeld viaduct, near Bremen, with a formation of Tallboy-armed Lancasters following. Crews behind Calder noticed how his bomber's wings arced upwards at the tips in a graceful curve as they took the strain of the bomb's weight. The weapon itself was recessed into the bomb bay, the bomb doors having been removed.

The Grand Slam speared into marshy ground thirty yards away from one of the viaduct's arches, producing a spurt of mud. It detonated 100 feet below the

The shattered remains of the Bielefeld Viaduct after the attack by No. 617 Squadron. (IWM)

surface, blasting a huge underground cavern into which 500 feet of the viaduct collapsed. A shower of Tallboys completed the work of destruction.

Forty Grand Slams went down on enemy targets before the end of the war, all of them dropped by 617 Squadron. Bridges were the main objectives, but the 10-ton bombs were also aimed at U-boat pens in northern Germany and heavy gun positions on Heligoland. One of the final missions was flown against Germany's last pocket battleship, the *Lützow*, on 13 April 1945, but although it had been originally planned to sink her with a Grand Slam it was in fact a Tallboy that ripped out her bottom.

Towards the end of the war in Europe plans were made for the large-scale use of the Lancaster and its successor, the Avro Lincoln, against Japan. Plans were made to convert some Lancasters as flight refuelling tankers. The plan envisaged that the RAF contingent, known as Tiger Force, would be based on the island of Okinawa and drop its Tallboys and Grand Slams on the bridges that connected Kyushu to the main Japanese island of Honshu. Extensive trials were carried out by Flight Refuelling Ltd and a great deal of flight refuelling equipment had already been manufactured when the war ended and the project was abandoned.

Lancasters of No. 419 Squadron, RCAF, at RAF Middleton St George at the end of the war in Europe. (Herb Kellaway)

The second major production version of the Lancaster was the Mk.III, of which about 3,000 were built. The much-modified Lancasters IV and V became the prototypes of the Lincoln Mks I and II. The Lancaster Mk.VI, nine of which were converted from Mks I and III, was equipped for electronic counter-measures. The last production Lancaster was the Mk.VII, 180 of which were built by Austin Motors. The Mks VIII and IX were never built, and the Mk.X was a licence-built Mk.III, 422 being produced by the Victory Aircraft Company of Canada. Some Lancasters were converted as RAF and later BOAC transports, with faired-over turrets. Lancasters remained in service with RAF Bomber Command for some time after the Second World War until replaced by the Avro Lincoln, and RAF Coastal Command used the GR.3 maritime patrol version until this was replaced by the Avro Shackleton. Avro refurbished fifty-four Mk.1s and Mk.7s and converted them to the maritime patrol role for use by France's Aéronavale, and other Mk.1s were converted for photographic survey work as the PR.Mk.1. Some Lancasters were converted to the civil air transport role as the Lancastrian. Total Lancaster production, all variants, was 7,374 aircraft.

There are seventeen known Avro Lancasters remaining in the world, two of which are in airworthy condition, although limited flying hours remain on their airframes and actual flying is carefully rationed. One is PA474 of the Battle of Britain Memorial Flight and the other is FM213 of the Canadian Warplane Heritage Museum re-created as VR-A of No. 419 Squadron RCAF, the

One of the Lancaster's last tasks in the Second World War was to repatriate Allied prisoners of war, seen here about to board an aircraft of No. 149 Squadron. (Leslie Graham)

'Mynarski Memorial Lancaster' in honour of Canadian VC winner, Andrew Mynarski.

Mynarski was one of ten aircrew awarded the Victoria Cross during operations in Lancasters. His exploit is repeated here as a tribute to them all.

On the night of 12/13 June, Lancasters of No. 419 Squadron, Royal Canadian Air Force – operating out of RAF Middleton St George in County Durham – were engaged in an attack on marshalling yards at Cambrai. Shortly after midnight Flying Officer G.P. Brophy, the rear gunner of Lancaster A-Able, warned his captain, Flying officer Art Debreyne, that a Junkers Ju 88 was approaching from behind and below. The Lancaster was just beginning an evasive corkscrew manoeuvre when the port wing and aft section of the fuselage were hit by cannon shells. Fire broke out immediately between the mid-upper and rear gun turrets. Debrayne ordered his crew to bale out and managed to retain partial control while the forward crew members were leaving via the front hatch. Having remained at the controls for what he considered a long enough period to allow the others to get out, the pilot also jumped at a height of 1,300 feet.

Unknown to the captain, however – the intercom was dead – Brophy was still in the rear turret. As there was no longer hydraulic power to rotate the turret, he had to turn it by hand far enough to permit him to reach his parachute. Having obtained it he began to turn the turret beamwards, intending to bale out directly from his position, but the rotation gear handle came away in his hand and he found himself hopelessly trapped.

Meanwhile, the mid-upper gunner, Flying Officer Andrew Mynarkski, had recognised Brophy's plight while on his way to the rear escape-hatch. He unhesitatingly made his way through the flames to try to release him, and as he did so his parachute and clothing caught fire. All his efforts to free Brophy were in vain, and in the short time left it was impossible to do more. Brophy realised this and waved Mynarski away, indicating that he should try to save his own life.

Mynarski fought his way back through the flames to the escape hatch. There he paused, turned – and as a last gesture to his trapped friend – stood to attention in his burning flying clothing and saluted before jumping. On the ground, Frenchmen watched as he descended like a blazing torch, his parachute and clothing aflame. When they reached him he was beyond all help, and died of severe burns shortly afterwards.

Miraculously, the only man who had witnessed Mynarski's courage lived to tell the story. The Lancaster struck the ground in a flat attitude and skidded

The Lancaster and its civilian derivative, the Lancastrian, were widely used as engine test-beds. This aircraft, VH742, was used to flight-test the Rolls-Royce Nene jet engine. (Rolls-Royce via John Gregory)

along for a considerable distance. The vibration freed the rear turret and Brophy was thrown clear. He was knocked out for a while, but regained consciousness to find that he had not suffered serious injury. He succeeded in contacting the French Resistance and returned to England early in September. He at once made the facts of Mynarski's heroism known to the authorities, testifying that his colleague could almost certainly have left the aircraft safely had he not paused to try to effect the rescue. Mynarski must have been fully aware that in trying to free the rear gunner he was sacrificing his own life, but he seemed unaffected by any instinct of self-preservation. On 11 October, 1946, Pilot Officer Andrew Charles Mynarski was posthumously awarded the Victoria Cross.

CHAPTER THIRTEEN

The Gloster Meteor

I t has often been stated, quite erroneously, that Germany's Messerschmitt 262 was the world's first operational jet fighter. In fact, that honour fell to the British Gloster Meteor, which became fully operational a full two months before the first Me 262 *Staffel* was formed in October 1944.

The Gloster Meteor, the RAF's first operational jet fighter, traced its lineage to the first British experimental jet, the Gloster E.28/39. Fitted with the fully operational W.1 engine, this aircraft made its first fight from Cranwell, Lincolnshire, on 15 May 1941, with Gloster's chief test pilot Gerry Sayer at the controls. The flight lasted seventeen minutes and on this occasion Sayer kept the speed down to about 16,500 rpm in order to hold back the turbine inlet temperature. This gave a thrust of 860 lb, which was considered adequate for Sayer to ascertain the control qualities of the airframe; the engine had already run for twenty-five hours on the bench. Within days the aircraft was reaching speeds of up to 370 mph at 25,000 feet, with the engine set at 17,000 rpm, exceeding the performance of the contemporary Spitfires. Two E.28/39s were built, but the second aircraft was destroyed on 30 July 1943 when its ailerons jammed and it entered an inverted spin. The pilot, Squadron Leader Douglas Davie, baled out at 33,000 feet (10,065 m), the first pilot to do so from a jet aircraft. The first prototype E.28/39, W4041, is today on display in the Science Museum, Kensington, London.

In August 1940, well before completion of the experimental E.28/39, George Carter, Chief Designer of the Gloster Aeroplane Company, had submitted a preliminary brochure to the Air Ministry, outlining his proposals for a turbojet-powered fighter. Realising that it would take too much time to develop a turbojet of sufficient thrust to power a single-engined fighter, Carter selected a twin-engine configuration, the design having a tricycle landing gear and high-mounted tailplane, with the engines housed in separate mid-mounted nacelles on the low-set wings. In November 1940 the Air Ministry issued Specification F.9/40, written around this proposal, and design arrangements were finalised in the following month. On 7 February, 1941, Glosters received an order from the Ministry of Aircraft Production for twelve 'Gloster Whittle aeroplanes' to the F.9/40 specification. The planned production target was eighty airframes and 160 engines per month.

Apart from the fact that it was jet-powered, the Gloster Meteor, as the new fighter was eventually named, was entirely conventional in design. Eight aircraft were completed initially, the first flying on 5 March 1943. The aircraft was powered by two 680 kg (1,500 lb) thrust Halford H.1 turbojets, but the first

Britain's first jet aircraft, the Gloster E.28/39.

Meteor F.I EE223/G was the first to be fitted with Rolls-Royce Derwent I turbojets in short-chord nacelles. (Corinne Moore)

twenty production aircraft were fitted with the 771 kg (1,700 lb) Rolls-Royce Welland.

It was in June 1944 that the Royal Air Force entered the jet age, and the squadron selected to pioneer its entry into the new era was No. 616, based at Culmhead, near Taunton in Somerset. Since the spring of 1944 there had been strong rumours that No. 616 was to rearm with a radical new aircraft; most of the pilots however believed that if re-equipment did take place it would be with Griffon-engined Spitfire Mk.XIVs, and this belief was strengthened when, early in June, two of these aircraft arrived at Culmhead. Then, suddenly there was fresh speculation when, in the middle of June, No. 616's commanding officer, Squadron Leader Andrew McDowall, and five of the squadron's pilots were sent on detachment to the Royal Aircraft Establishment at Farnborough. It was not until they arrived that McDowall and his colleagues learned what awaited them: a conversion course to Gloster Meteor Mk.1 jet fighters.

Twenty production Meteor F.Mk.1s had been ordered to meet the urgent demand for a jet fighter for the RAF. The aircraft was basically a military version of the F.9/40, powered by Rolls-Royce W.2B/23 Welland engines each developing 1,700 lb.s.t. The two Meteor F.1s at Farnborough, EE213 and EE214, proved delightful aircraft to fly and conversion progressed smoothly once the pilots had got used to the novelty of not having a propeller in front of them. McDowall and the other five pilots on the initial conversion course were enthusiastic about the new aircraft and when they returned to Culmhead early in July their eagerness quickly infected the rest of the squadron.

No. 616's first Meteor, EE219, arrived at Culmhead on 12 July 1944, the day on which, as a matter of coincidence, the German V-1 offensive began against Britain. During the next few days, eleven more Meteors were flown in from Farnborough and the task of converting the rest of the squadron's pilots to the new type continued. Without exception the pilots found the Meteor delightful to handle; the main problem, after flying for years in tail wheel aircraft, lay in getting used to the tricycle undercarriage.

On 21 July 1944 the squadron's Spitfires, accompanied by two Meteors, deployed to Manston in Kent, where they were joined by five more Meteors two days later. The pilots of the RAF's first jet flight were the newly-promoted Wing Commander McDowall, Wing Commander H.J. Wilson (McDowall's second in command), Squadron Leader L.W. Watts (McDowall's predecessor as 616 Squadron CO, who had elected to remain as a flight commander), Flying Officers Roger, McKenzie, Clark and Dean and Warrant Officer Wilkes. The establishment of a Meteor flight at Manston was kept a strict secret, a tight security cordon being thrown around the airfield.

On 27 July, No. 616 Squadron was ordered to mount its first 'Diver' patrol, as the sorties against the V-1s were codenamed. The first pilot to take off at 14.40 hours was Flying Officer McKenzie, but he landed forty-five minutes later without having sighted any of the enemy missiles. Seven more sorties were flown in the course of the day with the same negative result. The week that followed was full of frustration and disappointment. In order to increase the time on patrol it was decided to decrease the distance between the squadron base and the approach path of the flying bombs by moving the Meteors to a dispersal aerodrome near Ashford, the aircraft carrying out their Diver patrols from this location and returning to Manston at the end of the day's flying.

It was while flying from Ashford on 29 July that Squadron Leader Watts and Flying Officer T.D. ('Dixie') Dean became the first of 616's pilots to sight a V-1. Watts spotted the missile after only ten minutes on patrol and closed in on it, but as he attacked his four 20 mm cannon jammed after only two rounds had been fired. Helplessly, he could do nothing but sit in his cockpit and watch while the V-1 flew on towards its target (Later that day the same thing happened to another pilot, and it was subsequently established that the cause of the jamming was updraught in the cartridge case ejection slots under the fuselage). Dean also attempted to attack a V-1, but failed to get within cannon range before the missile entered a restricted zone, reserved for the barrage balloon defences, and he had to break off.

In the evening of 4 August, Dean sighted a V-1 only minutes after taking off from Ashford. Gaining speed in a dive, he made a head-on attack, but his guns jammed after just a short burst. Determined not to let the V-1 escape, he pulled round hard and closed in from astern, bringing his Meteor alongside. With infinite care he slid his wingtip under that of the missile, holding them just a few inches apart. The turbulent airflow disturbed the V-1's equilibrium; its wing rose sharply and its gyro toppled, sending it out of control. Dean watched it as it hurtled down, pulse jet still going flat out. Seconds later it exploded in open country.

Dean had become the first British jet pilot to destroy an enemy aircraft, albeit by unconventional means, but although there was an element of danger in his method it was nevertheless much safer than attacking a V-1 at close range, where there was a real danger that the fighter might be damaged by debris from the exploding missile. On landing at base Dean learned that another pilot, Flying Officer J.K. Roger, had also attacked and destroyed a flying bomb minutes after Dean's own victory. Roger's cannon had worked satisfactorily and the V-1 had dived into the ground and exploded near Tenterton. From now on the frequency of the Diver patrols was stepped up considerably. No. 616 had two Meteors airborne continuously throughout the day, flying in relays in patrols of thirty minutes' duration. By 10 August Dean had destroyed two more V-1s to complete his hat-trick and the squadron's score mounted steadily. The busiest days were on 16 and 17 August, when five V-1s were destroyed by the Meteor pilots. By 31 August 1944, the date when the V-1 sites were finally overrun by Allied ground forces, the squadron's score stood at thirteen destroyed. Although it was only a very small fraction of the total number of missiles destroyed by the air defences, it nevertheless proved the Meteor's capability in action against small high-speed targets.

For the remainder of 1944, 616 Squadron settled down to a steady and somewhat boring routine of demonstration flights for the benefit of Allied military dignitaries and air exercises in conjunction with RAF Bomber Command (which was now flying daylight missions in growing numbers) and the US Eighth Air Force. The object of these exercises was primarily to assist the Allied bomber commands to develop defensive tactics against the German Me 262 jet fighters which were appearing in action against the daylight bomber formations, and against which the piston-engine Allied fighter escorts were virtually power-less.

On 18 December 1944 No. 616 Squadron received its first two Meteor F.3s, EE231 and EE232. The Meteor F.3 was a much better proposition than the F.1, using the 906 kg (2,000 lb) thrust Rolls-Royce Derwent I engine. Three more, EE233, 234 and 235 arrived on the twenty-fourth and in January 1945, following a move to Colerne in Wiltshire, the squadron exchanged all its remaining F.1s for F.3s. On 20 January 1945, a flight of 616's Meteors flew to Belgium to join No. 84 Group of the RAF 2nd tactical Air Force at Melsbroek. Because of the danger that anti-aircraft gunners and fighter pilots might confuse the Meteors with the Messerschmitt 262, the British fighters, which had been camouflaged in the normal RAF grey-green day fighter colours (lacking the black and white identification bands which were borne by most aircraft of the Tactical Air Force) were finished in a glossy white paint scheme overall.

The Meteor pilots, who had been looking forward to the move to the Continent and the action it promised were to be sadly disappointed, and the next few weeks were remarkable only for their lack of activity. Because of the risk of a Meteor falling into enemy hands the pilots were given strict instructions not to fly over enemy-held territory and instead they were assigned to fly standing patrols over Nijmegen and other allied air bases in the vicinity. To vary the boring routine the pilots set themselves unofficial competitions to see who could achieve the fastest scramble time, climb to altitude and so on. On one of these occasions, during a competition to see who could get his wheels up the fastest during a formation take-off, Warrant Officer Wilkes retracted his undercarriage a split second too early with the result that the wheels came up before the Meteor was off the ground and the aircraft flopped down on its belly. Operations from Melsbroek were flown from semi-prepared grass strips or PSP matting, a fact that considerably alarmed representatives of Glosters who visited the unit. Nevertheless the Meteor proved itself fully capable of operating under these conditions, and on one occasion an aircraft was successfully flown out of a ploughed field after making an emergency landing.

The remainder of 616 Squadron arrived on the Continent on 1 April 1945, deploying to Gilze-Rijen in Holland, and the Air Ministry now authorised the jet fighters to assume a more offensive role. Although the Meteors made short forays into enemy air space, however, they failed to make contact with the *Luftwaffe* and it was decided to employ them on armed reconnaissance and ground attack. On 17 April, Flight Lieutenant Cooper became the first Meteor pilot to fire his guns in anger over enemy territory when, in the course of an armed reconnaissance, he sighted a large enemy truck near Ijmuiden. After one firing pass the vehicle slewed off the road and burst into flames.

For 616 Squadron the last weeks of the war in Europe was marked by feverish activity as the unit moved from airfield to airfield in the wake of the Allied advance, carrying out its armed reconnaissance and attack sorties under considerable pressure. On 20 April the squadron was established on German soil at Quackenbruck near Bremen; four days later, four Meteors led by Wing Commander McDowall attacked the enemy airfield of Nordholz near Cuxhaven, diving out of the sun from 8,000 feet. In a single firing pass McDowall destroyed a Junkers 88 on the ground and sent some cannon shells through a motor vehicle. Flying Officer Wilson attacked two petrol bowsers, which he set on fire, and raked airfield installations with his remaining shells. Flying Officer Moon strafed a dozen railway trucks on the airfield perimeter and destroyed an anti-aircraft post while the fourth pilot, Flying Officer Clegg, shot up a large vehicle full of German troops who waved as the jet fighter bore down on them, no doubt mistaking it for a Me 262. They were still waving when Clegg opened fire.

Up to now No. 616 Squadron had suffered no casualties while flying Meteors. It was a record that lasted until 29 April, when two Meteors flown by Squadron Leader Watts and Flight Sergeant Cartmell took off on an offensive patrol. Some minutes later the aircraft entered cloud and soon afterwards Allied troops on the ground observed a large explosion followed by debris fluttering down. Both pilots lost their lives.

Although the Meteor pilots still half hoped that they might have a chance to test their aircraft in combat against the *Luftwaffe*'s latest fighters, by the beginning of May it was apparent that this was not to be. Nevertheless ground attack work was exciting enough, for enemy flak was still heavy and several Meteors returned to base with battle damage. The squadron's final day of combat operations came on 4 May 1945, and marked the climax to a week of intense ground attack activity. During the day's operations the Meteor pilots destroyed one enemy locomotive and damaged another, knocking out ten trucks and two half tracks as well as strafing a number of installations. At 17.00 hours, the squadron received a signal to the effect that all offensive operations over Germany were to be suspended.

The second RAF Fighter Command unit to convert to Meteors was No. 504 (County of Nottingham) Squadron, Auxiliary Air Force. After a short working-up period on the new aircraft it was declared operational in April 1945, but it was not deployed to the Continent. It retained its Meteor 3s until August 1945, after which it successively flew Mosquitoes and Spitfires before rearming with Meteor Mk.4s in 1949.

Meanwhile, the second British jet fighter to become operational had made its appearance. Design work on the DH.100 Vampire had begun in May 1942, the prototype flying on 20 September 1943, and in the spring of 1944 it became the first Allied jet aircraft capable of sustained speeds of over 500 mph over a wide altitude range. The first production Vampire flew in April 1945. It was not until 1946, however, that the first examples were delivered to operational squadrons. The Vampire was powered by the 2,300 lb.s.t. Halford H.1 engine, now named the Goblin.

The Meteor Mk.3, which eventually equipped fifteen squadrons of RAF Fighter Command in the immediate post-war years, was followed into service by the Meteor F.Mk.4. Powered by two Rolls-Royce Derwent 5s, the F.Mk.4 first flew in April 1945 and subsequently, in November, set up a new world air speed record of 975 km/h (606 mph).

The de Havilland Vampire was the Meteor's contemporary. Seen here are Vampire FB.5s of No. 608 Squadron, RAuxAF, at RAF Thornaby. (via Ken McCreesh)

A Meteor Mk.4 undergoing deck landing trials on the aircraft carrier HMS Illustrious. (Royal Navy)

Rolls-Royce Chief Test Pilot Wing Commander Harvey Heyworth making a high-speed pass over Farnborough in a Meteor F.4, September 1949. Seen in the background are the DH Comet and Armstrong Whitworth Apollo airliners. (Rolls-Royce via Corinne Moore)

The Meteor Mk.5 was a photo-reconnaissance version of the Mk.4; only a few were built. The Mk.6 was a swept-wing Meteor project that never left the drawing board, while the T.Mk.7 was a two-seat trainer variant, of which 640 were built. To improve the range and performance of the F.4, Glosters designed a new high-speed tail unit, lengthened the forward fuselage, installed an extra internal fuel tank and introduced a one-piece sliding cockpit canopy over a Martin Baker ejection seat, the modified aircraft emerging as the Meteor F.Mk.8 in October 1948. The F.8 was the most prolific of the meteor variants and formed the mainstay of RAF Fighter Command in the early 1950s, equipping thirty-two regular and eleven R.Aux.AF squadrons. The Meteor F.8, which was supplied to both Egypt and Israel, saw considerable action during the Arab–Israeli war of 1956; it was also used by No. 77 Squadron RAAF in Korea.

The Australians' experience with the Meteor in air-to-air combat with the greatly superior MiG-15 was not a happy one. The squadron flew its first operational mission with the Meteor on 30 July 1951, a sweep by sixteen Meteors south of the Yalu. The Meteors flew in finger fours between 30,000 and 35,000 feet, with sixteen F-86 Sabres 10,000 feet lower down. No contact was made with the enemy. Several more sweeps were flown in the first three weeks of August, with the same negative result. During one of them, on the 20th, two Meteors

Meteor F.8s of No. 77 Squadron, RAAF, in their blast-proof revetments at Kimpo, Korea.
(RAAF)

collided during a formation change and crashed north of the Han river. Both
pilots – Sergeant Mitchell and Flight Sergeant Lamb, the latter an RAF instructor – were killed.

On four or five occasions during August the Meteors were detailed to escort
B-29s and RF-80s to Sinanju, and it was while escorting a flight of Shooting
Stars with two sections of four Meteors on the 25th that MiGs were sighted for
the first time. Two enemy jets were spotted south of Sinanju and one of the
Meteor flights gave chase; the leader, Flight Lieutenant Scannell, opened fire at
extreme range but no hits were claimed. The first real test came four days later,
on the 29th, when eight Meteors were detailed to escort B-29s and another eight
to carry out a diversionary sweep north of Sinanju. At 11.20 the latter flight, led
by Squadron Leader Wilson, spotted six MiGs at 40,000 feet over Chongju,
5,000 feet higher than themselves. Keeping the enemy in sight Wilson manoeuvred his formation up-sun, but as he did so two more MiGs appeared a few
thousand feet below. Wilson decided to attack and went into a dive followed by
his number two, Flying Officer Woodroffe. As the two Meteors levelled out,
however, Woodroffe's aircraft suddenly flicked into a spin (an unpleasant
tendency of the Meteor 8, caused by the effects of compressibility, if the aircraft
exceeded Mach 0.8 at altitude) and dropped away; the pilot managed to recover
several thousand feet lower down, but now Wilson had no one to cover his tail.
As he began his approach to attack, a MiG jumped him out of the sun, un-

noticed in the thirty-degree blind spot caused by the dural structure at the rear of the Meteor's cockpit. The first warning Wilson had of the danger was when cannon shells passed over his wing; he immediately put his aircraft into a maximum-rate turn in a bid to shake off his pursuer. He was rescued by Flight Lieutenant Cedric Wilson and Flying Officer Ken Blight, who spotted his predicament and drove the MiG away – but not before cannon shells had shot away Squadron Leader Wilson's port aileron and punched a three-foot hole in his port wing, puncturing a fuel tank. Despite the damage Wilson reached base safely, touching down at 30 knots above normal landing speed. Meanwhile, a fierce air battle had developed over Chongju as the other Meteors were hotly engaged by thirty MiGs. The weight of the attack fell on 'Dog' section, led by Flight Lieutenant Geoff Thornton; one Meteor was shot down and its pilot, Warrant Officer Don Guthrie, baled out to spend the rest of the war in a PoW camp.

The Meteors continued to fare badly. On 5 September, six Meteors, escorting RF-80s at 20,000 feet in the Antung area, were bounced by a dozen MiGs, attacking from astern in pairs. During the five-minute battle that followed Warrant Officer W. Michelson was attacked by three MiGs which severely damaged his tail before he succeeded in shaking them off. Three Meteor pilots – Blyth, Cannon and Dawson – fired at MiGs, but with no result. There was another skirmish on the 26th, when twelve Meteors – once again escorting RF-80s – were attacked by more than thirty MiGs. One of the enemy fighters was cut off from the rest by Flight Lieutenant Thomas, who chased it well to the south of Pyongyang before its superior speed enabled it to escape. Another pilot, Flight Lieutenant Dawson, fired several bursts at a second MiG and saw pieces fly off it, but the cine film of the combat was over-exposed and this could not be confirmed. In this action Sergeant Ernest Armitt's Meteor was hit and damaged, but he returned to base safely.

On 1 December, twelve Meteors, led by Flight Lieutenant Geoff Thornton, were carrying out an offensive sweep at 19,000 feet when some fifty MiGs were sighted high above. At that height the Meteor pilots knew that they had no hope of holding their own in a turning fight; the odds would be better if they could draw the MiGs down to their own level, although the Australians were at a great tactical disadvantage. The MiGs saw them and came down in pairs to make a fast diving attack on 'Charlie' flight, which broke on Thornton's command. One pilot, Flying Officer Drummond, left it a little late and was hit in the fuel tanks. His call for help was answered by Flying Officer Bruce Gogerly, of 'Able' Flight, who got on the tail of a MiG and shot it down with a long burst of 20 mm fire – the Meteor's first confirmed combat victory in Korea. Gogerly was himself subjected to a series of head-on attacks by pairs of MiGs, as were some other pilots; a second MiG was shot down and was subsequently claimed by several pilots, so it was credited to the whole squadron.

Eventually, the Meteor was withdrawn from air combat operations in Korea and assigned to ground attack work, which it performed with creditable results until it was replaced by F-86 Sabres.

The Meteors FR.9 and PR.10 were reconnaissance variants, while the long-nose Meteor NF.11, NF.12, NF.13 and NF.14 were AI-equipped night fighters.

The NF.14, the last of the Meteor fighters, had a new clear-vision cockpit canopy, and deliveries to the RAF were completed in 1955. The T.7 was a two-seat trainer. Meteor production, all variants, totalled 3,545 aircraft.

In October 1955 Flight Refuelling Ltd began the conversion of a number of ex-RAF Meteor F.8s as target aircraft, 233 being converted between 1956 and 1969 with the designation U.Mk.15 and U.Mk.16. A further batch was converted for use by the RAAF with the designation U.Mk.21. The Meteor TT.20, converted from the NF.11, was a target tug.

The first Meteor mark to be exported was the Mk.4, which was supplied to Argentina (100), Holland (65), Belgium (48) and Denmark (20). The most prolific of the Meteor variants was the F.Mk.8, which equipped thirty-two regular and eleven R.Aux.AF squadrons in the early 1950s. This version was also the subject of major export orders, going to Egypt (8), Belgium (23, plus 67 licence-built), Denmark (20), Syria (19), Holland (5), plus 155 licence-built, Brazil (60) and Israel (11).

CHAPTER FOURTEEN

The English Electric Canberra

B y the end of 1948 development of the Rolls-Royce Avon engine had been given high priority, for the prototype of one of the aircraft it was to power – the English Electric A1, later to be named the Canberra – was nearing completion. From the outset, the new light jet-bomber was envisaged as a Mosquito replacement, to operate primarily in the radar bombing role at high altitude. Discussions on the aircraft's configuration were held between English Electric and the Ministry of Aircraft Production in the spring of 1945, and in May that year the concept was formalised by the issue of an MAP contract, E.3/45 (changed soon afterwards to B.3/45) covering the manufacture of four prototypes by the end of 1949. The limited time-scale meant that the aircraft would have to be conventional in design, although English Electric's policy, to quote the talented aerodynamicist F.W. (Freddy) Page, was to create an aeroplane that was 'the extreme in adventurous conventionalism'. That it would also be a compromise between old and new was also accepted, both by English Electric and the MAP.

The English Electric design team, under the leadership of W.E.W. Petter, held regular monthly meetings with Rolls-Royce, and by July 1945 it had been agreed that the bomber would be powered by two 6,500 lb thrust AJ.65 axial-flow turbojets, although the second prototype was to be fitted with two 5,000 lb thrust Nenes as an insurance against delays with the AJ.65. In fact, no one could have envisaged at the time how protracted the development of the AJ.65 Avon would be. Seven years were to elapse before the Avon became operationally acceptable to the RAF, and even then some snags remained to be eliminated. The problems had still not been solved when the first Canberra B.2s were delivered to the RAF, with the result that these early examples suffered from a plague of engine troubles.

By the early months of 1946 the number of people working on the design of the jet bomber had risen to 200, mostly working in a requisitioned garage in Corporation Street, Preston, known locally as Barton Motors or TC, because it had served as a government training centre during the war. Also during 1946, Petter set about recruiting a suitable man for the post of chief experimental test pilot, and by the end of the year he had found two likely candidates. One was Wing Commander Tony Martindale, a serving RAF officer who, as a test pilot with the RAE Farnborough, had amassed considerable experience in high speed flight during compressibility trials at high Mach values in piston-engined fighters; the other was Wing Commander Roland Beamont, who had a distinguished career as a wartime fighter leader and test pilot and who had since conducted high speed trials with the Gloster Meteor in preparation for the RAF's successful attempt on the world air speed record in 1946. It was Freddy Page who pointed out that a test pilot with operational experience was what was needed, and this tipped the balance in Beamont's favour. He joined the English Electric team in May 1947.

By this time, work on the English Electric A1 had progressed as far as a wood and cardboard mock-up at Barton Motors. The aircraft that was taking shape was a good deal larger than the Mosquito; the two jet engines were semi-buried in the wing, which was of symmetrical section with the centre of pressure well aft for a high usable Mach number. The aircraft was intended to operate at Mach 0.8 at high altitude (up to 50,000 feet), and therefore much attention was paid to the lightness and effectiveness of the controls. These were manually operated, with an electrically operated trimmer and an electrically operated variable incidence tailplane to compensate for strong trim changes at higher Mach values.

By the end of 1948 component assembly of the A1 prototype was nearly complete at Barton Motors and at Strand Road, English Electric's main factory in the middle of Preston. In the meantime, B.3/45 had been revised somewhat, emerging in 1947 as B.5/47. This made provision for a visual bombing station and added a third crew member as bomb aimer, which was to prove very useful to the RAF under operational circumstances some years later. This decision resulted from the fact that that the development of the ARI 5829 G-H radar bombing system intended for the A.1 was falling seriously behind schedule. Also included in B.5/47 was provision for two jettisonable wingtip fuel tanks of 250 gallons each.

Petter had now moved his design facility to Warton, a former USAAF maintenance base five miles from Preston, and final assembly of the A.1 first prototype, VN799, took place early in 1949. A major concern had been the late delivery of the flight engines due to development delays in the Avon RA.1 programme, and as a back-up measure the second prototype had been hurriedly re-engineered to take Rolls-Royce Nenes, but in the event the flight-cleared pair of RA.1s was delivered in March.

Meanwhile, Roland Beamont had been investigating the effects of compressibility at speeds of up to Mach 0.84 and altitudes of up to 45,000 feet in a clipped-wing Meteor IV, EE545, which had been loaned to English Electric on a Ministry contract for thirty hours of research. Forty-seven flights were made, and they provided valuable information on the effects of the phenomenon known as 'shock stall' at Mach numbers in excess of Mach 0.8. They also gave a clear indication that the new jet bomber, above 40,000 feet, would be extremely difficult to intercept by existing fighter aircraft.

With none of the fanfare that was to accompany the emergence of new combat aircraft in later years, the A1 prototype was rolled out at Warton on 2 May 1949, finished plate blue overall. Following satisfactory engine runs, taxiing trials began on 8 May and revealed no problems apart from some nose

The English Electric A1 prototype being rolled out at Warton on 2 May 1949. (BAe)

wheel shimmy. On 9 May Beamont made three short hops to check elevator, aileron and rudder response; these also proved satisfactory, within the manoeuvring constraints of the runway, and the decision was taken to make the maiden flight as soon as the weather conditions were favourable.

These conditions were met on 13 May (a Friday, to the apprehension of the more superstitious members of the English Electric team), and so that morning Beamont lifted VN799 off the Warton runway at 80 knots. During the subsequent climb at 120 knots the pilot encountered some yaw problems and went up to 10,000 feet off the Lancashire coast to check them out, throttling back to maintain 220 knots IAS. He was accompanied by a Vampire chase aircraft flown by J.W.C. (Johnny) Squier, English Electric production test pilot. The yaw problem persisted and so the flight was cut short. After reducing the IAS to assess the low-speed handling qualities, Beamont turned back to Warton and set up his approach pattern, joining the circuit downwind and making his final approach at 100 knots. The yaw problem again showed up as the aircraft ran through some turbulence on the approach, but Beamont touched down safely at 85 knots and brought the aircraft to a standstill in 800 yards.

The aircraft had proven crisp and pleasant to fly, apart from the yaw problem. It was clear that some modification to the rudder was needed, and so the decision was taken to reduce the area of the horn balance (the small balanced area at the tip of the control surface) progressively, each stage being tested in flight. After the first modification, Beamont flew VN799 on 18 May, taking the aircraft up to 15,000 feet and 420 knots IAS. Rudder response was better, but the pilot reported some flutter-type vibration at speeds of over 400 knots IAS. On the following day, flying at 20,000 feet and Mach 0.77, he reported some moderate directional 'snaking'; this was found to occur at this Mach value at any altitude, and the problem was eventually traced to wake turbulence behind the cockpit canopy. It was cured by a simple fairing. The vibration, known as 'eight cycle flutter' – caused by the instability of the tail structure vibrating at its natural frequency of eight cycles per second – was reduced by modifications to the elevator horns and mass balances. These were made between 1 and 5 July, after the prototype had made eleven flights. With its new rudder shape VN799 resumed flying on 6 July, and in the course of thirty-six further flights up to the end of August the aircraft reached 42,000 feet (on 11 August) and achieved its initial design speed of 470 knots on the last day of the month, exceeding the initial Service limit of 450 knots by a 20-knot margin. During this series of flights, for the first time, Beamont investigated the aircraft's aerodynamic characteristics and found no difficulty in looping and rolling it at speeds of up to 350 knots, although he had to exercise some strength above that figure.

The other three A1 prototypes all flew before the end of 1949, by which time the type had officially been named the Canberra. The second (Nene-powered) prototype, VN813, flew on 9 November from Warton, while the third, VN828, followed on 29 November. This was the first Canberra to fly from the English Electric facility at Samlesbury, where the company was then engaged in the licence production of de Havilland Vampires. The last of the four, VN850, flew on 20 December 1949.

Two of the first four Canberras to fly, VN813 and VN850, were subsequently allocated to Rolls-Royce for engine trials. VN813, the second A1 (B.Mk.1) was used for development flying by English Electric before being allocated to Rolls-Royce in 1950 to take part in the Nene engine development programme. VN850, the third B.Mk.1, was the first Canberra to have provision for jettisonable wingtip tanks, and trials with these were successfully completed in July 1950. Before this, it also became the first Canberra to give a display overseas, being flown from Warton in Lancashire to Paris/Orly on 11 June in fifty-four minutes. On 24 and 25 June it flew to Antwerp to be displayed at the Belgian International Air Show. The aircraft carried out several more demonstrations during 1950, twice at Farnborough (the first time at an RAF display in July and then at the September SBAC Show) and also before a US mission at Boscombe Down in August. Following the September SBAC Show, it was assigned to Rolls-Royce for Avon engine development work, and became the first Canberra to exceed 500 knots Indicated Air Speed (IAS).

While development work continued with the Canberra B.1 prototypes, production of the definitive version for RAF Bomber Command, the B.5/47 Canberra B.2, had been getting under way. Two B.2 prototypes were built, and the first of these, VX165, flew for the first time on 21 April 1950, followed by the second aircraft, VX169, on 2 August. Both were powered by 6,500 lb.s.t. Rolls-Royce Avon RA.3 (Mk.101) engines. The first production B.2, WD929, flew

Roland Beamont demonstrating the Canberra before assembled VIPs. (BAe)

from Samlesbury on 8 October 1950. All these aircraft carried out intensive trials, culminating in CA Release – which cleared the aircraft for RAF service – in the spring of 1951. Canberra B.2s allocated to Rolls-Royce for engine development work at various times were WD930, which had previously flown with the Handling Squadron at Boscombe Down and with the Royal Radar Establishment, WD943, and WD959.

The Canberra B.2 entered service with No. 101 Squadron at RAF Binbrook in May 1951. During its early career, the aircraft established a number of records. In 1951 it made the first non-stop crossing of the Atlantic by a jet aircraft, and between 1953 and 1957 it set up three altitude records, reaching 63,668 feet, 65,890 feet and 70,310 feet.

In the early 1950s, there was a good reason for placing emphasis on the Canberra's high-altitude capability, for the aircraft proved an excellent tool for

Canberra B.2 WD954 seen against the backdrop of Mount Kilimanjaro during tropical trials in Kenya. (BAe)

gathering strategic air intelligence. The Canberra's role as a photographic recon-naissance aircraft, one of the most important it was to fulfil over the years, was dictated by specification PR31/46, which in effect called for a PR version of the B.5/47 Canberra B.2. The main external difference between the B.2 and the PR variant, designated PR.Mk.3, was that the latter's front fuselage was extended by fourteen inches to accommodate a 415 gallon ventral fuel tank, a camera bay and a flare bay. For the day photography role the PR.3 was equipped with either four or six F.52 and one F.49 cameras, while equipment for the night role comprised two F.89 cameras, photocells and a 1.75 photoflash crate. The aircraft carried a crew of two. The prototype PR.3, VBX181, was flown for the first time from Samlesbury on 19 March 1950, but during subsequent test flying severe vibration problems – caused by the fuselage extension and consequent re-distribution of mass – were encountered, and a speed restriction of Mach 0.75 was placed on the aircraft (compared with Mach 0.84 for the B.2). The problem was eventually alleviated by increasing the elevator and tab mass-balances, but it was never cured completely. All this delayed the PR.3's CA (Comptroller Aircraft) Release, and it was not until 31 July 1952 that the first of an initial production batch of twenty-seven aircraft, WE135, took to the air. It was allocated to No. 540 Squadron at Benson for operational trials, and re-equipment of this unit with the PR.3 began in December. WE135 then went to the PR element of No. 231 OCU, the Canberra operational conversion unit. In March 1953 No. 540 Squadron moved to RAF Wyton, near Huntingdon, together with Nos 58 and 82 Squadrons. The latter began to re-equip with Canberra PR.3s in November 1953 and No. 58 Squadron followed soon afterwards, using Canberras reallocated from the other two units.

The next variant was the T.4 dual control trainer, which entered service in 1954; this was followed by the B.5, a converted PR.3 intended for target marking, but only a few examples were produced before it was superseded by the B.6, a version with more powerful Avon 109 engines The B(I)Mk.6 was an interim night interdictor version, while the PR.7 was a photo-reconnaissance variant. The Canberra B(I).8, which entered service in 1956, featured some radical modifications, the most notable being an entirely redesigned fuselage nose and an offset fighter-type cockpit, the navigator being buried in the starboard fuselage. In October 1955 Peru ordered eight B(I).8s, and a similar number, together with two T.4s, was ordered by Venezuela in January 1957.

The Canberra PR.9 high-altitude photo-reconnaissance variant also had an offset cockpit and an increased wing span, as well as RR Avon 206 engines. Although the Canberra PR.9 could not reach the same altitudes as the more

Canberra T.4s of No. 232 OCU, RAF Bassingbourn, in neat formation. (RAF)

The Canberra B(I).8 interdictor, with its high-mounted cockpit and belly gun-pack. (BAe)

famous Lockheed U-2, it was nevertheless an impressive aircraft, with an impressive performance, although the latter fell short of expectations. Although its Avon Mk.206 engines gave a good rate of climb to 50,000 feet it fell off rapidly above that altitude, and further tests revealed that the induced drag from the new wing centre section at high altitude was virtually cancelling out the increased thrust margin. On 18 September 1956 Roland Beamont reached 59,000 feet in a PR.9, but the aircraft would go no higher and it had used a great deal of fuel in getting there.

By July 1960 No. 58 Squadron at RAF Wyton had six PR.9s on strength, and now embarked on a period of intensive flying. The aircrews were impressed by the PR.9, and in particular by its rate of climb. It could reach 30,000 feet in two and a half minutes. High level operations meant the use of partial pressure helmets and jerkins, and crews had to attend a course on the theory of high-altitude flight and its effects on the human body at the RAF Aeromedical Centre at Upwood, where they were subjected to simulated high-altitude decompression. Most of the training flights undertaken by No. 58 Squadron were by single aircraft, flying 'Lone Ranger' sorties to El Adem, Cyprus, Nairobi and the Gulf, or 'Polar Bear' sorties to Norway. Frequent sorties were also flown to the 2nd Allied Tactical Air Force operational area in Germany. Typically, a Canberra would fly at high level to a point off the north coast of Germany, followed by a let-down into the recognised 2 ATAF low-level routes and a landing on a German airfield. On the way back to the UK from Germany a similar profile was used, the Canberra flying at high level and then descending to make use of the UK low level routes. Sometimes the PR Canberras, operating from Bodo or Andoya in Norway, ventured deep inside the Arctic Circle; one of the longest of such missions, in December 1960, involved an overflight of Jan Mayen Island, 500 miles north-north-east of Iceland.

The Canberra T.11 was a version for training AI observers, while the B.15, designed for service in the near and far east, was a modified B.6 with underwing hard points for bombs or rocket packs. The B.16, for service in Germany, was similar, but retained many of the B.6's radar aids. Other Canberra variants included the U.Mk.10 target drone (modified B.2), the T.17 ECM trainer, the E.15 electronic reconnaissance variant, the TT.18 target tug, the T.19 target facilities aircraft, and the T.22 trainer for the Royal Navy.

The Canberra was built under licence in the USA as the Martin B.57, and in Australia as the B.20 and T.21. India was a major export customer, while re-furbished Canberras were sold to Argentina (two being lost in the 1982

The Canberra was a very agile aircraft, as is demonstrated by this B.6 of No. 9 Squadron, RAF Binbrook. (BAe)

Falklands war), Chile, Ecuador, France, Peru, Rhodesia/Zimbabwe, South Africa, Sweden, Venezuela and West Germany.

During their lengthy career, Canberras saw action in many parts of the world. RAF aircraft operated against communist terrorists in Malaya and bombed Egyptian airfields during the Suez crisis of 1956, Australian Canberras and USAF B-57s were used extensively in Vietnam, while Indian Air Force aircraft fought in the Indo–Pakistan conflicts of 1965 and 1971. Refurbished Canberras were sold to Argentina (two being lost in the 1982 Falklands war), Chile, Ecuador, France, Peru, Rhodesia/Zimbabwe, South Africa, Sweden, Venezuela and West Germany.

A ceremony to mark the disbandment of the last Canberra Squadron in the Royal Air Force – No. 39 (PR) Squadron – took take place at RAF Marham on Friday 28 July 2006. The ceremony included a flypast by a Canberra PR9 on its last ever sortie. RAF Canberras made their final flights on 31 July when three were delivered to their new home with Delta Jets at Kemble. The withdrawal of the Canberra from RAF service left the Indian Air Force as the only full-time military operator, although Canberras are retained by the Air Force of Peru and several ex-RAF machines and RB-57s are flying in the US for research and mapping work. The Indian Air Force retired its last Canberras on 11 May 2007, when No. 106 (Lynx) Squadron flew its last sortie from Agra.

About ten airworthy Canberras were in private ownership in 2007 in various parts of the world.

CHAPTER FIFTEEN

The Vickers Viscount

I n 1943 with the war beginning to turn in the Allies favour, the UK Government, concerned about Britain's position in the commercial aircraft market in the post-war era, convened a body known as the Brabazon Committee to investigate the future needs of the British civil airliner market. A year earlier, the United States and the United Kingdom had agreed to split responsibility for aircraft construction: the US would concentrate on transport aircraft while the UK would concentrate on heavy bombers. It was recognised that this would leave the UK with little experience in transport construction by the end of the war, a worrying development given the production infrastructure that would now be useless. Moreover, the massive infrastructure in the US would allow them to produce civilian designs at low cost.

The committee, under the chairmanship of Lord Brabazon of Tara, studied a number of designs and technical considerations, and delivered a report calling for the construction of four general designs studied by the committee and members of the state-owned airlines, the British Overseas Airways Corporation (BOAC) and later British European Airways (BEA).

The report identified four main types of civil transport that would be needed after the war. The first, or Type I, would be a very large transatlantic airliner serving the high-density routes such as London–New York, and accommodating passengers in luxury during the twelve-hour flight. The Type II would be a short-haul feeder liner intended to replace the Douglas DC-3 and the de Havilland Rapide, although at the suggestion of BEA this was later split into two designs, the piston-engined Type IIA and the turboprop-powered Type IIB. Type III envisaged a larger medium-range airliner serving the air routes of the British Empire, while the Type IV, the most ambitious concept of all, called for a jet-powered 100-seat airliner. This resulted from the input of one of the committee members, Geoffrey de Havilland, whose company was involved in developing the DH.100 Vampire jet fighter.

Of these proposals, the Type I emerged as the Bristol Brabazon, which proved to be a white elephant. The biggest and most ambitious project ever undertaken by the British aircraft industry, the Brabazon 1 prototype flew for the first time on 4 September 1949, two years behind schedule, and plans were made to produce a Mk.2 version, but the project was abandoned in 1952 and the sole prototype was scrapped.

The Type IIA became the Airspeed Ambassador, while the Type III was developed into the Bristol Britannia. The contract for developing the Type IIB went to Vickers, who set about designing an airliner, originally named the

The Bristol Brabazon, seen here with a damaged wingtip after colliding with a hangar door at Filton, was never a viable proposition and was abandoned. (via Bob Sharp)

Viceroy, which was to become the most successful venture of them all. It was to be powered by four Rolls-Royce propeller-turbine (turboprop) engines.

During the late 1940s, the main emphasis at the Rolls-Royce Aero-Engine Company was on the development of the Avon family of engines and on the Dart turboprop, which was being evaluated in Wellington, Lancaster (for anti-icing tests) and Dakota test-beds. Two of the Dakotas (G-ALXN and G-AMDB) were flown by British European Airways (BEA) pilots, brought in to assist the Rolls-Royce test team. This was a valuable experience, because it injected the airline pilots' experience and knowledge into the development of the first turboprop engine specifically developed for commercial aircraft. The other Dakota, KJ829, was on loan from the RAF. The Wellington (LN715) flew early in 1948 and was the first aircraft to be powered exclusively by the Dart. The next aircraft to fly with Darts was the prototype Vickers Type IIB, which by then would be renamed the Viscount following India's independence, which made Viceroy no longer politically acceptable.

The choice of the Dart was not made without much discussion. As the Type IIB was a high-risk venture from the technical point of view, the Ministry of Supply also ordered the prototype of a rival design, the Armstrong Whitworth Apollo, which was to be fitted with four Armstrong Siddeley Mamba turbo-props. The Mamba was an advanced turboprop with an axial compressor,

Gloster Meteor EE227, the world's first propeller-turbine aircraft, was powered by Rolls-Royce Trents driving five-blade Rotol propellers and had additional fins on the tailplane. (Rolls-Royce via Corinne Moore)

whereas the Dart appeared to be a more primitive engine, with two centrifugal compressors derived from the Griffon supercharger and seven can-type combustion chambers around the outside. However, the centrifugal compressor was of proven reliability, and all the British industry's turbine experience had been acquired with this type of engine, so it was the Dart that was selected.

Once this decision had been taken, in March 1947, the construction of two V.630 prototypes began at Vickers' Foxwarren high security experimental shop. The second prototype, the V663, was experimentally fitted with Rolls-Royce Tay turbojets. This aircraft first flew on 15 March 1950 and spent its working life as a test-bed, being allocated the Ministry of Supply serial number VX217. It was originally fitted with manual controls, but was later used to test the power control system that was to be installed in the Vickers Valiant jet bomber. A third prototype, the V.640, was to have been powered by four Napier Naiad turboprops. This aircraft, G-AJZW, was funded by Vickers, but was never built.

The Viscount 630 prototype first flew on 16 July 1948, with Vickers' Chief Test Pilot Jeffrey 'Mutt' Summers at the controls. The aircraft, G-AMAV, was awarded a restricted Certificate of Airworthiness on 15 September 1949, followed by a full Certificate on 27 July 1950, and on 29 July British European Airways started a month's trial service on the London–Paris and London–Edinburgh routes using this aircraft. Although it never belonged to BEA, in 1953 it was named Endeavour as a member of the airline's 'Discovery' class, and with race number 23 on its tail it took part in the air race from London to

The Vickers Viscount 630 prototype pictured during an early test flight. (Source unknown)

Christchurch, New Zealand, in October 1953, averaging 290 mph over the 11,795-mile course.

BEA's immediate criticism of the Viscount was that the design was too small, the original version seating only thirty-two passengers, and too slow, with a cruising speed of 275 mph. These factors, which resulted in unacceptable operating costs, compelled BEA to reject the type in its present configuration.

Vickers went back to the drawing board and came up with the enlarged Viscount V.700, which could accommodate up to forty-eight passengers (fifty-three in some configurations), and a cruising speed of 308 mph (496 km/h). The new prototype first flew 28 August 1950. British European Airways ordered twenty V.701s, in August 1950, with a follow-on order for seven more. Of the original order, eighteen were built at Weybridge and the remainder at the new Vickers facctory at Hurn. The first production aircraft was delivered to BEA in January 1953, and after being awarded a passenger-carrying Certificate of Airworthiness on 17 April, this aircraft left Heathrow on the London–Rome–Athens–Cyprus route, inaugurating the world's first turboprop-powered service. Three Viscounts (V.702s) were ordered by British West Indian Airways (BWIA) in June 1953, and these were used to extend the airline's services to New York in the north and Georgetown in the south. After BWIA purchased more modern

Viscount variants, three of the V.702 fleet were released to Kuwait Airways after overhaul and conversion.

In November 1951 Aer Lingus ordered four Viscounts (V.707s), and these saw extensive service on the airline's routes with Collinstown Airport, Dublin, at the hub. Also in November, Air France placed an order for twelve V.808 Viscounts, which went into service on all the company's European routes until they were eventually replaced by the Sud-Aviation Caravelle. The V.720 was a version for Trans Australian Airlines, fitted with Dart Mk.506 engines; the order was placed in June 1952 and deliveries began with VH-TVA, the thirteenth Hurn-built aircraft. This aircraft was destroyed on a training flight at Mangalore, Melbourne, on 31 October 1954. A replacement was ordered in April 1955 and ther first service flown on 18 December 1954. The last of this batch was the first Viscount to be fitted with slipper auxiliary tanks.

Structurally, the 700 Series Viscount was a low-wing, cantilever monoplane of all-metal stressed skin construction. The wings, of modified NACA 63 aerofoil section, werew built around a single main spar which supported the main bending loads and, together with the leading and trailing edge members, was carried by three circular frames of the centre fuselage. The wing ribs were closely spaced chord-wise, an arrangement that dispensed with span-wise stringers, and the whole wing was covered with a stressed Alclad skin. Forward and aft of the main spar were the bag-type main fuel tanks accommodating 1,720 imperial gallons, rising to 1,950 gallons in the 700D model; slipper tanks, when fitted, held an extra 145 imperial gallons each.

The fuselage skin was flush-riveted to stringers carried on the lateral circular frames, and the entire fuselage was pressurised except for the flight deck

Viscount G-APPX seen at Newcastle Airport before delivery to Kuwait Airways. This aircraft was scrapped in 1973. (Source unknown)

under-floor compartment and the tail cone aft of the rear pressure bulkhead. Three of the Viscount's four engines drove cabin blowers for conditioning of the cabin to maintain sea level conditions up to an altitude of 15,000 feet, rising to the equivalent of 8,000 feet at an altitude of 30,000 feet. The main passenger cabin was 6 ft 5 in hight at the centreline, and 9 ft 5 in wide at its maximum width. Passengers normally entered by the rear port-side entrance, the front port door being used for the crew's entrance and baggage loading. Some Viscounts were fitted with electrically operated airsteps.

The normal first-class seating configuration was four abreast, and a cabin temperature in the range of 65 to 80 degrees fahrenheit was maintained, according to location. There were three freight compartments, one of 110 cubic feet ahead of the main passenger cabin, one of 204 cubic feet aft, with its own starboard access door, and a forward hold of 215 cubic feet beneath the floor of the passenger cabin, fitted with twin access doors. The air-conditioning plant and much of the aircraft's electrical installation was situated behind the latter hold. The airframe was thermally de-iced from the inboard engines, exhaust gas being fed through a heat exchanger through which ram air was passed and heated; the hot air was ducted to the wing and fin leading edges, and then vented to atmosphere through louvres situated about two-thirds of the way back on the wing and fin. In conditions of high outside air temperature, a water-methanol injection system was used in some Viscounts to sustain full take-off power, the system being energised automatically by opening the throttles.

The cockpit layout was straightforward and conventional, with the engine controls and instruments grouped centrally and full dual control for captain and co-pilot. The main radio panel was in the roof. The port and starboard consoles contained fuel pumps, pressurisation and de-icing controls. The consoles were deleted from the cockpit layouts selected by some operators, the ancillary controls being grouped instead in the roof, above the radio panel. Most aircraft were fitted with storm warning radar, installed in the extreme nose.

The Viscount's landing gear was of the forward-retracting twin-wheel tricycle type, and was operated hydraulically. Single shock absorbers supported each twin-wheel unit, and anti-skin brakes were fitted. Both hand and toe brake controls were fitted in the cockpit to facilitate ground manoeuvring.

For thirty years, between 1935 and 1965, the Vickers Viscount was the only aircraft that appeared on the scene to challenge American dominance of the world commercial aircraft market. The world's first true turboprop aircraft, the Viscount emerged as a superb design, offering comfort, reliability and efficiency, and consequently sold in large numbers on both sides of the Atlantic. After the production 700-series Viscount went into regular service from 18 April 1953, the major European and American airlines sought early delivery of their share of the 445 Viscounts that were built up to the beginning of 1959.

An order placed by TCA (later Air Canada) for the Viscount Series 700 in November 1952 was most significant. For the first time, a British company realised that an operator outside the UK might be able to improve the product and make it more acceptable in the world market.

The TCA order was secured following a long series of meetings between Sir George Edwards, Chief Designer of the Vickers-Armstrongs team and TCA engineers, which resulted in some 200 modifications being made to the basic Type 700 Viscount. The modified Viscount was known as the V.724, TCA placing an order for fifteen aircraft. On 12 December 1954, with the delivery of CF-TGI – which was built on the reopened Weybridge production line – TCA became the first operator of turboprop-powered airliners in North America. The inaugural service was on 4 April 1955, between Toronto and New York.

TCA's order aroused the interest of other companies in North America, and in June 1954 Capital Airlines, at that time one of the largest US short-haul operators, placed an initial order for three Type 744 Viscounts. The first of these was delivered exactly a year later, and was the forerunner of much larger orders from Capital. By 1956 there were more Viscounts flying in the USA and Canada than in the whole of Europe. The airliner was immensely popular because of its standard of passenger comfort, one factor of which was the quietness of its Dart turboprops, which were setting hitherto unheard-of standards of running and maintenance. The large elliptical windows, measuring 26 inches by 19 inches along the axes, were also a prominent factor in the Viscount's passenger appeal.

Capital placed repeat orders for the Viscount between 1954 and 1958, but then the airline ran into financial difficulties and was forced to merge with United Air Lines, who kept the existing Viscount fleet in service. Fifteen more aircraft intended for Capital were sold off to other customers.

Although there were many Viscount type numbers, signifying differences in interior layouts to suit customer requirements, there were basically only three models in the 700 series. These were the original 700, with Dart 505 or 506 engines; the 700D with Dart 510s and extra fuel tankage; and the 770D, the North American equivalent of the 700D. Some of the latter aircraft were fitted with slipper fuel tanks on the wing leading edges. Excluding prototypes, 287 Series 700 Viscounts were built. One of the most interesting was VP-YNC, a V.748 for Central African Airways (CAA) and the 100th Viscount built. Flown on 24 May 1956, it was delivered two weeks later and named Mlanje. Following the break-up of the Central African Federation it was transferred to Air Rhodesia on 1 January 1969, flying in blue camouflage after a SAM attack. Air Zimbabwe took the aircraft over in 1979.

A 'one-off' 700 Series Viscount was the V.763, which resulted from a personal interest in the airliner shown by Howard Hughes, the celebrated pilot, aircraft manufacturer and multi-millionaire owner of the Hughes Tool Company. The specification for the single V.763 was the longest ever drawn up, and the aircraft was subjected to minute inspections by Hughes engineers. In the end Hughes' interest waned and the aircraft, which by now was holding up the production line, was sold to TACA of El Salvador with the registration YS-09C.

In 1954, Vickers and BEA jointly reached a decision to stretch the Viscount by moving back the rear pressure bulkhead, creating a 111-inch internal extension while making the fuselage only 46 inches longer. This aircraft appeared as the V.802, twelve of which were ordered by BEA, but in 1955 Rolls-Royce offered an increase in power with the Dart 525 engine, which was installed in the considerably revised V.810 series. The V.810 sold well, the last order being placed by CAAC of the Chinese People's Republic – the first time that country had placed an order with a Western source. Typical of the smaller companies which recognised the value offered by the Viscount was Manx Airlines, which leased an 813 series aircraft, G-AZNA from British Midland airways; this particular airliner had then been in service for over a quarter of a century.

An important order for Viscounts was placed in December 1955 by Continental Airlines. This involved the purchase of twelve V.812s, followed by an order for three more in February 1956. The Continental Viscounts had an interior with fifty-two seats and a rear lounge. To comply with CAA requirements a fuel jettison system was installed. In March 1956, South African Airways (SAA) placed an order for seven 52-seat Viscount 813s, these aircraft eventually replacing the airline's Skymasters and Constellations on internal routes. Also in 1956, Lufthansa decided to replace their Convair 340/440 fleet with, initially ordering seven Viscount 814s.

The 444th and last Viscount was first flown on 2 January 1964, 438 of these being regular aircraft sold to airline customers. Several were bought new by executive owners (the first being the Canadian Department of Transport in 1954) and air forces, the first by the Indian Air Force in 1954. Every Viscount that appeared on the second-hand market was quickly snapped up.

The type continued in BEA and British Airways service until the 1980s, eventually being passed on to charter operators such as British Air Ferries (later British World). The last British-owned Viscounts were sold in South Africa.

In 1951 Vickers-Armstrong began design studies of an aircraft to succeed the Viscount in airline service. The result was the Type 951 Vanguard, which first flew on 20 January 1959. In the event only 44 Vanguards were built and these were operated by just two major airlines, BEA – which had placed an order for twenty Vanguards in July 1956 – and the Canadian airline TCA (later to become Air Canada). The Type 951 was followed by two more variants, the Types 952 and 953, which had a reduced range but increased payload, and twenty Vanguard 952s were ordered by TCA in January 1957, followed by three more at a later date. BEA, meanwhile, had revised its order to six Vanguard 951s and fourteen 953s; the first aircraft entered service with BEA on 17 December 1960, while TCA began Vanguard operations in February 1961. The Vanguard, however, was never a success, and as jet aircraft took over the passenger role it was relegated to freight duties.

In summary, it may be said that the Viscount, despite a somewhat shaky start, turned out to be the right airliner in the right place at the right time. Its successor, the Vanguard, was not.

CHAPTER SIXTEEN

The de Havilland Comet

I n 1948, there began a chain of events that would change the face of civil aviation for ever. In that year, two Rolls-Royce Nene turbojets were installed in a Vickers Viking airliner, making it the world's first jet-powered transport aircraft, and on 19 July Vickers Chief Test Pilot Jeffrey 'Mutt' Summers flew it from London to Paris in a record time of thirty-four minutes and seven seconds at an average speed of 348 mph, to mark the thirty-nineth anniversary of Louis Blériot's cross-Channel flight.

Just over two years later, on 27 July, 1949, de Havilland Chief Test Pilot John Cunningham lifted the prototype of the de Havilland Comet, the world's first jet airliner, off the runway of the company airfield at Hatfield on its maiden flight. Powered by four de Havilland Ghost turbojets mounted in pairs in the wings, the Comet underwent three years of flight testing before inaugurating the world's first jet passenger service with BOAC in May 1952 with a flight from London to Johannesburg.

The Comet that flew in BOAC livery was, in fact, the 'Type IV' airliner proposed to the Brabazon Committee by Geoffrey de Havilland, and was a far different aircraft from some of the original design concepts. During 1944 several unorthodox configurations were considered, including one with twin tail-booms and three de Havilland Goblin turbojets, a canard type with three Ghost turbojets mounted on the rear fuselage, and a tailless type with a swept wing and short fuselage. The three-ghost formula emerged as the favourite at this stage, and on 19 April 1944 the Brabazon Committee recommended an immediate start on the design of the jet airliner. However, the Committee agreed that it was not yet practicable to draw up a list of firm requirements for the jet transport, as had been done for more conventional types. Within the de Havilland Company itself, however, there was an instinctive feeling that the jet airliner concept was right, and that such an aircraft should not be restricted to short-range operations.

By August 1944, the formula placed before the Brabazon Committee by the de Havilland design team envisaged a 'three-Ghost Vampire mail carrier', with provision for six passengers and 2,000 lb of mail, and on 28 February 1945 a high-speed wind tunnel model was sent to RAE Farnborough to be tested. Meanwhile, thoughts were turning towards a less specialised airliner powered by four Ghost turbojets and of more conventional design, and two studies were put forward in March 1945, one involving an aircraft with a fuselage width of 8 ft 6 in and seating twenty-four passengers three abreast, and the other with a 10 ft wide fuselage seating up to thirty-six passengers.

A jet airliner would fly high and fast, although a lot of problems remained to be solved, not the least of which involved pressurising a large passenger cabin. There was also a good deal of discussion about the merits of the swept wing in delaying the onset of compressibility at high speeds, approaching the speed of sound. It was known that the Germans had carried out much research into swept wing, high-speed flight, and had applied it to two combat aircraft, the turbojet-powered Messerschmitt 262 and the rocket-powered Me 163. Aerodynamic research facilities in the United Kingdom, in the summer of 1945, were greatly inferior to those that existed in the United States; throughout the whole industry there was not a single transonic wind tunnel, because although working examples had been discovered in Germany at the end of the war these had been dismantled with astonishing speed and shipped back to the USA, along with a vast amount of data on high-speed aerodynamics and design.

On 1 October, 1945, de Havilland placed a progress report before the committee, based on all available aerodynamic knowledge then available in the UK. The report envisaged a tailless airliner of 75,000 lb all-up weight, powered by four de Havilland Ghost turbojets mounted under the wing and closer to the trailing edge. The wing was to be swept at 40 degrees.

It was, however, considered imperative that practical research needed to be conducted into swept-wing flight at high speeds, and for this it would be necessary to build a research aircraft. This emerged as the DH.108, which was basically a Vampire with swept wings attached. The aircraft had no tailplane, the fin and rudder being mounted on the fuselage nacelle. Three aircraft were built, each one with the specific task of testing the swept wing configuration at various speeds. The first of them, TG283, flew from Woodbridge in Suffolk (which had a long runway) on 15 May 1946, with de Havilland's son Geoffrey Jr at the controls. The third DH.108, VW120, was the high-speed aircraft of the trio, and on 9 September 1948, flown by test pilot John Derry, it exceeded Mach 1.0 in a steep dive between 12,000 and 10,000 m (40,000–30,000 feet). Despite conflicting claims that arose thereafter, the DH.108 appears to have been the first turbojet-powered aircraft in the world to exceed Mach 1. All three DH.108s were destroyed in fatal crashes, two after disintegrating in mid-air. Geoffrey de Havilland Jr was killed in one of them.

During an early stage of research flying with the DH.108, it was realised that the proposed sweepback of 40 degrees was unacceptable, and that a much smaller degree of sweep would result in a more economical and lighter aircraft. By November 1946 a complete weight and performance statement for the proposed jet airliner, which bore the company designation DH.106, had been prepared. At 100,000 lb all-up weight the aircraft was estimated to be capable of carrying a payload of 7,000 lb (twenty-four passengers) from London to Gander against a 100 mph headwind, with allowances for diversions, while for operations on the British Empire routes to the Middle East and India an all-up weight of 96,500 lb was envisaged, giving a stage length of 2,200 miles with a 10,000 lb payload (thirty-two passengers).

Detail design work on the DH.106 began in September 1946, and the first production orders were negotiated with BOAC for eight aircraft and British

South American Airways for six aircraft during the next few months. When BSAA merged with BOAC, the contract for all fourteen aircraft was finalised with the latter company. In June 1948 the de Havilland Ghost turbojet received civil type approval, the first jet engine to be certificated for public passenger carrying. By that time the Ghost had been flying for eleven months, mounted in the outboard engine positions of two Avro Lancastrian test-beds (aircraft of this type, incidentally, were also used as test-beds for the Rolls-Royce Nene). Between them the two engine development aircraft flew 425 hours. Much valuable information was amassed, but as the Lancastrian's ceiling was only 25,000 feet the engine's performance at the altitudes where the DH.106 would be in its natural habitat could not be measured. To plug this gap, a Vampire was fitted with special thin wings and a Ghost engine, and in 1948 test pilot John Cunningham flew this aircraft to a record altitude of nearly 60,000 feet.

Meanwhile, the first DH.106 Comet airliner, G-ALVG, one of two examples ordered by the Ministry of Supply, was taking shape under conditions of great secrecy in Hatfield's experimental shops. Even the weather was on the side of secrecy, for when the aircraft was pushed out on to the apron for engine runs on Saturday 1 April 1949, a heavy mist protected it from unwanted attention. The definitive DH.106 design was an all-metal 36-seater with a circular section fuselage mounted on a thin, moderately-swept wing with four de Havilland

The second DH Comet 1, G-ALZK, was delivered to the BOAC Comet unit at Hurn in April 1951. It was scrapped in 1957. (The Aeroplane)

Ghost 50 turbojet engines buried in the wing roots, a novel feature at the time and one that left the wing aerodynamically clean. Good handling characteristics at the lower end of the speed range were assured by the provision of general flaps, and by the use of Lockheed Servodyne hydraulically assisted power controls. This control system was tested on the DH.108 and a full-size rig was then set up in the factory, operating continuously for more than three years. Four crew occupied the flight deck in the extreme nose, the all-weather visibility having been carefully determined by fitting various nose configurations to a Horsa glider, which was towed by a Halifax. The tricycle undercarriage was equipped with large single main wheels which retracted outward into bulges in the under surface of the mainplane.

Structural testing of the DH.106 airframe had followed the usual procedure, with extra emphasis on the stresses that would be imposed by full cabin pressurisation. The first production wing was fixed to a section of the fuselage and subjected by hydraulic rams to upward and downward stresses that deflected the wings by 3 feet at the tips, this being repeated many thousand of times. Static loads were applied to the main undercarriage units mounted on this rig, the worst landing loads also being applied thousands of times to form a test of the undercarriage itself and of the surrounding wing structure. Drag and side-load tests were applied, and also drop tests and retraction tests. In all, 16,000 undercarriage retractions were made with the bearings being packed with a mixture of grease and sand. The DH.106's nose wheel steering was thoroughly tested, a nose wheel assembly complete with hydraulic gear and pilot's steering wheel being mounted on a commercial chassis which, suitably ballasted, was driven at speeds of up to 50 mph over a cumulative distance of 120 miles.

A decompression chamber was installed at Hatfield for testing structure and systems to limits of minus 70 degrees centigrade and the equivalent of 70,000 feet altitude. The first large section of the DH.106 to be tested in the chamber was the nose, which was subjected to 2,000 applications of a 9 lb pressure. Testing of pressurised sections to much greater stresses was done under water, so that when failure occurred the test specimen would not be ripped apart (Because water is virtually incompressible no energy is stored, when failure occurs the internal and external pressure equalises at once and the damage is localised, making it possible to examine the cause of the failure). Both the nose section and a section of the cylindrical fuselage were pressure tested under water, being subjected to 16.5 lb per square inch, double the pressure they might be expected to endure in service. Windows and window frames were subjected to exhaustive tests, including pressurising every working day for three years, with routine twice-weekly cleaning and polishing. One window was tested to 100 lb per square inch.

The structural testing programme was based on the belief that static testing would be more than adequate to reveal any fatigue stresses that might be present in the airframe, particularly the fuselage. As it turned out, the belief was to be tragically misplaced.

In the evening of 27 July 1949, John Cunningham's thirtieth birthday, de Havilland's Chief Test Pilot took the Comet 1 prototype off the Hatfield runway for its maiden flight. With Cunningham were J.W. Wilson, second pilot;

F.T. Reynolds, flight engineer; H. Waters, flight engineer (electrics); and A.J. Fairbrother (flight test observer). They took the Comet up to 10,000 feet, carried out a number of handling tests over the low and medium speed range, then returned to base, making a low pass along the runway at 100 feet before landing after a flight of thirty-one minutes. In the next eighteen working days the Comet amassed a total of thirty-two and a half hours of flight time, including display flying at Farnborough in September, the sleek silver airliner drawing much admiration. This was followed by a number of fast overseas flights to measure fuel consumption under simulated airline route conditions, beginning with a return trip to Castel Benito, Libya, at an average speed of 448 mph on 25 October 1949, with John Cunningham at the controls. The outward trip took three hours twenty-three minutes, the return trip three hours twenty-three minutes.

On 2 May 1952 BOAC used G-ALYP ('Yoke Peter') to inaugurate the first all-jet commercial service, between London and Johannesburg. The Comet brought unheard-of luxury to its élite clientele. Carrying thirty-six passengers at 12,190 m (40,000 feet) in near silence, it was twice as fast as contemporary piston-engine airliners. It carried 30,000 passengers in its first year of operations, by which time fifty examples had been ordered by BOAC and other airlines, beginning with Canadian Pacific Air Lines.

The next model after the Comet 1 was the 44-seat 1A, which was fitted with 2,268 kg (5,000 lb) Ghost 50 Mk.2 engines with water/methanol injection, increased tankage and which consequently had an increased range at higher all-up weights. During 1952–3 ten Comet 1As were delivered to Air France (three), Canadian Pacific (two), UAT (three) and No. 412 Transport Squadron of the RCAF (two). F-BGNX was the first of Air France's Comet 1As, although the French carrier UAT was actually the first to take delivery of the jet airliner. Air France opened Paris–Rome–Beirut services on 26 August 1953.

Then things began to go wrong. On 26 October, 1952, BOAC Comet 1 G-ALYZ with thirty-five passengers on board crashed on take-off at Rome/ Ciampino Airport, fortunately without loss of life; the accident was attributed to the captain having failed to notice that the aircraft had adopted an excessive nose-up attitude during the take-off.

The first fatal Comet crash occurred on 3 March 1953 and involved Comet 1A CF-CUN, on a delivery flight to Canadian Pacific Airlines via Karachi and Sydney. On take-off from Karachi, the aircraft's wing struck a bridge and it crashed and caught fire with the loss of all eleven people on board. Pilot error was initially blamed, but flight tests established that lift could be lost if the pull-up was made too quickly after take-off. The leading edge of the Comet's wing was redesigned as a result.

There was worse to come. On 2 May 1953, Comet 1 G-ALYV of BOAC disintegrated in a thunderstorm shortly after taking off from Calcutta on a flight from Singapore to London. All 37 passengers and six crew were killed. Two further crashes in January and April 1954, the first involving G-ALYP off the Italian island of Elba and the second G-ALYY off Stromboli, with no survivors and no apparent cause, led to the entire fleet being grounded for investigation. In

February 1955, the remnants of the Italian crashes were brought to the surface and shipped back to the UK for exhaustive testing, while a Comet airframe was tested to destruction. Analysis showed the cause of the crashes to be metal fatigue. After thousands of pressurised climbs and descents, the fuselage metal (which was thinner than standard due to the need to save weight, resulting from the aircraft's underpowered de Havilland Ghost engines) around the Comet's large rectangular windows would begin to crack and eventually cause explosive decompression of the cabin and catastrophic structural failure.

Despite their misfortunes, the Comet 1s and 1As flew over 30,000 revenue hours in less than two years of service.

While the ill-fated Comet 1 was still operational, de Havilland embarked on studies for a 'stretched' version, the Comet 3. Registered G-ANLO, this flew for the first time on 19 July 1954. By the end of 1954, with the full Comet 1 accident findings available, de Havilland decided to combine all the latest knowledge into a Mk.4 version, and a modified G-ANLO, now fitted with Avon 523 engines, began a flight test programme in February 1957. The first production Comet 4, G-APDA, flew on 27 April 1958 and was the first of nineteen ordered by BOAC. On 4 October 1958 BOAC inaugurated the first fare-paying transatlantic jet service (London–New York), beating Pan American's Boeing 707 by three weeks. The Comet 4A was a still-born version projected for Capital Airlines; from it was derived the Comet 4B.

Hawker Siddeley, into which the old de Havilland firm had been absorbed, ended its Comet 4 programme with the Mk.4C, produced by merging the long body with a large pinion-tanked wing. The Comet 4C was the most successful model of all, being bought initially by Mexicana, Misrair (Eyptair), Aerolineas Argentinas, MEA, Sudan and Kuwait. Altogether thirty of this series were produced, twenty-three of them at Hawker Siddeley's Chester factory, bringing total Comet production to 113. The final examples went to King Ibn Saud of Saudi Arabia, the Royal Air Force (five) and the Aeroplane and Armament Experimental Establishment (A&AEE) at Boscombe Down, Wiltshire (one). The last two went to Hawker Siddeley at Manchester for conversion to the prototype Nimrod MR.1 maritime patrol aircraft.

The Comet 5 was a proposed development that would have been a marked improvement over the previous models. Features of the design included a wider fuselage allowing five abreast seating, a wing with greater sweep, and pod mounted Rolls-Royce Conway engines, all producing a similar configuration to the Boeing 707 and Douglas DC-8 which were being developed on the other side of the Atlantic. Support from the Ministry of Transport was not forthcoming, and the project did not proceed. Ironically, BOAC, backed by the Department, went on to order Conway powered Boeing 707s.

The Royal Canadian Air Force and the Royal Air Force were both early recipients, two aircraft being delivered to No. 412 Squadron RCAF in 1953 and five Comet C.2s to No. 216 Squadron, RAF Transport Command, in June 1956. The Canadian aircraft remained in service until 1964. No. 51 Squadron RAF also took delivery of three Comet C.2s, modified for electronic intelligence gathering and designated Comet Mk.2R, in 1958. Two of these aircraft re-

Among the users of the Comet 4C was Mexicana, the Mexican national carrier. (BAe)

Comet 4C ST-AAW was used by Sudan Airways. (BAe)

An RAF Comet C.2 dominates the back row in this lineup of aircraft from the Air Museum at RAF Cosford in 1971. The Museum is now greatly expanded and is the 'other half' of the RAF Museum. (RAF)

The RAF was an early customer for the Comet, the C.Mk.2 equipping No. 216 Squadron at RAF Lyneham, Wiltshire. (RAF)

mained in service until 1974. Meanwhile, in February 1962 No. 216 Squadron had added five C.Mk.4s to its strength, and after the withdrawal of the C.2 s in March 1967 it continued to operate these aircraft on Air Support Command's routes around the world until it disbanded in June 1975.

The only complete surviving Comet 1 is a Comet 1XB on display at the RAF Museum Cosford. It is painted in BOAC colours and displays the registration G-APAS, although it never flew for that airline, having been delivered to Air France, and then to the Ministry of Supply after conversion to 1XB standard.

Comet 4C G-APDB, owned by the Duxford Aviation Society, was re-painted in its original BOAC colours in December 2006 in readiness for its inclusion in the new AirSpace hangar. It was this airliner, taken on by DAS on a 99-year lease from its last operator, Dan-Air, in 1974, that made the first transatlantic jet passenger flight from London to New York on 4 October 1958.

The nose of BOAC Comet 1A G-ANAV is displayed at London's Science Museum, while the fuselage of Air France Comet 1A F-BGNX is preserved at the De Havilland Aircraft Heritage Centre in Hertfordshire. The last Comet to fly, 4C XS235 Canopus, is kept in running condition at Bruntingthorpe aerodrome, and in 2007 there were plans to reurn it to flying condition.

CHAPTER SEVENTEEN

The Hawker Hunter

I n March 1948, the Hawker design team under Sydney Camm was studying a design for a swept-wing jet fighter in response to Air Ministry Specification F.3/48, which was dictated by the need for a fighter with a sufficiently advanced performance to enable it to intercept a new generation of jet bombers in the class of the Boeing B-47 Stratojet, the prototype of which had flown in December 1947. The advent of advanced aircraft such as the B-47 had resulted in a new Air Staff Operational Requirement, OR.228, and it was to this that F.3/48 conformed.

Several schemes for a swept-wing jet fighter had already been considered by Hawkers. Much depended on the selection of a suitable engine, and the most promising appeared to be the AJ.65 axial-flow turbojet then being developed by Rolls-Royce. Unfortunately, no one at that time envisaged how protracted the development of the AJ.65 would be. Seven years were to elapse before the AJ.65, by then named the Avon, would become operationally acceptable to the RAF.

The project that evolved around the AJ.65 was allocated the Company designation Hawker P.1067, which in 1948 underwent a number of changes to conform to OR.228. The new Operational Requirement called for a single-seat land-based fighter capable of carrying out day interception duties in any part of the world. Its primary role would be the interception of high-altitude, high-speed bombers as soon as possible after they were detected by radar, but it would also have a secondary ground-attack role. The OR was dictated by the need to intercept a fast, high-flying, nuclear-armed bomber as far as possible from its target area, and so the greatest importance was attached to time-to-altitude performance. The time from engine start to 45,000 feet, including taxi time, was not to exceed six minutes, while the rate of climb was not to be less than 1,000 feet per minute at 50,000 feet. The requirement also called for a maximum speed in level flight of at least 547 knots at 45,000 feet, with a desirable diving speed of at least Mach 1.2. The required endurance was seventy-five minutes, including the climb to 45,000 feet and ten minutes' combat at full power at that altitude. Armament was to be four 30 mm Aden guns.

In September 1948 Hawker received a contract to build three P.1067 prototypes. Two of these were to be powered by the Rolls-Royce AJ.65 Avon, the third by the Armstrong Siddeley Sapphire. To carry out high speed research, Hawker built two prototypes of an experimental aircraft, the P.1052, which had swept wings but a conventional tail. One of these was later modified and fitted with all-swept flying surfaces, and in this guise it became the Hawker P.1081.

The P.1067 prototype, WB188, flew for the first time from Boscombe Down on 20 July 1951, with Hawkers Chief Test Pilot Squadron Leader Neville Duke

The sheer grace and beauty of the P.1067 are apparent in this splendid shot of WB188, taken during an early stage of the flight test programme. (BAe)

at the controls. The second Avon-powered aircraft, WB195, flew on 5 May 1952, and the Sapphire-powered prototype, WB202, on 30 November that year. Intensive trials with all three aircraft continued into 1953, by which time there was no longer any doubt that Hawker had produced a very fine aircraft indeed. It now remained to be seen what experienced RAF fighter pilots thought of its characteristics, and how well the Hunter, as the aircraft was named, would stand up to high-g combat manoeuvres.

The Hunter sailed through its Service handling trials at Boscombe Down in the summer of 1953 almost without complaint. The first real problem occurred early in October, when two pilots from the Central Fighter Establishment's Air Fighting Development Squadron (AFDS) were cleared to fly the first production Hunter F.1, WT555. During a preliminary combat evaluation, a serious snag occurred almost immediately. When the wing trailing edge flaps were used as airbrakes in high-speed, low-level turns, the Hunter's nose pitched violently downwards, which was quite unacceptable. The problem was solved by fitting the aircraft with a ventral airbrake.

The second major problem was the tendency of the Avon engine to surge during high-g turns and rapid acceleration. This tendency was aggravated when the Aden guns were fired at altitudes above 25,000 feet as a result of shock waves entering the air intakes. The problem was later solved by Rolls-Royce through the introduction of a 'fuel-dipping' system, but it had not been cured by the time the Hunter entered service with RAF Fighter Command in the summer of 1954.

One problem with the Hunter F.1 that was never overcome was its lack of endurance, and this shortcoming was demonstrated when four F.1s from the Central Fighter Establishment at West Raynham took part in a series of annual air exercises. It was the first time the Hunter had been able to fly under simulated war conditions against fast, high-flying targets such as the English Electric Canberra, Boeing B-47 and North American B-45, and although it carried out successful interceptions on all of them, its restricted fuel resulted in none of the interceptions being made more than eighty miles from base.

Extending the endurance of the Hunter F.1 and the Sapphire-engined F.2 was the main concern of the Hawker design team in 1954, with both variants due to enter full RAF service in the course of the year. The obvious answer was to increase the fuel load without affecting the aircraft's performance, and so Hawker set about modifying the fuselage system of the F.1, deleting the rear fuselage tanks but increasing the other fuselage tank space as well as providing under-wing attachments for two 100-gallon drop tanks. In addition, eight small bag tanks were fitted into the inboard wing leading edges. These modifications were incorporated in the 114th Hunter F.1, and in this guise the aircraft was re-designated Hunter F.4, which made its first flight on 20 October 1954. Similar modifications were made to the F.2, which was then designated F.5. The first example, WN954, flew on 19 October 1954, the day before the F.4.

Meanwhile, the first Hunter F.1s had been delivered to No. 43(F) Squadron at RAF Leuchars, Scotland, beginning in July 1954, but the squadron continued to use its Meteor F.8s after that while personnel gained experience with the new fighter. From December 1954 the second squadron of the Leuchars Wing,

The third production Hunter, WT557, was allocated to the Royal Radar Establishment for radio trials. (BAe)

Hunter F.1s of No. 43 Squadron, seen from an accompanying Meteor T.7. (BAe)

No. 222, also exchanged its Meteor F.8s for the Hunter F.1. Meanwhile, No. 257 Squadron at Wattisham had begun rearming with the Hunter F.2 in September 1954, and re-equipment of No. 263 Squadron with F.2s began at the same base in February 1955. The last to rearm with the early marks of Hunter was the Odiham Wing, whose No. 54 Squadron received F.1s in March 1955 and No. 247 Squadron in June. Both the Odiham squadrons exchanged their F.1s for F.4s in the summer of 1954, this mark having first been delivered to No. 111 Squadron at North Weald in June.

All these units, in addition to working-up operationally on the new type, carried out a great deal of display and publicity flying. In February 1955, for example, Nos 43, 257 and 263 Squadrons laid on a major flypast at Wattisham, and in March No. 43 Squadron formed an aerobatic team with three Hunters. Also in 1955, the RAF's first four-ship Hunter aerobatic team was put up by No. 54 Squadron, and both teams represented the Royal Air Force during the year at home and on the continent.

In April 1955, No. 263 Squadron at Wattisham began to rearm with the Hunter F.5, the modified F.2 with a greater fuel capacity and wing hard points for stores. The F.5 was also issued to Nos 1, 41, 56 and 257 Squadrons before the end of 1955. The Hunter F.4/F.5 Squadrons, now having an aircraft with an

No. 43 Squadron's aerobatic team, the Fighting Cocks, seen over Scotland in 1955. (BAe)

Fine study of No. 54 Squadron's aerobatic team. (Crown copyright)

enhanced combat endurance over that of the F.1, used them to good effect in Exercise Beware, the annual Fighter Command air defence exercise which was held during the last week of September. In fact, this was the first major test of the Command's Hunter Squadrons in a simulated war situation, and the pilots were impressed. While flying Meteor 8s they had grown accustomed to the disconcerting experience of having Canberras out-turning them at 40,000 feet and converting mild-evasion-only tactics into perfect quarter attacks on the Meteors' exposed bottoms. The same pilots, now flying far superior aircraft, reported delightedly that the Canberra looked quite different when seen from above!

All the Hunter squadrons were engaged in comprehensive flying programmes during 1956. In May, the squadrons based in northern Britain took part in Exercise Rejuvenate, and made a very good showing against bombers attacking from the north-west at high level. These were mainly USAF Strategic Air Command B-47s, whose operational ceiling of 42,000 feet was well within the Hunter's limits. In September, the squadrons went over to their full operational roles in the annual Fighter Command exercise, Stronghold; the targets were once again B-47s, together with RAF Canberras and Valiants.

In October 1956, the two Hunter F.5 squadrons of the Tangmere Wing, Nos 1 and 34 (the latter having received Hunters early that year) deployed to Cyprus in support of Operation Musketeer, the Anglo-French occupation of the Suez Canal Zone. On 2 November 1956 the Hunters flew a number of top cover sorties over the Canal Zone in support of naval fighter-bombers, but their limited endurance did not allow sufficient time in the patrol area, and this, together with the fact that there was no opposition from the Egyptian Air Force, resulted in a decision not to use them in that role again. During the remainder of the operation the Hunters, together with Mystère IVAs of the Armée de l'Air, were kept on high alert states at Akrotiri and Nicosia in case the Egyptians attempted to use their force of Ilyushin Il-28 jet bombers to attack Cyprus.

At the end of 1956 RAF Fighter Command had sixteen Hunter squadrons at its disposal, based on ten airfields from Leuchars in Scotland to Tangmere in Sussex. Fighter Command's general policy in the 1950s was to concentrate two day-fighter squadrons and one night squadron to form a single wing on an operational airfield; the Leuchars Wing, for example, comprised Nos 43 and 222 Squadrons, with Hunters, and No. 151 Squadron with de Havilland Venom NF.3s. This policy was to remain in force until the early 1960s, when the squadrons of Fighter Command began to receive an integrated all-weather weapons system in the form of the English Electric Lightning.

There were two exceptions. At the Greater London fighter stations of Biggin Hill and North Weald, a single Hunter squadron shared the location with two Royal Auxiliary Air Force squadrons equipped with Meteor F.8s. It is interesting to note that during this period, RAuxAF pilots were regularly attached to the Hunter squadrons for conversion or continuation training on the Hunter. Apart from the fact that these pilots would have provided a considerable pool of reinforcements for the first-line squadrons in time of war, it was expected that the RAuxAF would re-equip with the Hunter when the first-line squadrons got more modern equipment and handed down their aircraft. That expectation was abruptly swept aside in 1957, when the flying units of the Royal Auxiliary Air Force disbanded.

At the end of 1954, the Second Tactical Air Force (TAF) in Germany had nineteen fighter and fighter-bomber squadrons at its disposal, nine equipped with the Canadair F-86E Sabre Mk.1 and the remainder with the de Havilland Venom FB.1. From the outset, it was intended that the Hunter F.4 would perform the dual function of air defence and ground attack in 2 TAF, replacing the Sabre completely and the Venom in part, and re-equipment with the Hunter was completed by May 1956. The Hunter was also used by the Belgian, Danish and Netherlands Air Forces.

The Hunter Wings in 2 TAF maintained very high alert states, with one squadron from each wing taking it in turns to maintain a Battle Flight of two Hunters on immediate standby and the remainder at fifteen minutes' readiness. In time of war, the requirement was for the whole of the fighter force to be airborne within one hour of the alert sounding. In the interests of operational efficiency there were frequent exercises and practice alerts. In the latter event the Hunter squadron on standby was required to be airborne within thirty-five minutes. The squadrons had slightly different air defence roles, depending on their geographical location. The primary task of the Bruggen and Geilenkirchen Wings was the air defence of the Ruhr, while the Jever and Oldenburg Wings were to secure air superiority over the North German Plain, engaging the enemy as far as practicable to the east.

In the mid-1950s the main threat was still expected to come from bombers attacking at high level, and a great deal of emphasis was consequently placed on practice combat at high altitude. This involved one-v-one, two-v-one, two-v-two and two-v-four combats between Hunters, or with the Hunters taking on Venoms. The Venom was a remarkably agile aircraft at high altitude, and at 45,000 feet or more it could out-turn the Hunter without too much effort, although its acceleration was poor.

The Hunter F.4's career in 2 TAF was relatively short-lived. In 1957, as part of an economic measure that involved sweeping cuts in the size of the British forces in Germany, it was decided to disband all the Venom squadrons and nine of the thirteen Hunter squadrons, the survivors being scheduled to convert to the latest Hunter fighter variant, the F.Mk.6.

In Fighter Command, the Hunter F.6 began to replace the F.4 from February 1958. The Rolls-Royce Avon 203 engine that powered the F.6 was free of any surge tendency, which at last eliminated many of the problems that had been associated with gun firing at high altitude. Up to 1958 the Hunter had not been cleared to fire all four guns at altitudes in excess of 48,000 feet, but in June that year a special exercise was arranged in which four Hunters of No. 43 Squadron each fired all four guns twice at 51,000 feet, setting a record which was never beaten by any other Hunter squadron.

The Hunter F.6 was very popular in squadron service. Although its maximum speed at all altitudes offered no real advantage over that of the F.4, because of airframe design limitations, its rate of climb at 45,000 feet was 1,700 feet per minute, compared with 1,000 feet per minute for the F.4, and the new automatic fuel system permitted the throttle to be banged open, closed and banged open again without any risk of a flame-out. Also, thanks to the Avon 203's isopropyl-nitrate starter system, which replaced the cartridge starter of earlier marks, the engine rotated up to self-sustaining rpm much more quickly, allowing a faster scramble time.

Training the Hunter pilots was the responsibility of two Operational Conversion Units, No. 229 at Chivenor in Devon and No. 233 at Pembrey in South Wales, which was equipped mainly with Hunter F.1s and F.4s that had been retired from the first-line squadrons. Pilots graduated to the Hunter after receiving initial instructional jet training in the de Havilland Vampire T.11 and carrying out live firing in the Vampire FB.5.

Although conversion from the two-seat Vampire T.11 to the single-seat Hunter proceeded fairly smoothly, with a commendably low accident rate, the RAF's requirement for a two-seat Hunter trainer became increasingly urgent, not least because of the need to train the pilots of foreign air forces which had agreed to purchase the Hawker fighter. This resulted in the two-seat Hunter T.7, which first flew on 8 July 1955, powered by a 7,500 lb thrust Avon RA.21 turbojet. Beginning with XL567, deliveries of the Hunter T.7 to No. 229 OCU began in 1958. The Hunter Mks 8, 12, T52, T62, T66, T67 and T69 were also two-seat trainer variants.

In 1959 RAF Fighter Command was eagerly anticipating the operational debut of the English Electric Lightning F.1. The initial order for this aircraft had been placed in November 1956 and a major airfield development programme had been initiated to accommodate the new type. The Lightning should have been in squadron service in mid-1959, but had been subjected to various delays and uncertainties which had set back the programme by about a year. All this meant that the Hunter F.6 had to continue as the RAF's first line of defence, together with the all-weather Gloster Javelin, for a good deal longer than had been anticipated. Moreover, in the wake of the Defence White Paper of 1957, which had cast doubt on the future of manned aircraft for the RAF and which

The Hunter T.7 two-seat trainer variant. (BAe)

had led to the abandonment of some airfields which were being prepared for the introduction of the Lightning, it was now certain that some of the Hunter squadrons would not be re-equipped, and would therefore be disbanded. At the end of 1959 the futures of only three Hunter-equipped squadrons in the United Kingdom seemed secure; these were Nos 1, 43 and 54 Squadrons, which were scheduled to rearm with the Hunter FGA.9 and assume a ground attack role.

The last two Hunter F.6 air defence squadrons in the UK were Nos 19 and 92 at Leconfield in Yorkshire. No. 19 Squadron received its first Lightning F.2s in December 1962, and No. 92 also began to rearm with the Lightning in the following April. Later, in 1965, these two squadrons took their Lightnings to Germany to form the RAF's air defence element of 2nd Allied Tactical Air Force.

The Hunter's day as the principal weapon in the air defence of the United Kingdom was over, but in other spheres, and other roles, the splendid Hawker fighter still had a long way to travel.

In 1958, Hawker Aircraft received a Ministry of Supply contract for the conversion of a number of Hunter F.6s to carry three nose-mounted cameras in place of the radar ranging equipment. The first conversion, XF429, flew for the first time on 7 November 1958, and forty-three F.6s were subsequently modified to this standard under the designation Hunter FR.Mk.10. The variant was basically similar to the FGA.9, although there was no provision for rocket armament and the Distance Measuring Equipment (DME) was deleted. The FR.10 had a radius of action of 250 nautical miles at low level and 750 nm hi-lo-hi.

On 31 December, 1960, No. 79 Squadron, which had been operating the Swift FR.5 in the fighter-reconnaissance role, disbanded at Gütersloh, but on the following day it was renumbered No. 4 Squadron. The Swifts continued in service for some weeks, carrying the insignia of both Nos 4 and 79 Squadron, until they were replaced by Hunter FR.10s. No. 2 Squadron continued to use the Swift FR.5 until March 1961, when it too became operational on the Hunter FR.10. Both units were based at Gütersloh before the end of 1961, forming RAF Germany's Tactical Reconnaissance Wing. Its primary role was low-level visual reconnaissance, the aircraft being controlled by a NATO-administered Tactical Operations Centre, and the squadrons could be tasked to operate anywhere within the NATO area from northern Norway to Greece. Pilots found the Hunter FR.10 a considerable improvement over the Swift in terms of ferry range; with 230-gallon drop tanks, it could fly from Germany to Malta non-stop.

In January 1960, No. 38 Group, originally formed in 1942 to provide airlift facilities for the British Army, was re-formed at Upavon in Wiltshire and two Hunter squadrons, Nos 1 and 54, based at Stradishall in Suffolk with Hunter F.6s, were designated to provide its offensive element. The planned role of the two squadrons required them to be rearmed with the Hunter FGA.9, but as priority was given to the re-equipment of squadrons in Malaya, Hong Kong and the Middle East with this variant, it was to be early 1961 before the two Stradishall squadrons received their first ground-attack Hunters. The squadrons were formally transferred from RAF Fighter Command to No. 38 Group in December 1961 and relocated at RAF Waterbeach, moving to West Raynham in August 1963. Throughout the 1960s, the West Raynham Wing continued to provide tactical support for No. 38 Group, taking part in frequent overseas deployments to Scandinavia and the Middle East. In July 1969, No. 1 Squadron moved to Wittering to begin conversion to the V/STOL Harrier; No. 54 Squadron disbanded on 1 September that year, its remaining Hunters and pilots becoming the United Kingdom echelon of No. 4 Squadron, which was also earmarked for conversion to the Harrier.

In the early 1960s, Hunter FGA.9s of No. 20 Squadron, which was based on Tengah, Singapore, became heavily involved in operations during the crisis period known as the Indonesian Confrontation. It began in December 1962, when an armed rebellion broke out in the Sultanate of Brunei, marking the beginning of four years of continuous operations in which British forces, predominantly Gurkha troops, fought against Indonesian attempts to prevent the British colonies of Sarawak and Sabah, later known as North Borneo, being incorporated into the State of Malaysia. The Indonesian Air Force made numerous incursions into Malaysian air space. As a result of this, HQ Far East Air Force decided to establish an Air Defence Identification Zone (ADIZ) around the borders of Sabah and Sarawak, extending to three miles offshore. To police the ADIZ, No. 20 Squadron deployed eight Hunters to Borneo on 20 February 1964, four aircraft positioning at Labuan and four at Kuching. In addition, two Gloster Javelin Mk.9R aircraft of No. 60 Squadron deployed to each of these airfields, so providing Eastern Malaysia with a permanent day and night, All-weather air defence system.

During the months that followed, No. 20 Squadron's Hunters were also called upon to attack groups of Indonesians who had infiltrated into Western Malaysia, mainly the province of Johore. Operations continued until mid-1966, when a peace treaty was concluded between Malaysia and Indonesia.

No. 20 Squadron remained at RAF Tengah until early in 1970. From 1967 the air defence commitment in Singapore had been taken over by the Lightning F.Mk.6s of No. 74 Squadron, and from that point No. 20 Squadron had been gradually reduced in size, its surplus Hunters being returned to the United Kingdom for refurbishing and eventual allocation to the Tactical Weapons Units. The squadron disbanded on 18 February 1970, later to re-form as a Harrier unit.

The other squadron to operate Hunters in the Far East was No. 28 Squadron, which received FGA.9s at Kai Tak, Hong Kong, in June 1962. It disbanded on 15 December, 1966.

The Hunter was licence-built in Holland and Belgium; principal customers for British-built aircraft were India, Switzerland and Sweden. Indian Hunters saw considerable action in the 1965 and 1971 conflicts with Pakistan, ten Hunters being lost in the three-week air war of 1965 and twenty-two in the 1971 battle, some of these being destroyed in the ground. The grand total of Hunter production, including two-seat trainers, was 1972 aircraft, and over 500 were subsequently rebuilt for sale overseas.

Hunter FGA.9s of No. 20 Squadron, Singapore. (Crown copyright)

The Swiss Air Force was a major Hunter customer. This Mk.58 has just touched down on a motorway, an exercise practised frequently. (BAe)

In August 1953 the prototype Hawker P.1067 was fitted with a Rolls-Royce RA.7R afterburning engine, in effect a 'racing' Avon, for an attack on the World Absolute Air Speed Record. Fitted with a sharply pointed nose cone fairing, the aircraft was flown to Tangmere, Sussex, at the end of August for practice runs. On 7 September, Hawker's Chief Test Pilot, Neville Duke, broke the record with an average speed of 1,171 km/h (727.63 mph). Twelve days later, the aircraft also established a 100 km closed circuit world record at an average speed of 1,141 km/h (709.2 mph).

CHAPTER EIGHTEEN

The Fairey Delta Two

I n the mid-1950s, the RAF Air Staff decided to take an enormous leap forward and go for an aircraft that would be capable of reaching a speed of Mach 2.0 at 60,000 feet. An Operational Requirement, OR.329, was issued, calling for an ability to reach that altitude within six minutes of take-off. A Specification, F.155T, was written around the OR and issued in February 1955.

Among the companies rising to meet the demands of F.155T was Hawker Aircraft, who already had considerable experience in the design of an advanced all-weather fighter. In the early 1950s, at a time when the de Havilland DH.110 and the Gloster Javelin were undergoing comparative trials and experiencing many teething troubles, the Hawker team had evolved a two-seat design, the P.1092, which featured a slender delta wing. Hawkers claimed that with an afterburning Avon engine this aircraft would have achieved a speed of about Mach 1.5 and, using airborne interception equipment then under development, could have been in RAF service by 1957. This project came to nothing, and when F.155T was issued Hawker responded with a new and much larger design, the two-seat P.1103, which was to have been powered by a de Havilland Gyron engine.

The other principal contender in the F.155T stakes was Fairey Aviation. This company, noted for its long association with naval aircraft, had entered the high-speed research field in 1947, when it built a series of small delta-wing models designed to be launched from mobile ramps. Tests with these rocket-powered designs continued at Woomera in Australia until 1953, when the Ministry of Supply lost interest in the vertical-launch concept.

In 1947, however, Fairey had received a Specification, E.10/47, for a manned delta-wing aircraft to investigate the full range of flight characteristics of a ramp-launched machine which could eventually be developed into a high-speed interceptor suitable for use from small ships or aircraft carriers. The result was the FD.1, which flew for the first time at Boscombe Down on 12 March 1951. The original plan was that the FD.1 would be fitted with large booster rockets for vertical or angled ramp take-off; control at take-off speeds was to be effected by four swivelling jet nozzles at the rear fuselage which could be operated by normal controls. With the waning of MoS interest in the ramp-launch idea, however, the FD.1 was fitted with a tricycle undercarriage. Powered by a Rolls-Royce Derwent turbojet, its estimated performance included a maximum speed of 587 mph at 40,000 feet and the ability to climb to 30,000 feet in four and a half minutes. Before its first flight, however, the aircraft was fitted with a small tailplane mounted on top of the fin, and this imposed an airframe limitation of 345 mph. The FD.1 undertook a great deal of test flying, investigating lateral and longitudinal stability, rolling performance and the effectiveness of braking parachutes. The test programme was terminated in 1953 and, sadly, this interesting little machine ended its days as a ground target.

Meanwhile, in February 1949, Fairey had been asked to investigate the design of a single-engine transonic research aircraft, which was covered by Specification ER.103. In December 1949 the company came up with firm proposals for a highly streamlined delta-wing machine that was, in essence, a supersonic envelope just big enough to house a pilot, engine and fuel. Frontal areas were cut to a minimum and all possible external bulges removed. Maximum clearance between the Rolls-Royce Avon RA.14R engine and the fuselage skin was less than six inches, while the delta wing, spanning 26 feet 10 inches, was as thin as possible, with a thickness-chord ratio of only four per cent. Leading edger sweep was 60 degrees.

Fairey received a contract to build two aircraft in October 1950, but considerable delay resulted from the fact that the Company was heavily involved in the super-priority production of the Fairey Gannet for the Royal Navy, and detailed design work did not begin until the summer of 1952. By this time, Fairey had a new Chief Engineer: he was R.L. Lickley, who had been head of the

The Fairey Delta 1 was used to test the flight characteristics of the delta wing. (Westland)

Department of Aircraft Design at Cranfield. Under his direction, the aircraft – now known as the FD.2, or Delta Two – gradually took shape, and the first drawings were released to the shops in September 1952.

The finalised FD.2 design differed from the original concept only in minor detail. The biggest modification involved the nose section. To improve the pilot's vision during the landing phase, Fairey's design team devised a 'droop snoot' whereby the whole nose section, including the cockpit assembly forward of the front bulkhead, could be hinged downwards at a ten-degree angle. The wing, despite its thinness, was of remarkably solid construction, being a light alloy structure with three main and two subsidiary spars forming a rectangular torsion box. Each wing contained four integral fuel tanks which, together with the fuselage collector tank, provided a total capacity of 322 Imperial gallons. The wing trailing edge carried inboard elevators and outboard ailerons, which were power-operated.

Fairey's chief test pilot was Group Captain Gordon Slade, but it was his deputy, a young ex-Fleet Air Arm officer named Peter Twiss, who took the FD.2 into the air for the first time at Boscombe Down on 6 October 1954. Before the flight, Twiss built up his experience of high speed flight with supersonic dives in Hunters, Swifts and Sabres, and by flight testing the little FD.1.

Right from the beginning, the FD.2 showed itself to be an aircraft of enormous potential. Twiss made thirteen flights, gradually building up his confidence in the machine, and plans were afoot to begin the real work of high-speed, high-altitude research when, during the fourteenth flight on 17 November, 1954, something went wrong. At 30,000 feet, thirty miles from Boscombe Down, the engine failed as a result of an internal pressure build-up which collapsed the fuselage collector tank. Twiss did some rapid calculations and worked out that he could just about glide home for a dead-stick landing. He scraped across the boundary fence, selecting undercarriage down at the last moment, but only the nose wheel extended. Twiss said later:

> I no longer doubted that we should finish up in one piece, although I believe it looked quite spectacular from the ground. The nose wheel touched first, and we dragged along on this and the tail end, with sparks streaming off the runway. Fortunately, the engine failure had been caused by a fuel stoppage, so there was no fuel near the engine and very little fear of fire. Anyway, we gradually lost speed. Eventually the starboard wing dropped and we began careering towards the control tower at about 100 knots. On the grass we slowed quickly and, at about 40 knots, the starboard wing dug in and brought us to a grinding standstill.

Twiss escaped with a severe shaking, and later received the Queen's Commendation for Valuable Service in the Air. The Delta Two, however, had sustained damage that put it out of action for eight months, and the test programme was not resumed until August 1955. In September the FD.2 prototype, WG774, took part in the SBAC Show at Farnborough, although Peter Twiss kept it throttled back for security reasons. The Fairey team, almost to their

The prototype Fairey Delta Two, WG774. (Westland)

surprise, were beginning to learn that the aircraft was capable of very high speeds, and as yet it had not even used its afterburner. The first supersonic flight was made on 28 October 1955, and further supersonic flights confirmed Fairey's view that the Delta Two was capable of speeds well in excess of 1,000 mph. Urged by Gordon Slade and Peter Twiss, the company began to think seriously of using the aircraft in an attempt on the world air speed record, which at that time was held by a North American F-100C Super Sabre at 822.26 mph.

The idea was put to the Ministry, whose initial attitude was one of disbelief that the FD.2 could fly at anywhere near 1,000 mph. Grudging approval was eventually obtained after a lot of hard work on Fairey's part, but the Ministry of Supply made it clear that it did not wish to be associated with the attempt. No finance was forthcoming, and Fairey had to pay for the necessary insurance cover as well as for the services of the team of recording specialists from the Royal Aeronautical Establishment, Farnborough.

The attempt on the record was prepared under conditions of stringent secrecy, and on 10 March 1956, Peter Twiss took WG774 to a new average record speed of 1,132 mph at 38,000 feet over a 9.65-mile course off the south coast between Thorney Island and Worthing. It was the first time that the record had been raised above the 1,000 mph mark, and it exceeded the previous American-held record by 37 per cent, the biggest leap so far.

The achievement astounded the rest of the aviation world, and Fairey felt secure in the belief that the Delta Two's design had proven itself to the point where proposals could be put forward for a family of supersonic fighters based on it. Two FD.2s were now flying – the second, WG777, having flown on 15 February 1956 – and between them the two aircraft had made well over 100 flights by the time Peter Twiss captured the air speed record.

As a first step towards the development of a supersonic fighter based on the Delta Two, Fairey proposed ER.103/B, a variant with a modified fuselage housing a de Havilland Gyron or a Rolls-Royce RB.122 turbojet with reheat. This was to be followed by ER.103/C, which would be a prototype fighter fitted with AI and armed with Firestreak missiles mounted on the wingtips. It was estimated that the aircraft's performance would include a speed of Mach 2.26 at 55,000 feet and Mach 1.8 at 60,000 feet, with a time to 45,000 feet of 1.9 minutes.

At the same time, Fairey considered various proposals to meet the demanding F.155T Specification for an all-weather fighter, and came to the conclusion that the weapons system required by the Air Staff was so complex that it could not be fully developed before 1962, at the very earliest. To bridge the gap, the Company proposed a simpler delta-wing fighter that would be capable of meeting any air threat that was likely to develop within that period; it would be powered by an afterburning Gyron, plus two de Havilland Spectre Junior rocket motors, and would be armed with Firestreak Mk.4 AAMs (later renamed Red Top) mounted at the wingtips. The aircraft would have a maximum level speed with reheat of Mach 2.5 at 59,000 feet. With optimum early warning the fighter would be capable of intercepting a target at 60,000 feet 118.5 nautical miles from base; even under the worst conditions, it would be able to reach an intercept point fifty nautical miles from base in 9.2 minutes, using reheat and one rocket in the climb and both rockets during the intercept manoeuvre.

Later in 1956, Fairey modified the design concept somewhat. The overall two-seat delta configuration was retained, but the single Gyron was replaced by two afterburning RB.128 engines and the rockets were deleted. Also considered was changing the armament to a pair of big Red Dean AAMs. As a further incentive, Fairey indicated that the design could be readily adapted to the medium/low level intercept, strike and reconnaissance roles.

It was all for nothing. On Monday, 1 April 1957, Fairey received a strong indication from the Ministry of Supply that they were favourites in the running for F.115T. The following Thursday, Defence Minister Duncan Sandys announced the immediate cancellation of the whole programme.

Meanwhile, as the result of a ban restricting supersonic flying over the United Kingdom to altitudes of over 30,000 feet, Fairey had asked the French Flight Test Centre at Cazeaux if the FD.2 might be based there for a time to undergo further high-speed trials. WG774 was accordingly flown to Cazeaux on 15 October 1956, and in the course of the following month it made fifty-two flights in a total of eighteen hours' flying. A third of the flying time was supersonic, the aircraft achieving Mach 1.04 down to 3,000 feet. The French looked on with interest, and gave new priority to the development of their family of delta-wing Mirage fighters. (It was afterwards hinted, somewhat spitefully in certain British government circles, that the French had copied the Mirage concept from the FD.2. This was quite untrue, and something of a slur on the technical ability of Marcel Dassault's excellent design team. In fact, the

The delta-wing Mirage IIAI-01, progenitor of the Mirage III series, taking off from an unprepared airstrip. (Dassault)

progenitor of the Mirage family, the Dassault MD.550 Mirage I, was conceived in 1954 and made its first flight in June 1955; the Mirage III made its first flight on 17 November 1956 and exceeded Mach 1.5 in level flight on 30 January 1957. There is little doubt, however, that the obvious capability of the FD.2 persuaded the French government to instruct Dassault to proceed with a multi-mission version of their design, the Mirage IIIA, the prototype of which [Mirage IIIA-01] flew on 12 May 1958).

Testing of the FD.2 continued, and in June 1958 one of the aircraft was flown to Norway for further low-level supersonic flight trials, intended to provide design information on the behaviour of an axial compressor over a wide range of flight conditions. Engine intake design had previously been dependent, to a great extent, on the testing of wind-tunnel models, and the main purpose of the trials was to record the pressure distribution in the engine intakes at various altitudes under subsonic and supersonic flight conditions up to the maximum speed of the aircraft, while taking simultaneous measurements of the stresses in the first-stage compressor blades.

Together, the two FD.2 prototypes made an enormous contribution to high-speed aerodynamic research. After its flying career was over, the second aircraft, WG777, went to the RAF museum at Finningley, Yorkshire, and later to Cosford, where it may be seen today. WG774 was almost completely rebuilt and, fitted with a model of the ogival wing planform that was to be used on Concorde, flew again as the BAC 221 in May 1964. It was retired in 1973 and is now on display at the Fleet Air Arm Museum, Yeovilton, alongside the British prototype of the Concorde SST. Both are on loan from the Science Museum, London.

CHAPTER NINETEEN

The Vickers Valiant

At the beginning of 1946, despite the obvious need for a strategic jet bomber capable of nuclear weapons delivery to replace RAF Bomber Command's piston-engine Avro Lincolns, the British Ministry of Supply had yet to issue a specification for such an aircraft. The only jet bomber specification for such an aircraft, in fact, was written around a tactical aircraft designed for the radar bombing role with conventional weapons; this materialised in the English Electric Canberra.

One of the problems that bedevilled British thinking on the design of a strategic jet bomber at this stage was that there was, as yet, no clear idea of the configuration of the weapon such an aircraft would have to carry. Despite the fact that British scientists had been instrumental in initiating the Allied atomic bomb project during the war, and had collaborated fully with the Americans in bringing an operational weapon to fruition, the Americans chose to make no exception in the case of the British when, in August 1946, they clamped down on the release of nuclear information to other nations. This meant, simply, that any nuclear weapons carried by future British bombers would have to be of British design.

Fortunately, Britain retained access to some uranium sources, including those of the Congo, and in 1945–46, under the auspices of Clement Attlee's new Labour government, work was begun on a new research and experimental establishment at Harwell, production reactors at Windscale and a low-separation diffusion plant at Capenhurst. The decision to go ahead with the design of British nuclear weapons was influenced by the belief of Attlee and his senior ministers that this would reconsolidate Britain's status as a world power. Although the East–West power blocs were already taking shape in 1946, there was no thought at this stage of using nuclear weapons as a deterrent, or even that they might be effective as such.

It was not until the beginning of 1947 that the decision to produce atomic bombs was made by the British government. In the meantime, however, the Air Staff, under the direction of Marshal of the RAF Lord Tedder, had drafted a requirement for a British nuclear bomb and the specification of an aircraft that would be capable of delivering it.

Tedder was a strong advocate of economy of force. There could be no question, in the nuclear age, of Britain becoming involved in a war of attrition; any future conflict must be fought by highly trained, highly mobile forces possessing great firepower. As far as Bomber Command was concerned, this meant the creation not of a bludgeon, but a rapier. The blade of the rapier was to be an advanced jet bomber capable of carrying a 10,000 lb 'special' weapon at

500 knots over a combat radius of 1,500 nautical miles, with a ceiling of 50,000 feet over the target.

Five aircraft companies submitted designs to meet the specification; the two eventually selected by the Ministry of Supply were those tendered by A.V. Roe and Co. Ltd, and Handley Page, respective manufacturers of the wartime Lancaster and Halifax bombers. A third design, the Type 660, submitted by Vickers, was less advanced in concept than the other two and was initially rejected. Later, when it was realized that the lower performance of the Vickers design was greatly outweighed by its ability to be developed more quickly than the others, it was decided to proceed with it as an 'interim' aircraft, a kind of insurance against the failure of the more radical bombers. It was a fortunate decision, and one which was to have far-reaching consequences. In March 1948, when a new specification (B9/48) was written around the Vickers Type 660, not even its designers could have envisaged the role this aircraft would play over the years to come. This was the aircraft that would form the backbone of the RAF's nuclear strike force during the dangerous years of the 1950s, and would pioneer the operational techniques of what would become the V-Force. In service, it would chalk up an impressive series of 'firsts', and would become the only British aircraft ever to release nuclear weapons. The name chosen for it was Valiant.

The aircraft that gradually took shape was highly streamlined and, for its size, remarkably elegant. The 108-foot fuselage was of circular section, with a large navigation and bombing radar installation occupying the whole of the nose forward of the cockpit. A blister under the nose accommodated the visual bomb-aiming station. The pressurised crew compartment was built by Saunders-Roe, one of nine major sub-contractors involved in the Type 660 programme, and accommodated five crew members: pilot and co-pilot, two navigators and an air electronics officer. The last three sat below and behind the pilots, facing aft, and had no ejection seats; in the event of an emergency they would have to unfasten their seat harnesses and various leads and open the main hatch, together with a metal windbreak that hinged out of the fuselage side ahead of the door. Without the windbreak, an exit from the hatch at high speed would have been virtually impossible. The two pilots would make their exit by first jettisoning the cockpit roof, which was blown off by a series of explosive bolts, and then using their Martin-Baker Mk.3A seats.

In all fairness, it should be mentioned that in its original Operational Requirement, the Air Staff had asked that the complete pressure cabin accommodating the crew should be jettisonable in an emergency and equipped with parachutes to form an escape capsule, but the contracting companies found the engineering problems associated with providing such a system to be insuperable. In 1948 Handley page actually tested such an escape system in model form, but the results were unsatisfactory and the idea was abandoned. Much later, in 1960, Martin Baker experimentally installed a rearwards-facing ejection seat in Valiant WP199, which had been modified for the purpose by Marshalls of Cambridge in 1959. There were delays in the programme because of pressure on Martin Baker for fighter aircraft ejection systems (they were developing one for the Lightning at the time) but trials eventually took place in mid-1960 and on 3 June that year a slave seat was successfully fired from the static aircraft at Chalgrove airfield. There was, however, no further development of the project, despite this initial success.

The Vickers Type 660's high-mounted wing had a mean sweep of 20 degrees, the angle being increased towards the wing root – at the thickest part – to improve lift/drag ratio. In this section the engines were buried. The structure of the wing, and indeed of the whole aircraft, was entirely conventional. In fact, the only major innovation lay in the electrical systems, with which the bomber was crammed.

The prototype 660, WB210, was powered by four Rolls-Royce Avon RA3 turbojets of 6,500 lb thrust. These were completely buried in the wing, with the tailpipes breaking the upper surface near the trailing edge. Early in 1951, the components of the prototype 660 were taken from the Foxwarren experimental shop to the new company airfield at Wisley, in Surrey, where final assembly took place. After a period of systems testing and pre-flight trials, WB210 made its first flight on 18 May 1951, with Vickers' chief test pilot J. 'Mutt' Summers as captain and G.R. 'Jock' Bryce as co-pilot. Conditions were gusty and the flight lasted only five minutes. As a precautionary measure the undercarriage was locked down and the flaps were left at their take-off setting of 20 degrees throughout. Four more flights were made from Wisley, but as this was only a grass airfield the 660 was subsequently moved to Hurn while a runway was laid at the previous location.

The name Valiant was officially adopted for the Vickers design in June 1951, and in 1952 it was decided that the Avro and Handley Page aircraft should have names beginning with 'V' as well. The Valiant flight test programme continued steadily with WB210 through the remainder of 1951, by which time a Royal Air Force officer, Squadron Leader Brian Foster, had been attached to the Valiant test team. On 12 January 1952 he was flying as co-pilot in the prototype, carrying out engine shutdown and relight trials over the Hampshire coast, when fire broke out in an engine bay as the result of a wet start. No fire detection equipment had been installed in the bay, and by the time the blaze was detected the damage was so advanced that the wing was on the point of collapse. The aircraft captain, Jock Bryce, therefore gave the order to abandon the aircraft and the three rear crew members went out first, followed by the two pilots. All the crew survived with the exception of Squadron Leader Foster, who was killed when his seat struck the tail fin while the aircraft was in a descending turn.

Fortunately for Vickers, the second prototype Valiant, WB215, was approaching completion at Foxwarren, and this flew for the first time at Wisley on 11 April 1952. It differed from its predecessor in having enlarged air intakes to feed the 7,500 lb thrust Avon RA7 engines with which it was fitted. This aircraft sustained the test programme for more than a year, and the Vickers team was joined by another RAF officer, Squadron Leader Rupert G.W. Oakley.

Meanwhile, on 8 February 1951, Vickers had received in Instruction to Proceed (ITP) with 25 production Valiant B.Mk.1s, confirmed by an order placed on 12 April. Five of these aircraft were to be powered by 9,000 lb thrust

XD823, a production Valiant B.Mk.1. (BAe)

Avon RA14 engines, while the remaining twenty were to have 10,500 lb thrust
Avon RA28s, with longer jet pipes. At about the same time, the company had
also received a Ministry of Supply specification for the development of a prototype target-marking version of the Valiant, which was to be specially strengthened in order to fly low and fast and was to have increased fuel capacity.

Bearing the type number 673, the designation Valiant B.Mk.2 and known
unofficially as the Pathfinder, this aircraft flew for the first time on 4 September
1953, just in time for that year's SBAC Show at Farnborough, where it was
displayed in a resplendent glossy black overall finish. The B.Mk.2's fuselage was
4 feet 6 inches longer than that of the B.1 and, because of major structural
redesign to the wings, a bogie-type main undercarriage was housed in two long
nacelles projecting behind the trailing edge.

The strengthened airframe, coupled with Rolls-Royce Avon RA14 engines,
gave the B.Mk.2 version an enormous performance advantage over the earlier
Valiant. It could, for example, attain a maximum speed at sea level of 552 mph,
whereas the B.Mk.1 version was limited by airframe considerations to 414 mph.
Performance of the production version, had it gone ahead, would have been
even more impressive, for this was to have been powered by the Rolls-Royce
RB80 by-pass engine, progenitor of the Conway, the world's first turbofan

engine. In the mid-1950s, however, the Air Staff decided that there was no longer a requirement for the role the Valiant B.2 was to have filled, and the sole example, WJ954, was eventually scrapped. Ironically, ten years later the whole of the V-Force was compelled to adapt to the low-level role, and the airframes of the Valiants then in service were found to be incapable of withstanding the stresses imposed by prolonged flight at low level.

The first production Valiant, WP199, flew for the first time on 21 December 1953, well within the deadline imposed by the Ministry. At the controls were Jock Bryce and Brian Trubshaw, who many years later was to be the first Englishman to fly the Anglo-French Concorde supersonic airliner.

While the early production aircraft were being put through their paces at the various development establishments, production of the definitive Valiant B.Mk.1 was getting under way. In 1954 came the first change in specification, with an order for eleven Valiants fitted with removable equipment for long-range, high-altitude photographic reconnaissance sorties by day and night and for aerial survey work. The first of these, WP205, designated Valiant B(PR)1, flew for the first time on 8 October 1954.

Meanwhile, in November 1952, Britain had exploded her first atomic device under water in the Monte Bello Islands, and a year later the first production bombs with this warhead – code-named Blue Danubes – were delivered to the Bomber Command Armament School at RAF Wittering, which had been designated as the first operational V-Force base. Eventually there were to be ten such bases, together with thirty-six dispersal airfields all over the British Isles to ensure that the V-Force would never be obliterated by a surprise attack.

Valiant B.1s of No. 138 Squadron at Luqa, Malta. (Bill Meadows)

In 1955 No. 232 Operational Conversion Unit was activated at RAF Gaydon, in Warwickshire, with the tasks of carrying out Valiant intensive flying trials and training crews for the V-Force. The first course to graduate formed the nucleus of No. 138 Squadron, which moved to Wittering with six Valiants in July. By the summer of 1956 No. 138 Squadron had been joined by another Valiant unit, No. 49 Squadron, while Nos 148, 207 and 214 Squadrons formed a second Valiant Wing at RAF Marham, in Norfolk. No. 49 Squadron was heavily involved in nuclear weapons trials, and on 11 October one of its Valiants (WZ366, Squadron Leader E.J.G. Flavell) made the first live drop of a Blue Danube during a series of trials code-named 'Buffalo' at Maralinga, South Australia. The Blue Danube detonated at between 500 and 600 feet. The fissile material had been loaded into the nuclear capsule in flight and the weapon had a modified fusing system. Because of fears that the fusing system might fail, resulting in a 40 kT ground burst and unwanted contamination, a low-yield (3 kT) version was used, rather than a standard production bomb. Nevertheless, this was the climax of the development effort, bringing together the bomb and the V-bomber in an operational configuration.

Soon afterwards, all the Valiant squadrons with the exception of No. 49 deployed aircraft to RAF Luqa, Malta, as part of the Anglo/French response to the Suez Crisis. On 31 October, these aircraft joined Canberras of RAF Bomber Command in a series of attacks on Egyptian airfields as part of the air offensive that preceded the Anglo-French landing in the Suez Canal Zone. The Valiants bombed singly from 40,000 feet, their targets being marked by 'pathfinder' Canberras, and were easily able to outclimb the few enemy night fighters sent up to intercept them. In fact, the Valiant had already shown its prowess in this respect during air exercises in the UK, evading Hawker Hunter fighters that had no difficulty in intercepting B-47 Stratojets operating at lower altitudes.

On 15 May 1957, Valiant XD818 of No. 49 Squadron, captained by Wing Commander K.G. Hubbard, successfully dropped the first nuclear weapon in the 'Operation Grapple' series of trials over Malden Island in the south-west Pacific. The bomb, which consisted of a Blue Danube ballistic case, was armed with a 'Short Granite' physics package that detonated at an altitude of about 8,000 feet, producing a yield of 100–150 kT. It was later publicised as a 'megaton-range device', which it was not. It was a so-called 'fall-back' fission device, a lightweight fission bomb producing a considerably higher yield than the first-generation atomic bombs.

The 'Grapple' trials continued on and off for the next eighteen months, the first phase being completed in June 1957. It was clear that all had not gone well with the tests, and that further experimentation was needed to provide a greater understanding of the triggering mechanisms that were needed to produce high-yield thermonuclear explosions. To this end, a series of tests called 'Antler' was set up at the Maralinga range in Australia, taking place in September–November 1957.

Testing at the Pacific Range, based on Christmas Island, resumed on 8 November 1957, when Valiant XD825 flown by Squadron Leader B.T. Millett dropped a fission device. The explosion produced a high yield, possibly as high

Valiant XD818 pictured during its days as 'gate guardian' at RAF Marham. It is now in the Cold War exhibition at the RAF Museum, Cosford. (RAF)

as 300 kT, according to some estimates, and was probably the first really successful test to have taken place at the Pacific Range.

An Air Staff Requirement (OR1136), calling for the development of a British air-dropped thermonuclear bomb, had been issued in July 1955, and by the spring of 1956 drawings and a mock-up of the bomb, code-named 'Yellow Sun', had been completed at RAE Farnborough, while another bomb, a kiloton-range weapon called 'Red Beard', was also under development as a potential replacement for Blue Danube. In October 1956, the Director General of Armament and Weapons at the Ministry of Supply suggested that an interim bomb with a megaton warhead might be brought into service before Yellow Sun, and that if the Grapple trials were successful the production of a form of megaton warhead could begin in August 1957.

The suggestion was adopted, and in March 1958 the first such interim weapon, known as 'Violet Club', was assembled at the Bomber Command Armament School at Wittering. It was identical to the Blue Danube except for its warhead, which was a pure fission type called 'Green Grass'. It was not really a megaton weapon at all, the warhead having a yield of around 300 kT, but the British conveniently defined 'megaton range' as a few hundred kilotons to several megatons. It was cheating a little, but it did not matter. The RAF would soon have its true megaton weapon, and in the meantime Violet Club – a very sensitive weapon that was very difficult to handle – increased the British deterrent capability. Very few were delivered, and they were withdrawn from service in 1959, with the issue of the first Yellow Suns.

The first truly successful test of a British thermonuclear bomb took place on 28 April 1958, when Valiant XD824 (Squadron Leader R.N. Bates) dropped a bomb with a 'Granite'-type physics package that detonated with an estimated yield of two megatons (2 mT). On 2 September, Valiant XD822 (Squadron Leader G.M. Bailey) dropped a 2.5 mT bomb by radar, the error from 45,000 feet being only 95 yards. On 11 September a bomb of similar yield was dropped by Valiant XD827 (Flight Lieutenant S. O'Connor), confirming that Britain was now a full member of the thermonuclear club.

Although 1957 and 1958 saw the introduction of the first Vulcan and Victor squadrons, it was the Valiant that continued to form the mainstay of the RAF's Medium Bomber Force (MBF) until the end of the decade, the aircraft being armed with the Red Beard or Blue Danube bomb; the more powerful Yellow Sun Mks 1 and 2 was reserved for the Vulcan and Victor. At the beginning of 1961 the Valiant still equipped nine squadrons and No. 232 OCU. The Valiant squadrons still operational as part of the MBF were Nos 7 and 18, the latter tasked with providing electronic countermeasures support for the MBF Squadrons 49, 90, 138, 148 and 207. No. 543 Squadron, at RAF Wyton, continued to perform its strategic reconnaissance role, while No. 214 Squadron at RAF Marham, which had pioneered flight refuelling techniques since 1958, now operated exclusively in that role and was joined by No. 90 Squadron, which became part of the tanker force at Marham from 1 October 1961.

During 1960–61 three Valiant squadrons, Nos 207, 49 and 148, were assigned to NATO in the tactical bombing role under the control of the Supreme

A photo-reconnaissance Valiant B(PR)Mk.1. Note the camera ports in the underside of the fuselage. (BAe)

Valiants, camouflaged for their low-level tactical role, on an Operational Readiness Platform. (RAF)

Allied Commander, Europe (SACEUR). For this task the Valiants could be armed with either conventional bombs (a full load comprising twenty-one 1,000 lb in three clutches of five and two of three) or the American Mk.28 and Mk.43 tactical nuclear weapons.

In 1963, the Valiants lost their white anti-flash paintwork and were camouflaged for the low-level role. Although the airframe had never been designed to withstand the stresses imposed by this type of work, it was thought that its useful life could be extended by a further five years. During 1964, however, a fracture occurred in the rear spar of a Valiant, and when other aircraft were inspected indications of metal fatigue were found. The last Valiant sorties were flown in December and the force was withdrawn from service in January 1965.

Appropriately, one of the last Valiants to fly operationally was XD818 of Operational Grapple fame, which took off from Marham on its last training sortie on 9 December 1964. In the following month, work began on reducing all Valiants with the exception of XD818 and four others – the latter engaged in special trials – to scrap. XD818 was preserved, first as gate guardian at RAF Marham and then in the Royal Air Force Museum at Hendon, from where it was moved in 2005 to the Cold War Exhibition at the RAF Museum, Cosford, where it may be seen today, the last survivor of its breed.

The last Valiant to fly was XD616, which had been on extended loan to the British Aircraft Corporation since September 1964 and which, on 29 April 1968, took part in a flypast to mark the disbandment of RAF Bomber Command and the inauguration of its successor, Strike Command. For the aircraft which had formed the core of Britain's nuclear deterrent for so long, it was a fitting swan song.

CHAPTER TWENTY

The English Electric Lightning

We know that we can catch the bombers and, going on past experience, we know that we can outfight any fighter equivalent to the US Century-series. The performance of the aircraft, coupled with the ease with which it is flown, gives the pilots confidence, and the fact that it is felt to be the best fighter in operational service in the world today gives our Lightning pilots the highest possible morale.

Squadron Leader John F.G. Howe

The man who made this statement to members of the Press at RAF Coltishall, Norfolk, in the spring of 1961 knew what he was talking about. He was the Officer Commanding No. 74 Squadron – the first unit of RAF Fighter Command to arm with the English Electric (BAC) Lightning F.Mk.1 fighter.

The aircraft that was to become the Lightning was conceived by the English Electric Company just after the Second World War, at a time when RAF Fighter Command had one jet fighter, the Gloster Meteor, in operational service and another, the de Havilland Vampire, scheduled for delivery in 1946. Early in that year both Hawker and Supermarine were studying schemes for swept-wing jet fighters which would eventually materialise as the Hunter and Swift and which would just be capable of exceeding Mach 1.0 in a dive. Experimentation with a truly supersonic design then centred on the Miles M.52, an aircraft that would theoretically have been capable of 1,000 mph at 36,000 feet. Miles aircraft were on the point of starting to construct a prototype when, in February 1946, the M.52 project was cancelled.

It was at this point that English Electric's talented young design team, under the leadership of their chief engineer, W.E.W. 'Teddy' Petter – already heavily occupied in bringing the Canberra jet bomber design to reality – began turning their thoughts to designing an aircraft that would not only be capable of sustaining supersonic flight, but also of reaching Mach 2.0.

The preliminary sketches they produced showed a radical design: an aircraft with a wing swept at 60 degrees, powered by two engines mounted one above the other in a slab-sided fuselage with a single-seat cockpit perched on top, advanced avionics, missile armament, powered controls and an all-moving tailplane. Perhaps the most amazing thing about the design was that the Ministry of Supply, which had begun to have serious doubts about the practicability of sustained supersonic flight while the M.52 project was in being, decided that it merited further investigation, and in 1947 issued an experimental study contract, ER.103.

This was followed, two years later, by a contract – F.23/49 – for two prototypes and an airframe to be used for static testing. In planform, the aircraft's sharply swept wings resembled a notched delta with a leading edge sweep angle of 60 degrees to ensure that the vortex flow would be fully developed. To ensure maximum effectiveness, the ailerons were mounted normal to the airflow on the cut-off tips. The wing also had trailing-edge flaps and (on production aircraft) a fixed but detachable leading edge. The latter was entirely clean except for a small saw-cut notch at around two-thirds span This was added to cure uneven airflow around the ailerons, a problem encountered during low-speed flight testing of the Short SB.5 research aircraft, built specially to test the wing configuration. The notch was fitted in place of a wing fence, which would have created higher drag, and was found to have the additional beneficial effect of re-energising spanwise airflow, and thus increasing vortex-derived lift. The wing was joined at the aircraft centreline and was installed as a one-piece unit, making removal of the wings difficult and time-consuming after manufacture was complete. The wing was built around two primary spars, to which were affixed closely spaced ribs and stringers. The wing torsion boxes formed the aircraft's primary internal fuel tankage, this being restricted by the space taken up by the main undercarriage wells. The SB.5's test programme proved that the English Electric design team had got their figures right, and construction of the two experimental prototypes, designated P.1 and P.1A, continued. The first of these, WG760, was flown at the Aeroplane and Armament Experimental Establishment (A&AEE) Boscombe Down on 4 August 1954 by Wing Commander R.P. Beamont, English Electric's Chief Test Pilot. The aircraft was powered by two Bristol Siddeley Sapphire turbojets and reached supersonic speed on its third flight.

Later in 1954, English Electric received a contract for the construction of three P.1Bs, which were effectively to be the prototypes of the operational version. The P.1B, which was the first British aircraft to be designed as an integrated weapons system, was powered by two Rolls-Royce Avon RA24 engines delivering 15,000 lb sea level static thrust each, and the first example, XA847, flew on 4 April 1957 – ironically, the very day that the British government published a White Paper forecasting the end of piloted combat aircraft and their replacement by missiles.

The original intention was that operationally, the P.1B – which was given the name Lightning – was to form a mixed interceptor force together with the Saunders-Roe SR.177, a target defence aircraft powered by a jet engine and a rocket motor. Along with other promising military aircraft projects, the SR.177 fell victim to the 1957 policy changes, leaving the Lightning alone to make the jump from subsonic to supersonic flight. And a considerable jump it was: unlike American fighter designs of the 1950s, which had progressed from the high subsonic F-86 Sabre via the 'Mach One plus' F-100 Super Sabre to the Mach Two F-104 Starfighter, the Lightning was to catapult the RAF straight from the

For security reasons, it was some time before photographs were released that showed the distinctive wing planform of the prototype P.1A. (BAe)

English Electric Lightning F.3 armed with Firestreak AAMs. (MoD)

era of the subsonic Hunter into the truly supersonic future, with no transitional phase.

There was no doubting the Lightning's potential. The first P.1B, XA847, reached Mach 1.2 in dry thrust on its first flight, and on 25 November 1958 Roland Beamont took it up to Mach 2.0 in level flight off the Welsh coast.

The first production Lightning F.Mk.1 flew on 29 October 1959, by which time its weapons system, comprising the AI23 radar and de Havilland Firestreak air-to-air missiles, had been developed to operational standard. Three armament combinations could be carried by the aircraft: two Firestreaks and two 30 mm Aden guns, two packs of twenty-four 2-inch unguided air-to-air rockets and two 30 mm guns, or four 30 mm guns. In practice, the Firestreak/gun combination was the normal weapons fit.

In December 1959 the first Lightning F.1 was delivered to the Air Fighting Development Squadron at RAF Coltishall, and it was there, on 29 June 1960, that No. 74 Squadron became operational with the new type. To say that the Lightning represented a leap of 100 per cent in performance over its predecessor, the Hunter F.6, was no exaggeration. Pilots coming to it from the latter aircraft were impressed by its apparent immense size, accentuated by the need to climb a 10-foot ladder before entering the cockpit. The cockpit and its associated equipment provided revelations too, and in some ways it was simpler than the Hunter's. For a start, a personal equipment connector was used to connect the pilot to oxygen, g-suit air, air ventilated suit supply and R/T lead in a single easy operation, while the newly-designed combined seat and parachute harness made strapping in a lot simpler. The height of the ejection seat itself could be adjusted by operating an electric switch.

The most revolutionary change in cockpit instrumentation was the elimination of the traditional artificial horizon and compass; instead, the Lightning was equipped with a master reference gyro that fed electrical signals continuously through 360 degrees in azimuth, pitch and bank. These signals were in turn fed to an attitude indicator which indicated pitch and bank, and to a heading indicator which showed direction. The master reference gyro also supplied information to the radar fire control system and the automatic pilot. The altimeter was different, too, being a new electrically-operated design with a simplified presentation by counters appearing in small windows to indicate the altitude. A single hand swept the dial every 1,000 feet, and since the Lightning's initial climb rate was in excess of 50,000 feet per minute, the hand rotated at over 50 rpm.

For a pilot new to the Lightning, one immediately noticeable aspect of take-off was the high nose-up attitude and the inertia that took the aircraft on a flight path parallel with the ground for some distance at unstuck, giving slight negative g or a sinking sensation. However, acceleration after unstuck was rapid, the speed building up to 400 knots at which point a further slight backward pressure on the stick established a climbing angle of 22 degrees on the attitude indicator. Optimum climbing speed was 450 knots (It is interesting to compare this with the McDonnell Douglas F-15 Eagle's optimum climb performance of 250 knots at a 65–70 degree climbing angle, giving a rate of climb of 33,000 feet per minute).

The Lightning's angle of climb was quite steep and pilots had to guard against a tendency to lower the nose, when it was quite easy to exceed Mach 1.0 in the climb. When levelling off, the throttles had to be moved back quickly to 85 per cent power in order to keep the aircraft subsonic. Pilots were enthusiastic about the reserves of power available from the Lightning's excellent Avon engines; towards the end of a sortie, with most of the fuel used up and the aircraft light, there was more thrust available in reheat than the weight plus drag, enabling the aircraft to climb vertically in the classic end-of-display manoeuvre that thrilled many an air show crowd.

A full reheat climb would take the Lightning to 30,000 feet in a little under two minutes, and even in cold power it was capable of reaching the tropopause in between three and four minutes from the start of the take-off roll. The Lightning's phenomenal climb performance, and its ability to accelerate rapidly to supersonic speed at the tropopause gave it an advantage over any other interceptor in service in the early 1960s. Pilots of Lockheed U-2 reconnaissance

A Lightning of No. 56 Squadron, RAF Wattisham, pulling up into a battle climb. (Crown copyright)

aircraft, which hitherto had easily evaded aircraft like the Hunter during their high-level transit flights through the United Kingdom Air Defence Region, were now somewhat disconcerted to find a pair of Lightnings sitting on their tails at altitudes in excess of 60,000 feet.

The standard Lightning intercept aimed to approach the target on a reciprocal (head-on) course and slightly below, so that the radar looked up, displaced laterally by 13 km (8 miles), with the Lightning turning in to roll out behind the target at about 2 km (1.5 miles). Conveniently, the Lightning's turn radius at Mach 0.85 and 7,620 m (25,000 feet) was 6.5 km (4 miles). In such an intercept, the pilot had to remember that the blip should be 20 degrees off the nose at 40 km (25 miles), 25 degrees at 32 km (20 miles), 32 degrees at 24 km (15 miles) and 40 degrees at the turn point (19 km/12 miles). Turn radii varied with height and speed, which meant more curves for the pilot to memorize. As if this were not difficult enough, the Lightning pilot had to calculate the target's inbound heading by measuring change of displacement over 8 km (5 miles) of closure, and calculated the target height at 16 km (10 miles) by multiplying scanner elevation by 10. This was vital, since the height difference between target and fighter had to be reduced to within 609 m (2,000 feet) to stand any chance of success, preferably with the fighter just below the target. Locking on to the target, the radar provided range and azimuth information, but no closure rate. If a missile was fired, the Lightning then had to roll inverted and pull inverted, in order to avoid debris from the target.

The Lightning F.1's most serious shortcoming was its very limited endurance. It burned 20 gallons of fuel per minute in the cruise and this rose to about 200 gallons per minute in the climb with full afterburner. To alleviate the problem, a flight refuelling probe was fitted to the aircraft, which was then designated Mk.1A, and thereafter Fighter Command's Quick Reaction Alert (QRA) Lightning force operated in conjunction with the Vickers Valiant B(K)1 tankers of the Marham Tanker Wing, these aircraft later being replaced by Handley Page Victor B(K)1As and B(K)2s.

Lightning F.Mk.1As equipped Nos 56 and 111 Squadrons at RAF Wattisham early in 1961, and two years later No. 56 Squadron was the RAF's premier aerobatic team, showing their nine red-and-silver F.1As at displays all over Europe. The Lightning F.1A was followed into service by the F.Mk.2, which had some very minor equipment changes and equipped Nos 19 and 92 Squadrons at Leconfield early in 1963. Two years later, both squadrons moved to Geilenkirchen and Gütersloh, Germany, to cover the Second Allied Tactical Air Force sector of the Air Defence Identification Zone, the 'buffer' between east and west. They retained their Lightnings until 1976–77, when the type was replaced by the Phantom FGR.2.

In June 1962 a Lightning Conversion Squadron was established at RAF Middleton St George, near Darlington in County Durham. At first, this relied on aircraft borrowed from the first-line squadrons, but on 1 June 1963 it was designated No. 226 Operational Conversion Unit and received some Lightning F.1s that had belonged to No. 74 Squadron, together with the first of eleven

The Lightning T.4 trainer. (BAe)

Lightning T.4 trainers. This two-seat variant had first flown on 6 May 1959 and, as well as the OCU, examples were allocated to each UK-based Lightning Wing.

Three more Lightning squadrons joined the RAF Order of Battle in the mid-1960s: No. 5 Squadron at Binbrook and Nos 11 and 23 Squadrons at Leuchars. By this time the UK Lightning squadrons had received the F.Mk.3, which had Rolls-Royce Avon 301 engines with full variable reheat and carried either Firestreak or Red Top AAMs. The combination of Red Top and the AI23B Ferranti Airpass airborne radar meant that the Lightning F.3 could make beam attacks on a target instead of the pilot having to manoeuvre into position astern of it, a significant step forward. To familiarise pilots with the F.3's systems, a modified version of the Lightning T.4 trainer, the T.5, was produced in small numbers.

The final version of the Lightning was the F.Mk.6, which was first issued to No. 5 Squadron in December 1965. The F.6 had a greatly enlarged ventral fuel tank and also provision for two overwing ferry tanks in order to meet an Air Staff requirement for rapid deployment overseas. With this new system the Lightning made some remarkable endurance flights. In June 1967, thirteen F.6s of No. 74 Squadron, using flight refuelling and with three stops en route, became fully operational at Tengah, Singapore, only five days after leaving their former base at Leuchars, in Scotland. The F.6's refinements were incorporated in RAF Germany's Lightning F.2s, which then became F.2As.

Although designed as a high-altitude missile-armed interceptor, the Lightning had a sturdy airframe and good low-level handling qualities that made it readily adaptable to the ground-attack role. The Lightning F.Mk.53, developed for service in Saudi Arabia and Kuwait, could carry two 1,000 lb HE bombs of 36 SNEB 68 mm rockets in two packs, in addition to forty-four 2-inch rockets in the front fuselage pack and two 30 mm Aden guns in the ventral pack. Saudi Arabia took delivery of 32 F.Mk.53s, as well as some two-seaters, while ten F.53s were supplied to Kuwait.

In the RAF, the Lightning's air defence role was gradually assumed by the Phantom and, later, the Tornado F.3. The last operational Lightning unit was No. 11 Squadron at Binbrook, which retained its aircraft until April 1988 when it, too, went over to Tornados. The last three working Lightning F.6s were used as target facilities aircraft in the Tornado F.3 radar development programme and made their last flight from British Aerospace's Warton airfield on 16 December, 1992.

The day of the Lightning as a combat aircraft was over, but it left a considerable legacy. In its heyday it could out-turn anything except the Harrier, and even then its rapid acceleration enabled its pilot to select an opportune moment for attack or to disengage without penalty. Until the advent of the F-15 Eagle, the Lightning was the world's only supersonic pure fighter aircraft, contemporary types like the MiG-21 and the Mirage III being designed for multi-role tasks, and by the time the Eagle flew in prototype form, the Lightning had already been in RAF service for twelve years.

All Lightnings shared the same engine layout, which gave the type its characteristic slab-sided appearance. The two engines were mounted one above the other and staggered, with the lower engine forward. This gave the smallest possible fuselage cross-section, but necessitated the use of different-length jet pipes, and made the engines vulnerable to collateral damage if one failed. Both engines received air from a nose intake, via complex, horizontally bifurcated internal ducts. The top engine was removed upwards (after removal of the jet pipe, which rolled out aft) while the lower engine was dropped down. An engine change could theoretically be achieved in four hours, although in practice it usually took days. Complex and inaccessible systems on the aircraft, coupled with a poor logistics system, meant that the early Lightnings had a poor utilisation rate. This was greatly improved with later marks of Lightning, but the systems were far from popular with engineers and ground crews. From the aircrew point of view, the Lightning was a true fighter pilot's aircraft, demanding and difficult to master, yet ultimately highly rewarding.

Many Lightnings are conserved in museum collections where they delight visitors with their clean sleek lines, evocative of the high speeds that they once attained. The Short SB5 and a P1.A are at the RAF Museum, Cosford. The Civil Aviation Authority refused a licence for the surviving airworthy examples to perform at airshows in the UK but a civilian company in South Africa, Thunder City, maintains two Lightning F.5s and two F.6s in flying condition.

CHAPTER TWENTY-ONE

The English Electric TSR-2

I n May 1951, when the English Electric Canberra first entered squadron service, it was beyond doubt the world's finest light jet-bomber. With some justification, the Air Staff felt that Bomber Command possessed a tactical aircraft that would remain capable of delivering a wide variety of weapons against targets in Eastern Europe with a high probability of survival for the best part of a decade.

Only a year later, the picture had changed. The fighter squadrons of the Soviet Union and its allies were rearming with the MiG-15, which had already proved itself in combat in Korea, and there was an unvoiced but growing feeling that, if the Canberra had to go to war – especially in daylight – the tragedy of May 1940, when the RAF's Fairey Battle light bombers were shot out of the sky over France by the *Luftwaffe*'s fighters, might be repeated.

In 1952, therefore, the Ministry of Supply issued Specification B.126T, calling for design studies of a bomber capable of carrying a 6-ton nuclear store over a combat radius of 1,500 nautical miles (2,800 km) at very low level and high subsonic speed, not less than Mach 0.85. Several firms submitted proposals, but the requirement was well in advance of existing technological capabilities and it was shelved. However, the contest remained open for a low-level naval strike aircraft capable of operating from existing aircraft carriers and delivering a kiloton-range nuclear weapon against land and sea targets by the toss-bombing method. This requirement was covered by Specification M.148T, which was written around Naval Air Staff Target NAST.39, and in 1955 the design competition was won by Blackburn Aircraft with their B.103. A development batch of twenty aircraft was ordered in July that year, and the robust B.103 went on to enter service with the Royal Navy as the Buccaneer.

On the face of it, the Buccaneer might have seemed the ideal aircraft to meet the RAF's requirement for a Canberra replacement. In fact, although its airframe was quite adequate for the kind of low-level precision strike work envisaged by the RAF, its systems as they existed at the time were not. Admittedly, there was plenty of scope for further development, but the Buccaneer was not fast enough. By 1956 the Air Staff had modified B.126T, which had been resurrected, to include an over-the-target speed at low level of Mach 1.3 and the incorporation of an inertial nav/attack system that would enable the aircraft to deliver conventional weapons with pinpoint accuracy.

A year later, in the aftermath of the 1957 Defence White Paper, the RAF's requirement was formalised as General Operational Requirement (GOR) 339. Eight firms were invited to submit tenders by the end of January 1958; the eight did not include the Hawker Siddeley Group, which had already submitted preliminary drawings of the P.1125 project and was well in the running with its P.1129 variant. The other firms were left in no doubt that they would have to get together and submit joint proposals if they were seriously to contest Hawker Siddeley; GOR.339 was likely to be the only major British military aircraft project in the foreseeable future, and it was too complex to be tackled by the resources of any single company. GOR.339 spelt the beginning of the end for the traditional structure of Britain's aircraft industry.

English Electric, who had already done a lot of research into a Canberra replacement, had a head start with the design if a two-seat delta-wing project known as the P.17A, which was powered by two Rolls-Royce RB.142 engines. In collaboration with Short Brothers, English Electric's proposal envisaged a vertical take-off assembly in which the P.17A would be mounted on a Short-designed VTO platform designated P.17D; this was to be powered by forty-four fixed RB.108 lift engines, sixteen swivelling RB.108 lift engines and ten RFB.108 engines for forward propulsion. Together, the P.17A/17D combination would weigh somewhere in the region of 150,000 lb (68,000 kg). In addition to its primary role of getting the P.17A into the air and so dispensing with vulnerable runways, the P.17D could be used to transport freight and fuel to forward operating locations. The idea was by no means as far-fetched as one might think. Shorts were at that time heavily involved with pioneer VTOL techniques and their SC.1 VTOL research aircraft had already flown in conventional flight. Apart from technical considerations, the main drawback to the P.17D was that its development costs were likely to be prohibitive. As well as the low-level strike version of the P.17A, English Electric also proposed a long-range interceptor variant, the P.22.

Bristol Aircraft and Vickers-Armstrong also submitted their proposals for OR.339. The Vickers entry, the Type 571, was an advanced twin-engine design incorporating an integrated terrain-following nav/attack system; the aircraft was, in fact, a complete weapon system, and although the Air Staff were coming down heavily in favour of English Electric's P.17A they were sufficiently impressed by the Vickers design to want to incorporate certain features of it in the finalized OR.339 requirement. As a result of this a new Air Staff Requirement, ASR.343, was issued in the spring of 1959. It dispensed with the vertical take-off concept, which brought about the end of Short Brothers' participation, and virtually demanded the amalgamation of Vickers and English Electric to bring the required aircraft to fruition. Together with the Bristol Aeroplane Company, they were eventually to form the British Aircraft Corporation in February 1960.

On 1 January, 1959, it was announced that Vickers-Armstrong and English Electric had been awarded the contract to develop a new tactical strike and reconnaissance aircraft, known as TSR-2, to replace the Canberra. Its airframe was to be developed from that of the P.17, and it was to be powered by two afterburning Bristol Siddeley Olympus 22R engines. The choice of power plant was pushed through in the face of severe criticism from the Vickers and English Electric design teams, who wanted a Rolls-Royce engine, and as events were to prove it was an unfortunate choice. Nevertheless, at the time the Olympus 22R was the only engine available for immediate development as a massive reheat unit to provide up to 33,000 lb (146.8 kN) s.t. with an acceptable specific fuel consumption, and with a configuration suitable for installing twin engines in the rear fuselage.

By May 1959 the contractors, the Air Ministry and the Ministry of Supply had all agreed exactly what was required and what was feasible. The most notable of the changes required under ASR.343 was that the low-level height was defined as 200 feet (60 m) or less, speed at 40,000 feet (12,000 m) was to be Mach 2.0 instead of Mach 1.7, electronic countermeasures (ECM) equipment was to be added, ferry range was to be increased to 2,500 nautical miles (4,600 km) and the aircraft was to be able to operate from firm grass, to allow it to be dispersed away from the large airfields that would inevitably be targets for an enemy early in any confrontation.

Development work proceeded at Weybridge and Warton, and a Management Board comprising representatives of the RAF, the Ministry of Aviation and BAC was set up to control the entire project and sort out any problems. In fact, the very opposite was to be achieved. Throughout its development, TSR-2 was to be bedevilled by the Board's decisions and compromises. In effect, it was the first time in the history of British aviation that decisions affecting the design of an aircraft were taken away from the design team and placed in the hands of a committee.

While the TSR-2 airframe gradually took shape, various sub-contractors were given the responsibility for developing associated systems. The contract for the automatic flight system went to Elliott Automation, who had amassed an enormous amount of experience in developing the inertial navigational system (INS) for the V-Force's Blue Steel stand-off missile; Ferranti was given the task of developing the terrain-following radar and nav/attack system, and EMI the sideways-looking radar, while Marconi was made responsible for avionics such as the Instrument Landing System (ILS).

By the spring of 1960, it was apparent that the cost of developing the aircraft's advanced electronic systems was greatly to exceed the estimated figures, and this was the first of a series of cost escalations that would contribute to the project's eventual downfall. Funds were diverted from other cancelled projects to keep TSR-2 going, but there was little slowing in the overall upward trend.

By the autumn of 1962 the design of TSR-2 had been finalised and the British Aircraft Corporation was able to provide the Ministry of Aviation with realistic simulated performance figures. These included a cruising speed of between Mach 0.9–1.1 at sea level and Mach 2.05 at altitude. Combat radius with external fuel would be 1,500 nautical miles (2,800 km), or 1,000 nm (1,850 km) with a 2,000 lb (900 kg) internal bomb load on internal fuel only. Initial rate of climb at sea level would be 50,000 feet per minute (15,000 m/min). A variety of flight profiles was envisaged, most involving lo-lo-sorties at heights of not more than 200 feet (60 m) at Mach 0.9. The aircraft could carry a formidable range of weapons, in both the conventional and nuclear strike roles.

TSR-2's main function, had it entered RAF service, would have been to carry out deep reconnaissance and attack missions against targets that required deep penetration of enemy territory, such as large bridges, airfields, missile and radar sites, marshalling yards, communication centres and depots. As a deep penetration system, TSR-2 was years ahead of its time. It was also the only strike aircraft in the world capable of a true short-field performance, which would have enabled it to operate in areas of the globe where large stretches of concrete did not exist, as well as increasing its own chances of survival in the event of an enemy attack on its bases. The use of an all-moving tailplane, replacing conventional elevator and aileron control, allowed maximum use to be made of full-span blown flaps as a high-lift device for short take-off and landing; this permitted the aircraft to operate from semi-prepared or low-grade surfaces only 3,000 feet (900 m) long. Another feature was the TSR-2's long-stroke undercarriage with low-pressure tyres, specifically designed for operation from rough surfaces. The nose wheel strut could be extended during take-off to position the aircraft in take-off attitude and so shorten its run.

The nav/attack system incorporated in the aircraft, the most advanced of its type anywhere, exploited the latest developments in radar/computer flight control techniques. Briefly, the system comprised a Doppler/inertial dead reckoning navigational system of very high accuracy which was corrected every 100 miles or so by fixes obtained from the sideways-looking radar. A forward-looking radar enabled the aircraft to follow the contours of the terrain either automatically or manually and regardless of weather at a pre-selected height above the ground, the pilot having the benefit of a head-up display. Data from the navigation and TFR systems was fed by a complex of digital and analogue computers into an automatic pilot that was capable of flying the aircraft to and from a pre-determined target, the flight plan being fed into the digital computer on punched tape. Throughout the flight, the ground position of the aircraft was displayed to the crew on a moving map. The particular attack mode required could be pre-selected and carried out automatically, without visual reference to the target.

In the reconnaissance role, TSR-2 was designed to carry a very complete reconnaissance pack in a pannier in the weapons bay. Its equipment included the EMI sideways-looking radar, moving target indication that could blot out all returns from stationary objects to disclose any movement in the area, and linescan, which took a TV-type picture by day or night and could be used to transmit information direct from the aircraft to a ground station in the forward area to provide real-time intelligence.

Because of the requirement that called for TSR-2 to be capable of supersonic flight at both high and low altitude, much attention was given in design to reducing the aircraft's response to gusts in order to make working conditions for the crew tolerable at very high speed and low altitude. During the initial design phase of TSR-2, research into low-level turbulence using Canberras over the Libyan desert at speeds of about Mach 0.7 (Operation Swifter) had shown that bumps of 1/2 g could be expected, on average, twenty-seven times a minute, which was more than twice the rate regarded as tolerable for the operating crews. Gust response is a factor of wing loading, and broadly speaking the lower the wing loading is, the rougher the ride for a given speed. The optimum solution is variable sweep, but TSR-2's designers opted for a delta planform and a small wing area, a leading edge sweep of 60 degrees and a very thin wing section, mounted as high as possible on the fuselage. To minimise the low-speed 'Dutch roll' characteristic of sharply swept wings (in a Dutch roll the aircraft begins to yaw due to a gust or other input, and this develops into a roll) the tip sections were given a sharp anhedral of 23 degrees.

A lot of thought was given to safety and crew comfort in the TSR-2's design. The windscreen, for example, which was made of alumino silicate, was designed to withstand a 1 lb (0.45 kg) bird strike at speeds in excess of Mach 1.0, and the cockpit incorporated a first-class air conditioning system, including refrigeration for high-speed flight. Both crew members had rocket-powered Martin-Baker ejection seats, capable of safe operation through very phase of the flight envelope from the take-off roll.

A contract for nine development TSR-2s had already been placed in October 1960, and this was followed by a preliminary order for eleven pre-production aircraft in June 1962. At this stage, it was still hoped to fly the first prototype in the autumn of 1963, with delivery of the first pre-production batch to follow two years later. Research and development costs were estimated at £90 million in 1960, but by the beginning of 1963 this figure had doubled and the whole schedule had slipped by two years. The problem of too many committees, each responsible for its own slice of the development work, still dogged the project, and even the setting up of a Steering Committee in 1963 to co-ordinate matters more closely did nothing to alleviate it.

Moreover, the project was now beset by worrying technical problems, mainly to do with the Olympus 22R engines. The fifth Avro Vulcan B.1, XA894, had been allocated to Olympus development work; the engine, fuelled from two tanks in the bomb bay, was mounted in a nacelle beneath the Vulcan's fuselage. The first flight with the Olympus 22R was made on 23 February 1962, and later in the year XA894 was fitted with the more powerful Olympus 22R-1, featuring a high-performance reheat system. All went well until 3 December 1962 when, during a full reheat ground run, the Low Pressure (LP) shaft failed and the engine disintegrated, spewing out metal fragments that ruptured both the bomb bay and main fuel tanks. Such was the force of the break-up that the LP turbine was hurled for half a mile in bounds of 150 yards, narrowly missing the Bristol 188 research aircraft. There were no casualties, but the Vulcan was completely burned out.

The cause was resonance, which led to the failure of the LP shaft at a certain rpm, but it was a long time before Bristol Siddeley established what had gone wrong, and in the meantime other Olympus 22R engines failed, fortunately on the ground. Modifications were made but these, together with other engine design changes, caused severe problems in marrying the Olympus to the TSR-2 airframe. The LP shaft problem had not been completely cured when the aircraft made its first flight, and failures were still occurring when the engine was run up to high rpm from a cold start – a procedure that was very necessary in a military aircraft, especially one whose whole effectiveness relied on becoming airborne in the minimum time.

By the end of 1963, the writing was already on the wall for TSR-2, although neither the Government nor BAC would admit it. Escalating research and development costs had made the project the subject of heated political controversy. The Labour Party, influenced by 'advisors' who had a minimal knowledge of military aviation and even less of the RAF's operational requirements, made political capital out of the funds that were being diverted to keep TSR-2 alive, and left the electorate in no doubt about what they would do to the project if they got into power. But there were sinister forces at work within the Ministry of Defence, too. The Chief of the Defence Staff, Lord Mountbatten, made no secret of the fact that he favoured a land-based version of the Buccaneer to meet the RAF's requirement, while the Ministry's Chief Scientific Advisor, Sir Solly Zuckermann, told everyone concerned that he thought TSR-2 a waste of public money and that better value might be obtained by buying aircraft from the United States.

Predictably, in-fighting such as this had an adverse effect on Government attempts to promote the TSR-2 overseas. The Australians, in particular, had shown an active interest in the aircraft since 1960, and two years later were favouring the British machine as a Canberra replacement. The requirement for a new RAAF bomber, as defined by Air Staff requirement ASR 36, was that the aircraft should have an all-weather capability in both its primary strike and secondary reconnaissance roles, a capability for delivering both conventional ordnance and 'special stores' (in other words, nuclear weapons), a speed of Mach 2.0 at 50,000 feet (15,000 m), a desirable radius of action of 1,100 nautical miles (2,000 km), and an in-service date with the RAAF of June 1966.

In May 1963 the Australian Government sent an RAAF evaluation team abroad to investigate possible alternatives to TSR-2. The evaluation team defined two basic missions for the new bomber. These involved, firstly, joint operations under American command against targets in southern China and North Vietnam, and secondly, providing a credible deterrent against Indonesia, which in practical terms meant operating from overseas and Australian bases against any Indonesian target (It should be remembered that, in 1963, British Commonwealth forces were involved in serious armed confrontation with Indonesia on the island of Borneo).

Between June and August 1963 the evaluation team investigated the French Mirage IV and the USA's McDonnell F-4C Phantom, North American RA5C Vigilante and General Dynamics TFX, which was later re-designated F-111.

Yet there was no sales drive aimed at convincing the Australian Government that TSR-2 was the aircraft the RAAF needed, so it was hardly surprising that Australian interest began to wane after Lord Mountbatten, during a tour of South-East Asia, expressed the opinion that mounting costs and complexity would prevent the aircraft ever coming into service.

It was not until the end of 1963 that a British Government delegation led by Hugh Fraser, the Secretary of State for Air, went to Australia to mount a sales drive, but by that time it was too late. Soon afterwards, the Australians decided

The prototype TSR-2, XR219, turning on to final approach at Boscombe Down at the conclusion of its first flight. (BAe)

to meet the RAF requirement by ordering twenty-four General Dynamics F-111As. The first of these, designated F-111C in RAAF service, were delivered in 1973.

The prototype TSR-2, XR219, made its maiden flight from Boscombe Down on 27 September 1964 with Roland Beamont at the controls, after carrying out twelve taxi runs. The flying qualities were good, but the pilot experienced strong lateral vibration on touchdown, which interfered with his vision at that critical moment. The problem lay with the complex undercarriage, which had remained down on this first flight, and it took over four months and nine flights before the undercarriage could be retracted successfully. The aircraft went supersonic for the first time on 21 February 1965, and high-speed low-altitude trials began in March. By this time a second aircraft, XR220, was scheduled to join the flying programme and a third, XR221, had successfully completed an initial ground run of the avionics fit. Work was progressing on six more development aircraft, five of which were partly complete.

The Labour Government that had taken office under Prime Minister Harold Wilson shortly after TSR-2's first flight had kept the project going so that the aircraft could be evaluated against the General Dynamics F-111. At that time, Wilson – acting on faulty advice – seriously believed that some

£300 million might be saved by buying the American aircraft. His Cabinet thought so too, and the final nail in TSR-2's coffin was hammered home on 6 April 1965, when Chancellor James Callaghan, during his budget speech, announced that the project was to be cancelled forthwith. The assassination was to be complete; no trace of the project was to survive. Orders were issued for the destruction of the completed prototypes and those on the assembly line, and of all the jigs and tools used by the manufacturing companies.

It is fair to say that the decision to cancel TSR-2, in its stage of development, was probably the most ill-advised ever made by a British government involving the aircraft industry. Admittedly, there were still snags to be overcome, but fewer snags than those that afflicted the F-111, for which the British Government now opted. Soaring costs and technical problems in the F-111 development programme eventually led to the cancellation of the British order, at considerable cost.

The gap was filled, in 1969, by the Buccaneer S.2, which Blackburn had wanted the RAF to have ten years earlier, and an admirable job it subsequently did. But it was not until 1982, with the debut of the Panavia Tornado, that the strike squadrons of the Royal Air Force at last possessed an aircraft capable of carrying out all the tasks for which the TSR-2 had been intended.

Of the TSR-2 airframes, XR219, XR221 and XR223 were taken to the gunnery range at Shoeburyness to be destroyed as 'damage to aircraft' targets. XR220 was kept at Boscombe Down for a year or so and then placed in storage

The Buccaneer S.2, originally a naval strike aircraft, filled the gap left by the cancellation of TSR-2. (BAe)

at RAF Henlow after it had had all its internal equipment ripped out. Even the wires to equipment were severed rather than disconnected. It was later transferred to the Aerospace Museum at RAF Cosford, near Wolverhampton. It was initially planned to scrap XR222, but the aircraft was instead allocated to the College of Aeronautics at Cranfield and later saved for restoration and moved to the Imperial War Museum at Duxford.

All the other airframes were scrapped. All tooling was destroyed. On the production line, as workers completed the assembly of some airframes prior to their transport to the scrap yard, the tooling was being destroyed with cutting torches behind them. Even a wooden mock-up of the TSR-2 was dragged out of the BAC factory at Warton and burned while the workers looked on. All technical publications, even photographs of the aircraft in its various stages of construction, were destroyed. Boscombe Down's official records of test flights were 'lost'. It was an act of vandalism unparalleled in the history of British aviation.

CHAPTER TWENTY-TWO

The Harrier and
Sea Harrier

The story of the vertical take-off application to air combat really begins in 1944, when Germany made plans to mass-produce a rocket-powered target defence interceptor, the Bachem Ba 349 Natter (Viper). One of the most extraordinary aircraft ever built, the Ba 349 was conceived as a rocket-powered target defence interceptor. Basically a piloted rocket armed with a battery of 73mm unguided rockets in the forward fuselage, the aircraft was launched from a vertical ramp with the aid of four jettisonable solid-fuel rocket boosters and climbed to altitude under the control of an autopilot, the human pilot only taking control during the attack phase. After firing his salvo of rockets into a formation of bombers, the pilot was then supposed to bale out. Several unpowered gliding test flights were made before the first and only manned vertical launch took place in February 1945. The Natter crashed, killing its pilot.

Other wartime German VTOL (vertical take-off and landing) projects, which never left the drawing board, included the Focke-Achgelis Fa 269 carrier-based fighter that was designed to use thrust vectoring – a single BMW radial engine in the fuselage driving two large-diameter propellers aft of the wing, which could be rotated downwards to provide vertical thrust and rearwards for horizontal flight – and the Focke-Wulf Triebflügel, a jet-powered fighter project that featured small turbojets mounted at the end of three long arms which, in turn, were mounted at about the mid-section of the aircraft's fuselage, the idea being that when the arms rotated they would act like a helicopter's rotor blades and lift the device, which sat on its tail.

The main problem confronting designers researching the vertical take-off concept was to find a foolproof means of ensuring stability during the critical transition phase between vertical and horizontal flight. However, in 1951, when the US Navy issued a requirement for a small fighter aircraft capable of operating from platforms on merchant ships for convoy protection, Convair and Lockheed both launched into a research programme that was to produce surprising long-tern results. Each company developed an aircraft of roughly similar configuration, a 'tail-sitter' using a powerful turboprop engine with large contra-rotating propellers to eliminate torque. The aircraft, using a simple, two-axis auto-stabiliser, would be flown vertically off the ground and then bunted over into horizontal flight. During lading it would hang on its propellers, which would then perform the same function as a helicopter's rotor and lower it to a landing on its tail castors.

Both aircraft, the Lockheed XFV-1 and the Convair XFY-1, flew in 1954. The XFY-1 was the more successful design and underwent a comprehensive flight test programme, but in 1956 the US Navy withdrew its requirement and abandoned VTOL research. The reasons given were technical ones, such as

The Lockheed XFV-1 was a possible US Navy solution to the vertical take-off problem. (Lockheed)

instability during the transition phase, but the real reason was that a powerful lobby of senior officers in the US Navy saw the development of the VTOL concept as a threat to the production of newer and larger aircraft carriers. It was to be many years before the VTOL concept returned to the US Navy as an operational reality, and it was a British design that made it possible.

In the United Kingdom, practical experiments based on the VTOL concept began in 1953 with the first vertical flight trials of the Rolls-Royce Thrust Measuring Rig. Known popularly as the 'Flying Bedstead', it had two Rolls-Royce Nene turbojets installed horizontally at opposite ends of the assembly, their tailpipes directed vertically downwards near the mass centre. While these trials were in progress, the Ministry of Supply issued Specification ER.143 for a research aircraft which could take off vertically by jet lift and then accelerate forward into normal cruising flight.

The thinking behind this specification was that VTOL might have an application in the design of future transport aircraft rather than in combat aircraft designs. The same train of thought was also being followed in the United States and resulted in VTOL research types such as the Lockheed Model 330 Humming Bird, which was built as part of the US Army Transportation Research Command Program.

The design submitted by Short Brothers, the PD.11 – a small tailless delta aircraft with five Rolls-Royce RB.108 engines, four for lift and one for forward propulsion – was judged to be the most promising, and in August 1954 Shorts received a contract to built two prototypes under the designation Short SC.1. The first SC.1, XG900, was initially not fitted with lift engines and made a conventional maiden flight on 2 April 1957; it was the second prototype, XG905, which began tethered hovering trials in May 1958. On 6 April 1960, at the Royal Aeronautical Establishment (RAE) at Bedford, test pilot Tom Brooke-Smith achieved the first complete transition from level flight to vertical descent and vertical climb, following a conventional take-off. That summer, XG900 now having had its battery of lift engines fitted, both SC.1s developed short, rolling take-off techniques from unprepared surfaces, the objects of which were to avoid ground erosion and to allow flights at increased take-off weights.

In April 1961 XG900 was handed over to RAE Bedford, while XG905 went to Belfast to be fitted with a new auto-stabilisation system, designed to compensate for gusts. More than 80 flights were made with the new system, starting in June 1963. The development pilot was J.R. Green, who had joined Shorts from the RAE. On 2 October, Green was returning to land when the gyros failed, producing false references which caused the auto-stabiliser to fly the aircraft into the ground. The failure occurred at a height of less than 30 feet, giving Green no time to revert to manual control. XG905 hit the ground upside down and Green was killed. The aircraft itself was repaired and flew again in 1966, carrying out trials with the Blind Landing Experimental Unit.

At no time was the Short SC.1 intended to lead to the development of a more advanced combat aircraft. Indeed, when the SC.1 began its trials in 1958 the Air Ministry was showing little or no interest in the concept, the general feeling being that the use of four or five engines solely to provide lift would result in a prohibitive weight penalty. What was needed was a different solution, and it came from an unexpected source.

In 1956 Michel Wibault, a French engineer, approached Bristol Aero engines with a proposal for a short take-off and landing (STOL) aircraft in which the thrust could be moved through an arc or 'vectored' from horizontally rearward to vertically downward. The power unit for Wibault's 'Ground Attack Gyropter' consisted of an 800 hp Bristol Orion turboprop driving four centrifugal blowers, the exhaust casings of which could be rotated to direct the jet of compressed air, and hence the reaction, or thrust, through ninety degrees. Although the Gyropter was too heavy to be practical, the concept of thrust vectoring – being able to direct all the thrust from the horizontal to the vertical and at any angle in between – had many practical advantages over the thrust deflection devices under investigation at that time.

Following engineering studies at Bristol, the thrust vectoring idea was developed into the first BE53 configuration of 1957, using the Orpheus engine as a central power generator. It was this form of the BE53 that was first studied by the Hawker design team at Kingston. Since only part of this engine's thrust output could be vectored, it did not provide a satisfactory basis for a useful V/STOL military aircraft. However, research discussions between the aircraft and engine design teams rapidly resulted in the BE53 configuration being changed in order to make the concept more adaptable to a practical V/STOL fighter. It was given the designation P.1127.

Within about a year of the P.1127 studies starting at Kingston, Hawker's factory in the Thames valley, the engine had evolved considerably, with four principal changes. First, a common air intake for the fan and high pressure (HP) compressors had been introduced, the fan thus supercharging the HP spool; second, contra-rotation of the two shafts had been introduced to minimise gyroscopic coupling forces; third, the turbine discharge had been split to give two further swivel nozzles, thus allowing all the engine's thrust to be vectored; and fourth, the use of compact, cascaded nozzles at all four outlets in lieu of the original large-radius bent pipes reduced external drag and swivelling torque. The last three of these changes came about directly as a result of ideas and pressure from the aircraft team. The engine was named Pegasus, after the inspiration of poetry, or the winged horse of the Muses.

It was in this form that the engine first ran, in September 1959, at 9,000 lb thrust. However, a decision to use HP instead of low pressure (LP) air for aircraft control forces in V/STOL flight demanded the use of a higher mass flow compressor. Thus modified, the Pegasus 2, of 11,000 lb thrust, ran in February 1960, and was cleared for flight in the prototype P.1127 in the late summer of that year.

The Pegasus was a simple, robust and reliable two-shaft turbofan. Thrust was produced from four separate nozzles which could be rotated through 100 degrees, from fully aft to about 10 degrees forward of vertical. The engine had two compressor/turbine systems, which contra-rotated in order to eliminate gyroscopic forces in V/STOL flight. The Pegasus had an installed thrust-to-weight ratio of nearly 6:1, among the highest for non-afterburning engines.

By the end of 1958, the first flight configuration of the P.1127 had been defined. However, although 75 per cent of the funding for the engine was supplied by the US Government through the Mutual Weapons Development Agency in Paris, no service sponsor could be found for the aircraft. It was not until early 1960, when the British government finally decided to support the project, that funding was made available. At this stage, the first prototype P.1127 was about half complete.

Two Pegasus 2-powered P.1127 prototypes were built, XP831 and XP836, making their first flights on 21 October 1960 and 7 July 1961 respectively. The first hovers took place in October 1960 and the first conventional flights in March 1961. Transitions to and from wingborne flight were accomplished in September 1961, and in December that year the P.1127 became the world's first V/STOL aircraft to go supersonic in a dive. A development batch of four aircraft followed, the first of these, XP972, making its first flight on 5 April 1962.

Hawker did not consider that the subsonic development was the ultimate V/STOL aircraft, and studies were already under way for a supersonic derivative, the P.1150, which in its finalised form became the P.1154. Using the same configuration, but fitted with a vectored thrust Pegasus 5 engine with plenum chamber burning (PCB), it looked like a stretched and refined P.1127. Plenum chamber burning involved the combustion of fuel in oxygen-rich air and at higher pressures than in most reheat systems. Using this arrangement, it was estimated that the P.1150 would reach Mach 1.7. However, the P.1150 design was quickly overtaken by events.

The NATO Basic Military Aircraft Requirement No.3 (NBMR3) competition of 1961 called for a V/STOL attack fighter, and it was the P.1154 proposal that emerged as the technical first choice of the multi-nation assessment team, sharing overall first place with France's Mirage IIIV. The Royal Air Force and the Royal Navy, in the knowledge that the successful NBMR3 design was likely to become the standard NATO strike/attack aircraft, wrote separate Operational Requirements around the P.1154, and further project studies went ahead at Kingston from 1962. The programme soon became embroiled in inter-service and political wrangles and a maze of conflicting demands.

Meanwhile, the Royal Navy had begun to show an interest in the P.1127. The first substantial reference to the potential of operating V/STOL fighters from ships had been made in a 1959 Hawker P.1127 document that bore a 'Secret' classification. This summarized the anticipated operational benefits and flexibility of V/STOL deck flying, although there was little in it that could not have been deduced by any aviation enthusiast who knew something of the principles of vertical take-off and landing. Yet, when the first P.1127 carried out its initial precarious hovers at Dunsfold in 1960, it was generally regarded as just one more of the V/STOL prototypes which, around this time, were aimed at reconciling the engineering problems of combining the flexibility of the helicopter with the combat performance of a jet attack fighter, so it was perhaps understandable that the P.1127 generated no special excitement in the hearts and minds of the Naval Staffs at the time. Nor was there any greater enthusiasm for its battlefield potential among the Air Staffs. It was subsonic; it was not planned to carry a range of sophisticated electronics; it had a pitifully small payload-radius performance compared with contemporary competing projects using conventional take-off and landing; and it did not replace any existing service aircraft which were on the verge of becoming obsolescent.

From 1960 to 1964, many problems were overcome in the development of the P.1127. The military services continued to show little more than polite interest in the aircraft's puny operational capability, although by this time the programme had the benefit of considerable government support, mainly on the basis of research contracts.

All this faint and distant interest among the Air and Naval Staffs changed positively, however, when the Hawker P.1154 – the first practical supersonic fighter design to feature vectored thrust – was NBMR3 early in 1962. The UK government of the day advised the RAF and RN to take a serious look at this aircraft to meet their future needs ashore and afloat, anticipating that a basic common design could be evolved with the aim of economising in future defence procurement.

The Royal Navy received a practical demonstration of V/STOL potential on 8 February 1963, when Bill Bedford, at that time Hawker's chief test pilot, flew the P.1127 prototype, XP831, to a deck landing on the aircraft carrier HMS *Ark Royal* in Lyme Bay, off Portland. Between 8 and 13 April 1963, Bedford and fellow test pilot Hugh Merewether, neither of whom had any carrier experience, took XP831 through the full range of vertical and short take-offs and landings without experiencing any difficulties. Contrary to naval preconceptions, the P.1127 met no 'cliff-edge' downdraught effects in hover crossing the catwalks, island turbulence produced no problems and the deck neither buckled nor got red-hot.

Unfortunately, the Royal Navy regarded the whole demonstration as something of a non-event. The Fleet Air Arm's senior admiral commented that for the first time in his experience of a new jet coming aboard, the 'fright factor increment' was negative. Normally, aircraft undergoing deck trials for the first time were heavier, faster and more heart-stopping than their predecessors. The observers aboard *Ark Royal* failed to appreciate the importance of XP831's significant reversal of this trend; the most significant misjudgement was betrayed in the subsequent naval PR handouts, which accorded only passing mention of the fact that the aircraft had been flown from the *Ark Royal* by two pilots who had never before landed on or taken off from a carrier.

The deck trials with the P.1127 did little to change the opinions of the Royal Navy. They stuck determinedly to their requirement, in the P.1154, for a two-seat, radar-equipped, supersonic all-weather fighter to be catapult-launched from the decks of the carriers *Victorious, Eagle, Ark Royal* and the projected new 50,000-ton carrier CVA-01. The RAF's needs in the P.1154 programme were for a single-seat strike/attack aircraft with a secondary supersonic intercept capability. However, the Royal Navy's interest in the P.1154 ultimately foundered. For eighteen months following the completion of P.1154 project studies for the Royal Navy and the RAF at Kingston in 1962, design studies were conducted in an attempt to incorporate the conflicting requirements of the two services into the P.1154 design. The resulting compromise was unacceptable to either. After 1963, the Royal Air Force initiated a separate programme for the design, development and prototype manufacture of a definitive P.1154RAF, but the Royal Navy went its own way towards the Rolls-Royce Spey-powered McDonnell F4k Phantom II. With that, the Royal Navy's interest in V/STOL became moribund, and was to remain so while it still possessed the carriers that could accommodate the aircraft it wanted.

The RAF's P.1154 fared no better. The reappraisal of British defence commitments which followed the accession to power of the labour Government in October 1964 led, in February 1965, to the cancellation of the P.1154 when the first aircraft was about one-third complete. It was some consolation to the RAF that they were permitted immediately to embark on the development of a fully operational version of the subsonic P.1127. Additional F-4 Phantoms were to be acquired for the RAF, and Britain also began a development venture with the aim of acquiring a variable geometry multi-role aircraft. After following a long and tortuous route via the F-111 and the Anglo-French VG project, this was eventually to result in the multi-national Panavia Tornado.

For the Royal Navy, the decisive blow fell in 1966, when a further revision of UK defence policy dictated that tactical air power at sea, from then on, would be provided by land-based aircraft provided by the Royal Air Force, a senseless decision if ever there was one. With that came the cancellation of CVA-01, leaving the Royal Navy with a fleet of ageing carriers whose expiry in the 1970s would effectively eliminate Britain's seaborne, fixed-wing combat aircraft capability.

Meanwhile, more restrained and immediately practical developments had been taking place. In the spring of 1962, the governments of the United Kingdom, the United States of America and the Federal Republic of Germany negotiated a tripartite agreement to continue the P.1127 development programme and to provide nine aircraft and eighteen engines for a joint evaluation of V/STOL operations in the strike fighter role, using the aircraft in the field, away from conventional air bases. British Ministry of Defence FGA D&P was produced to define the requirements for the Evaluation Squadron aircraft, of which the sixth P.1127, XP984, was extensively modified during its manufacture in 1963 to become the prototype. The new aircraft was given the name Kestrel, after the common European falcon. It was the first jet V/STOL aircraft to be granted a Release for Service Flying, in 1964.

The Kestrel looked similar to the P.1127 but incorporated many different features as a result of experience with the earlier machine. A swept wing of new design was fitted, as was a tailplane with a pronounced anhedral and wider span to improve longitudinal stability, and a longer fuselage, revised air intakes and a repositioned engine were other major changes. The power plant was the 15,000 lb thrust Pegasus 5. Two wing hard points, each able to carry a 100 Imperial gallon fuel tanks, were installed and a small gunsight was fitted to allow tracking evaluation. The Kestrel could reach Mach 1.25 in a dive.

The Tripartite Kestrel Evaluation Squadron was formed at RAF West Raynham with pilots and ground crew from the RAF, the US Air Force, the US

A Kestrel of the Tripartite Evaluation Squadron at the hover. (BAe)

Navy, the US Army and the *Luftwaffe*. During 1965, some 650 flying hours of testing were conducted in England, to evaluate the practical merits of jet V/STOL, developing operational concepts where the aircraft was used in the field and away from conventional air bases. These trials were a considerable success. In 1966, after the evaluation programme, six Kestrels were shipped to the United States, where they were used for US tri-service and individual service trials on land and at sea under the designation XV-6A. These made a particular impression upon the US Marine Corps, who became seriously interested in the XV-6A as a land- and ship-based tactical aircraft. At Langley, NASA used the XV-6A for flight research into the early 1970s.

Even as the P.1154 programme was being wound up early in 1965, Hawker Siddeley at Kingston was instructed by the British government to modify the Kestrel to take a 19,000 lb thrust version of the Pegasus, fit the avionic systems then being developed for the P.1154, less the radar, change the aircraft to accommodate a considerable weapons load and deliver the resulting attack fighter to the RAF in four years' time. The result was the Harrier, which, representing a more than 90 per cent redesign of the Kestrel, was committed to production in 1967. In its single-seat close support and tactical reconnaissance version, the aircraft was ordered into production for the RAF as the Harrier GR.Mk.1, the first of an initial order of seventy-seven machines flying on 28 December 1967. On 1 April 1969 the Harrier entered service with the Harrier OCU at RAF Wittering, and the type subsequently equipped No. 1 Squadron at Wittering and Nos 3, 4 and 20 Squadrons in Germany. After the formation of

Harrier GR.1As of No. 3 Squadron, Wildenrath, Germany. (Crown copyright)

the first RAF squadron many changes were subsequently made to the aircraft. Notable among these was the engine performance, which was raised from the 19,000 lb of the Pegasus 101 through the 20,000 lb of the 102 to the 21,500 lb of the 103 and 104.

The weapons system was extended and augmented by the addition of a passive radar warning system and, later, laser ranging and marked target seeking equipment. RAF Harriers were subsequently deployed in the ground attack, reconnaissance and close air support roles, aiding UK ground forces on the flanks of NATO (Norway to the Eastern Mediterranean) and on the NATO Central Front. They spent over 75 per cent of their time flying at low level (500 feet or less above the ground) and at high speed, in the region of 400 to 500 knots. The aircraft was designed to operate away from the vulnerable bases it used in peacetime. Low-pressure tyres, self-contained starting, simple systems check-out procedures, rapid turn-round between sorties, low maintenance demands and many other features which facilitated forward deployment were all the result of deliberate engineering choices in the design.

The first variant of the Harrier for the US Marine Corps was the AV-8A. It was McDonnell Douglas who developed the aircraft into a truly formidable fighting machine, the AV-8B Harrier II, which became the GR.5 in RAF service. (BAe)

The RAF had its Harriers, and although the Royal Navy had lost interest in V/STOL with the demise of the supersonic P.1154 project and acquired the conventional F-4 Phantom, when the idea of a seaborne Harrier was resurrected at a later date the Navy's interest was reawakened, although there were those who said that such an aircraft would simply serve as a stop-gap until something better came along. They were wrong.

Developed from the basic Harrier airframe, the Sea Harrier FRS.1 was ordered to equip the Royal Navy's three Invincible class aircraft carriers. The nose was lengthened to accommodate the Blue Fox AI radar, and the cockpit was raised to permit the installation of a more substantial avionics suite and to provide the pilot with a better all-round view. An initial production batch of twenty-four aircraft, plus three development aircraft, were ordered to expedite testing and clearance, and while the first Sea Harrier neared completion in the summer of 1978 the testing of its entire range of operational equipment was under way in two specially-modified Hawker Hunter T.8 aircraft. The first Sea Harrier FRS.1 took off for its maiden flight from Dunsfold on 20 August 1978; this aircraft, XZ450, was not in fact a prototype but the first aircraft of a

The Harrier GR.3 was fitted with laser ranging equipment in the nose. (BAe)

production order that had now risen from twenty-four to thirty-one. On 13 November it became the first Sea Harrier to land on an aircraft carrier, HMS *Hermes*.

The second production Sea Harrier, XZ451, flew on 25 May 1979 and became the first example to be taken on charge by the Royal Navy, being accepted on 18 June 1979 for service with the Intensive Flying Trials Unit. No. 800A Naval Air Squadron was commissioned at Royal Naval Air Station, Yeovilton, Somerset, on 26 June 1979 as the Sea Harrier Intensive Flying Trials Unit (IFTU), and on 31 March 1980 this unit was disbanded and re-formed as No. 899 Headquarters and training squadron. A second Sea Harrier squadron, No. 800, was commissioned on 23 April 1980, and was followed by No. 801 Squadron on 26 February 1981. The planned peacetime establishment of each squadron was five Sea Harriers; No. 800 was to embark on HMS *Hermes*, while No. 801 was to go to HMS *Invincible*. Meanwhile, an additional batch of ten Sea Harriers had been ordered from British Aerospace; the first of these flew on 15 September 1981 and was delivered to No. 899 Squadron.

Armed with Sidewinder AAMs, the Sea Harrier FRS.1 distinguished itself in the 1982 Falklands war. At the height of the campaign, on 21 May 1982, Sea Harriers were being launched on combat air patrols at the rate of one pair every twenty minutes. The Sea Harrier force was later upgraded to FA.2 standard, the forward fuselage being redesigned to accommodate the Ferranti Blue Vixen pulse-Doppler radar. The avionics suite was wholly upgraded and the aircraft armed with the AIM-120 AMRAAM medium-range air-to-air missile, enabling it to engage multiple targets beyond visual range. Deliveries of the thirty-eight converted aircraft began in 1992, followed by twenty-eight new-build machines; all were withdrawn from use in 2006. The following months saw the formation of the Joint Force Harrier, composed of RAF and Royal Navy personnel.

Perhaps the most fitting tribute to the Harrier came from Sir Tom Sopwith, who died aged 101 after literally witnessing a century of flight. His Sopwith Aviation Company produced the Camel, of which the Harrier, via Hawker Aircraft and Hawker Siddeley, is a direct descendant. When Sopwith saw the Harrier flying for the first time, his comment was: 'Now I've seen everything.'